Architects of Anthropology in India

Architects of Anthropology in India

(Volume - II)

Edited by

Sarthak Sengupta

GYAN

ISBN : 978-81-212-6146-3

Published, 2022

Published by

Gyan Publishing House
5, Ansari Road
Daryaganj, New Delhi-110002
Phone: 011-47034999, 9811692060
www.gyanbooks.com
E-mail: books@gyanbooks.com

Printed at: Gyan Press, Delhi.

Dedicated
in remembrance of
Late **Manomohan Sen**,
my grandfather,
an unsung poet and children's
litterateur of Bengal

Contents

Preface

In India, anthropology was introduced by Sir William Jones, who established the Royal Asiatic Society of Bengal at Calcutta in 1774 to study Nature and Man. However, the teaching of Anthropology in Indian Universities introduced in the University of Calcutta in 1918 as part of the curriculum of Ancient History and Culture and as a holistic study of humankind began in the same University in 1920 when it was given the status of an independent subject for study at the post-graduate level leading to a postgraduate degree. Thereafter, a separate Department of Anthropology was established in 1921. The year 2020, thus, marks the glorious completion of hundred years of teaching Anthropology in India, and such an important landmark calls for remembrance.

What is most striking about the discipline is that it is still deficient in having a documented volume on its history and development. It is a matter of great concern that a hundred-year-old academic discipline at the level of postgraduate teaching, which is devoted to the study of the biological and cultural evolution of human beings covering millions of years, could not reconstruct its history. The doyens of anthropology, how through the utmost devotion for the discipline and their obsession to imprint its huge implication in understanding the life of the humans, diligently persisted teaching and research of anthropology in India that deserve proper documentation highlighting a truthful and interpretive assessment of their contributions. Thus, we decided to celebrate this auspicious occasion deliberating upon the contributions of the founding stalwarts of the discipline who break new ground in the field of anthropological research in India. In this treatise, a modest attempt has been made to prepare a repository documenting the life and research contribution.

The first volume of the compilation – *Architects of Anthropology in India* – consisting of twenty-five chapters is devoted to the academic life and research contribution of doyens like L.K. Ananta Krishna Iyer, Sarat Chandra Roy, Bhupendranath Dutta, Tarak Chandra Das, N.K. Bose, Verrier Elwin, P.C. Biswas, D.N. Majumdar, Irawati Karve, H.D. Sankalia, Stephen Fuchs, C von Furer Haimendorf, Dharanidhar Sen, M.N. Srinivas, S.C. Dube, N.C. Choudhury, Surajit Chandra Sinha, Indera Pal Singh, Asok K. Ghosh, Gopala Sarana, K.S. Singh, Satadal Dasgupta, Amitabha Basu, D.K. Bhattacharya, and V.C. Channa.

The chapter in the present treatise (Volume II), attempts to cover twenty-five more distinguished scholars of anthropology, namely, J.P. Mills, B.S. Guha, K.P. Chattopadhaya, A.K. Mitra, S.S. Sarkar, M.C. Goswami, P.K. Bhowmik, Tulika Sen, H.K. Rakshit, K.S. Mathur, T.C. Sharma, Abhimanyu Sharma, D.N. Majumdar, S.R.K. Chopra, D.P. Mukherjee, R.S. Negi, Biswanath Banerjee, B.M. Das, B.N. Sahay, Priyabala Das, R.M. Sarkar, A.K. Haldar, H.C. Sharma, Surinder Nath, and Abdulla Ali Asraf. All the write-up is chronologically arranged as per their year of birth. A similar sequence is also maintained in photographs used in the jacket.

This comprehensively edited volume is dedicated with deep veneration to my grandfather Late Monomohan Sen, an almost forgotten poet and children's litterateur of Bengal before partition. He was the eldest son of renowned Ayurvedic practitioner Kaviraj Pyarimohan Sen of Sonarong village of Dhaka district and was born on 29th July 1865. Manomohan started his early education in Comilla and Chittagong and his later life settled in Mymensing town. He established himself as an eminent poet and contributed a lot to children's literature like *Shishutosh* (first published in 1904 and its 66 edition published within a span of 40 years); *Khokar Daptar; Mohonbhog*, which has fetched him wide recognition. Besides literary works, he has the talent of a good stage performer, dramaturge, composer, and earned fame for his devotion to various social works. His untimely demise on 2nd April 1913 at the age of 47 years only created a void in the Bengali children's literature.

I shall consider my efforts to be amply rewarded if this volume in any manner arouses interest and encourage the budding anthropologist of India.

Dibrugarh, 6th November 2021 **Sarthak Sengupta**

Acknowledgements

The editor of *Architects of Anthropology in India* records a deep sense of appreciation towards the intellectual existence shown by all the contributors to this volume. They made sincere efforts contributing their mite in the form of a write-up within the stipulated date for incorporation in this volume. It is their academic generosity that enabled this project to be completed successfully.

M/s Gyan Publishing House, New Delhi has earned sincere appreciation and made me indebted through their initiative in bringing out these volumes in a minimum possible time.

I extend my heartfelt greetings to Dr. Monimugdha Bhuyan of the Department of Anthropology, Dibrugarh University for arranging a few photographs and designing the jacket. Thanks are also due to Dr. Nabakumar Duary and Prof. Nadeem Hasnain for arranging a few photographs to use in the jacket.

Words fall short to express my sincere thanks to my wife Kabita, sons Sushruta and Samrat, daughter-in-law Surovee, and granddaughter Shinjinee for their loving support while I worked for the compilation.

Dibrugarh, 6th November 2021 **Sarthak Sengupta**

List of Contributors

Anamika Gogoi Duarah, Associate Professor, Department of Anthropology, Arya Vidyapeeth College, Guwahati, Assam, 781 017.

Anup K. Kapoor, Former Vice-Chancellor, Jiwaji University, and Formerly Professor of Department of Anthropology, University of Delhi, India, 110007.

Atul Chandra Bhowmick, Formerly Professor of Department of Museology. University of Calcutta, Kolkata, West Bengal, 700027.

Bhabani Kumar Borah, Museum Curator, Department of Anthropology, Gauhati University, Gopinath Bordoloi Nagar, Jalukbari, Guwahati, Assam, 781014.

Deepali Jain, Assistant Professor, School of Forensics, Risk Management and National Security, Rashtriya Raksha University, Lavad, Gandhinagar, Gujarat, 382305.

Indu Talwar, Formerly Professor of Department of Anthropology, Panjab University, Chandigarh, Punjab,160014.

Kakali Chakrabarty, Formerly Deputy Director (Cultural) of Anthropological Survey of India, Eastern Regional Centre, Salt Lake, Bidhan Nagar, Kolkata, West Bengal, 700091.

Maitreyee Sharma, Assistant Professor, Department of Anthropology, Dibrugarh University, Dibrugarh, Assam, 786004.

Monimugdha Bhuyan, Research Assistant, Department of Anthropology, Dibrugarh University, Dibrugarh, Assam, 786004.

Nabakumar Duary, Anthropological Survey of India, Government of India, Eastern Regional Centre, Salt Lake City, Kolkata-700091.

Nadeem Hasnain, Former Pro-Vice-Chancellor, Mahatma Gandhi International Hindi University, Wardha, Maharashtra, India, and Formerly Professor of Department of Anthropology, Lucknow University, Uttar Pradesh, 226007.

O.P. Jasuja, Professor, Department of Forensic Science, Chandigarh University, Gharuan, Mohali, Punjab, 140413.

Palash Chandra Coomar, Formerly Joint Director of Operations of Directorate of Census Operation, Ministry of Home Affairs, Government of India, West Bengal,700106.

Pradip K. Bhowmick, Formerly Associate Professor of Rural Development Centre, Indian Institute of Technology, Kharagpur, and Secretary, The Institute of Social and Applied Anthropology, Bidisha, Narayangarh, West Midnapore, West Bengal, 721437.

Prasanta Kumar Chattopadhyay, Formerly Professor of Department of Forensic Science, Punjabi University, Patiala, 147002

Ragini Sahai, Associate Professor, Amity Institute of Anthropology, Amity University, Gautam Buddha Nagar, Noida, Uttar Pradesh, 201313.

Rajendra Prasad Athparia, Formerly Superintending Anthropologist of Anthropological Survey of India, Government of India, North East Regional Centre, Mawlai, Madan Raiting, Shillong, Meghalaya,793024.

Richa Negi, Director, North East Regional Centre of Indira Gandhi National Centre for the Arts. Guwahati, Assam, 781001.

Rumjhum Ray Chaudhuri, Independent Consultant, Community Health and Social Development, Kolkata, West Bengal.

Sarthak Sengupta, Formerly Professor of Department of Anthropology, Dibrugarh University, Dibrugarh, Assam, 786004.

Sekh Rahim Mondal, Formerly Charu Chandra Sanyal Chair Professor of Centre of Himalayan Studies, and Department of Anthropology, University of North Bengal, Raja Rammohanpur, Siliguri, Darjeeling, West Bengal, 734013.

Sikha Chatterjee, Formerly Assistant Anthropologist of Anthropological Survey of India, Government of India, Eastern Regional Centre, Bidhan Nagar, Kolkata, West Bengal,700091.

Sovanjan Sarkar, Assistant Professor, Department of Anthropology, Vidyasagar University, Midnapore, West Bengal, India, 721102.

Sukanya Sharma, Professor, Department of Humanities, Indian Institute of Technology, Guwahati, Assam, 781039.

Sumahan Bandyopadhyay, Professor, Department of Anthropology, Vidyasagar University, Paschim Medinipur; West Bengal, 721102.

Tilak Bagchi, Formerly Assistant Keeper of Anthropological Survey of India, Western Regional Centre, Udaipur, Rajasthan, 313001.

Upala Barua, Formerly Associate Professor of Department of Anthropology, Cotton University, Panbazar, Guwahati, Assam, 781001.

Chapter - 1

J.P. Mills: An Administrator Who Pursued Anthropology as a Hobby

Monimugdha Bhuyan

Introduction

James Philip Mills, popularly known as J.P. Mills, was a noted architect of Indian Anthropology. He was a pioneer in undertaking remarkable anthropological investigations among the uncontacted tribal populations of Northeast India, particularly in the Naga Hills. James Philip was the younger son of Mr. James Edward Mills and Mrs. Ada Smith and was born on 18th February 1890 in Stockport city of Cheshire, United Kingdom. Mills started his early education in the public school at Winchester College, Hampshire, and later at Corpus Christi College of Oxford University, London. While reading the Greats at Oxfords, J.P. Mills had the opportunity to get introduced to Anthropology, as the diploma in Anthropology was initiated in Oxford in 1905, a few years before he began his degree studies (Jhala, 2019). In 1913, he joined the Indian Civil Service (ICS) and served as a colonial administrator in North-east India till 1947. In the year 1930, Mills was appointed as the Honorary Director of Ethnography of Assam. In the same year, he had established the nuptial knot with Pamela Vesey Fitzgerald. In 1942, the Royal Anthropological Institute (RAI) of Great Britain and Ireland conferred the prestigious Rivers Memorial Medal to J.P. Mills. This award was given in memory of the late President of RAI and renowned anthropologist W.H.R. Rivers for

Anthropological works in the field among the Nagas of Assam. Mills was also awarded a Gold Medal by the Asiatic Society of Bengal in 1945, for *Contributions to the Study of Cultural Anthropology in India* (Hobson, 2005:7).

After Mills retired from the Indian Civil Service in 1948, he left India and joined the School of Oriental and African Studies (SOAS) at the University of London. In SOAS, Mills was first appointed as Lecturer and later as Reader in Language and Culture with special reference to South-East Asia. The Department of Cultural Anthropology was initiated in SOAS in the year 1950, where he had the opportunity to work along with his old friend Christoph von Furer Haimendorf until his retirement in 1954, due to his ill health. Mills was elected to the Council of Royal Anthropological Institute in 1948 and served as its President from 1951 to 1953 (Hobson, 1996:1).

As an administrator

J.P. Mills started his career as a colonial administrator and got posted in Assam province of North-east India, after joining the Indian Civil Service (ICS) in 1913. In the year 1916, Mills was assigned as the Sub-divisional Officer (SDO) at Mokukchung of Naga Hills District of Assam (a former District of Assam province under British India) up to 1924, and then as the Assistant Commissioner. His close friend, J.H. Hutton was the Deputy Commissioner (DC) of the whole area based at Kohima at that period (Hobson, 1995). Around 1933, Mills was promoted to Deputy Commissioner of Naga Hill District and posted at Kohima, the administrative headquarters of Naga Hills. In 1943, he was appointed as the Advisor to the Governor for Tribal Areas and States with the overall responsibilities to handle the tribal matters of North-east India. This position enabled him to travel towards the Tibetan frontier and study tribal people, including the Mishmi, Dafla, and Apa Tani, living north of the Brahmaputra, then known as North East Frontier Agency (NEFA), now Arunachal Pradesh (Hobson, 2005:7). Mills could help his good friend Christoph von Furer Haimendorf, Ursula Graham-Bower, and her husband to enter those closed and politically sensitive areas that empower them to carry out many pioneering anthropological studies there (Hobson, 1996:1).

As an administrator, Mills never imposed alien western values on the local people; instead, he tried to understand the culture and values of the people he was appointed to administer. He realized that the strenuous assignment to administer the uncontacted tribal people could only be possible through the knowledge of Anthropology. Mills was able to gain the trust of the tribal people because he tried to understand their customary laws like that of the village elders. Even the punishments he executed were according to the tribal custom, like imposing a fine of *Mithun* (*Bos frontalis*). Because of his amicable nature, people approached Mills, with their cases to be heard, from distant areas, even from the territory beyond his administered boundary (Hobson, 2005:9). In the obituary of Mills, Haimendorf (1960:960) wrote about his sympathetic and non-bureaucratic approach to the Nagas and their problems that suited the administration of a loosely controlled frontier region to perfection.

Mills always tried to maintain a friendly relationship with the Naga village headman or the Chiefs. He believed that the Chiefs were an essential part of administering justice in the tribal disputes and also instrumental in protecting them from uncertain harms. In 1936, J.P. Mills carried out the famous Pangsha Expedition to abolish slavery in the Naga Hills when he was the Deputy Commissioner. Haimendorf also accompanied Mills in the expedition upon his invitation. This hazardous expedition was successful because Mills received enormous help from Chingmak, the Chief of Chingmei village of an inner unadministered area. Long before the expedition, Chingmak used to visit Mokukchung to meet Mills many times. Mills always received him with honour and respected his chiefly status. From that time, they were good friends. During Pangsha Expedition, Mills and his small force had to pass through Chingmei to rescue child slaves abducted by a truculent headhunting village called Pangsha. They could safely pass through Chingmei as his friend Chingmak, provided an escort of warriors to protect Mills and his companions throughout the expedition (Hobson, 2005:7; Mills, 1995).

The British annexation of the Chittagong Hill Tracts (now in Bangladesh) in 1860 resulted from prolonged disputes and fights over land between peasants of the plains and those of the hills and British tea planters. During the first decades of the 20th century, administration in the Chittagong Hill Tracts reached a critical state primarily because of the mismanagement of the Chiefs. This forced the government to transfer the collection of plough rent to their hand, which led the Chiefs to perceive becoming useless (Jhala, 2019). Colonial administrators were confronted with people of different ethnic origins who were unknown to them and where the administration tools employed in the plains failed. Civil servants in the administration realized this very soon and removed the area from the laws applicable to the plains of Bengal. J.P. Mills was assigned the duty to examine the Chittagong Hill Tracts and provide recommendations for running administration to Bengal Government. Mills went there in 1926 with a mission to bring the Chiefs under the demands of the British administration. In the beginning, Mills made an in-depth study of the Chiefs' history, status, privileges, and duties. There he toured almost five hundred miles on his foot and prepared his admirable and exhaustive report (Rizvi, 2003:65). Based on his experience of two months residence at the Hill Tracts, Mills recommended the Bengal Government how the Chiefs could be best utilized in the administration by assigning them a task in line with their status and history (Mey, 2009:16)

Anthropology as a hobby

J.P. Mills was an amateur in the field of Anthropology when he was posted in the Naga Hills as an administrative officer. However, he could make significant anthropological contributions, particularly during his Civil Service in India, only because of his hobby. In his Presidential Address to the Royal Anthropological Institute in 1953, entitled *Anthropology as Hobby,* Mills discussed the enthusiastic role of missionaries, travelers, and the administrators who had tried to record the people and their culture of the past. Those amateurs could accomplish such painstaking tasks without any formal knowledge of Anthropology because they considered Anthropology as their Hobby, even without knowing anything about the subject of Anthropology (Mills, 1953:1). J.P. Mills pursued the same hobby. He was a trained administrator but had chosen anthropology as his hobby during his extended stay among the tribal people of Naga Hills. According to

Mill (1953:1), as the amateur gardener has his pet flowers and methods, the same applies to anthropology. However, Mills pursued only Social Anthropology as his hobby and said that he was not competent to make Physical Anthropology his hobby. Regarding Archaeology, he mentioned that a person without proper training should never attempt to excavate a site (Mills: 1953:5).

A particular area is explored first by the travelers long before it is administered, and therefore their accounts are of great value, although scanty in volume. Exploration is an ongoing process, and after the travelers, the resident amateurs consisting of administrators and missionaries penetrate the untouched localities. Such contributions of the amateurs towards anthropology could not be overlooked as they unconsciously provide a base for the trained anthropologist to study such areas later on. Mills, therefore, mentioned about such amateurs in the same Presidential Address that, many of them came to, and lived in, distant lands in very early days and were able to record a way of life which had vanished or been profoundly modified by the time trained anthropologists were in the field to investigate it. Their accounts were often, and necessarily, incomplete and imperfect; but let us be profoundly thankful for them all the same. The pioneers and those who followed them have, let us remember, done valuable work by indicating, even if sometimes unconsciously, problems demanding study so that the trained anthropologist from home with limited time at his disposal can often go straight to a promising site, so to speak, and begin work at once without wasting weeks on a preliminary survey (*ibid*, 1953:2).

J.P. Mills believed that his service had provided him the privilege to spend a long duration among the people he studied. The trained anthropologist often lacked such opportunities as they had to face many hurdles like limited period, lack of wide choice of informants, etc., for their study. A resident overcomes such obstacles in the field as he has no time boundary and can include a wide range of informants. Such leisurely methods used by the amateur residents even helped them to collect and record their wide varieties of material culture. During his field tours, J.P. Mills collected a considerable amount of material culture specimens from the Naga villages and captured many beautiful photographs of them in their original milieu.

To fulfill the hobby of Anthropology, Mills mentioned his master key, which an amateur must use in the field and that is friendship, or more precisely, he said real friendship. According to Mills, the hobby brings you friends, and without friends, it cannot be properly pursued. Real mutual trust and confidence must be established, and if you show your interest in and appreciation of their institutions, your friends will in turn reveal to you their pride in them and tell you things you might not otherwise learn. Everywhere people are fully aware that the old ways of life are disappearing and your attitude, your genuine attitude, should be that of recording them not only for scholars at home but also for the community among which you are working, that the memory of them may be preserved when those who lived in them are gone. If you adopt this attitude and it is understood, as quickly is, your work does not lose in care and accuracy (1953:3).

As an ethnographer

J.P. Mills was a magnificent ethnographer who had contributed notable ethnographies of the lesser-known tribes of North-east India. Although he was an administrator, he always tried to study the culture of the people he was assigned to administer. Mills is best known for his three classic monographs written on three different Naga tribes. His first monograph entitled *The Lotha Nagas* was published in 1922, by the Government of Assam. When Mills was working as the Assistant Commissioner at Mokukchung of Naga Hills, for three years, he had the opportunity to acquaint himself with the customs and habits of the Lotha people. With the continuous encouragement and advice received from J.H. Hutton, one of his close friends and then the Deputy Commissioner of Naga Hills and the Director of Ethnography of Assam, Mills could complete his monograph on the Lotha Nagas. J.H. Hutton had also penned the preface of the book. Mills elaborately discussed the domestic life of the Lothas, who were a sedentary group cultivating rice through *jhum* cultivations. They were also good at spinning and making pottery. He also discussed their house type, including the youth dormitory *morung*, their customary laws, religion, folktales, songs, and language. The second monograph on Nagas by J.P. Mills was *The Ao Nagas,* published in

1926. He collected data for this book during his stay at Mokukchung as the Sub-divisional Officer (Vidyarthi, 1978:64). The pattern of writing this monograph was similar to that of Lotha Nagas. Beginning with the basic introduction of the people, Mills discussed their domestic life, laws and customs, religion, language and folktales, and folksongs. Henry Balfour of Pitts River Museum wrote the foreword of the monograph, who had the privilege to have an extended tour of Naga Hills with Mills in 1922. In this monograph, Mills tried critically to examine the changing aspects of the Ao pristine culture due to the impact of Baptist Missionaries. He was one of the first to record the peoples' reactions regarding the changes in their traditional culture (Vidyarthi, 1978:66). His third and last monograph on the Naga tribe was *The Rengma Nagas* published in 1937. The Government of Assam published this monograph, and by that time, Mills was the Honorary Director of Ethnography of Assam. This monograph was also written in the same style as the two other monographs on Nagas. However, in this monograph, Mills tried to make a comparative study of the same group, living in two different settings (Vidyarthi, 1978:66).

Besides these three classic monographs, Mills had published numerous short papers on the Naga tribes. Among them, a few significant articles are *Certain Aspects of Naga Culture*, published in the *Journal of the Royal Anthropological Institute of Great Britain and Ireland* in 1926; *Among the Head-Hunters of Naga Hills* published in the journal *Sphere* in 1926; *Folk Stories in Lotha Nagas* published in the *Journal and the Proceeding of the Asiatic Society of Bengal* in 1926; *The Naga Head-hunters of Assam* published in the *Journal of the Royal Central Asian Society* in 1935; *The effects of Rituals upon Industries and Arts in the Naga Hills* published in the journal *Man* in 1935 and *Lotha Naga Apotia Death* published in the *Journal of Indian Anthropological Institute* in 1938.

Mills had also given celebrated Presidential addresses to the Royal Anthropological Institute like *Mishimis of Lohit Valley* in 1952 and *Anthropology as Hobby* in 1953, which got published in the *Journal of the Royal Anthropological Institute* in the same year respectively. He had even contributed ethnographic notes of different tribes in the *Census of India 1931*, edited by J.H. Hutton in 1935 (Rizvi, 2003:73).

While Mills was on tour, he always used to write tour diaries and letters. These tour diaries and letters were of great value, which contained critical ethnographic pieces of information. Many letters of J.P. Mills, primarily written to J.H. Hutton and Henry Balfour, are now preserved in the Cambridge University Library archive and can be digitally accessed by browsing: https: // www. lib.cam.ac.uk /nagas/ coll/18/ records/ list/ coll/ index.html. The letters written to his wife during the Pangsha Expedition were published in 1995, by the Pitt Rivers Museum of Oxford in the form of a book entitled *The Pangsha Letters: An Expedition to Rescue Slaves in Naga Hills* with an introduction by his daughter Geraldine Hobson.

As a collector of museum specimens

Mills had another hobby, or rather, he would like to say it as a sub-hobby, of collecting unique material culture specimens (Mills, 1953:5). His friend Henry Balfour, a British archaeologist and the first curator of Pitt Rivers Museum of Oxford University, greatly influenced this hobby. The material culture specimens collected by Mills from Naga Hills contributed a rich treasure to many museums, like the Pitt Rivers Museum, the British Museum, and the Museum of Archaeology and Anthropology of Cambridge University. Pitt Rivers Museum was set up in Oxford University in 1884, by Augustus Pitt Rivers, primarily for displaying archaeological and anthropological objects. The collection of Pitt Rivers Museum significantly increased during the curatorship of Henry Balfour (1891-1939), who managed to increase the initial museum specimens from fifteen thousand to one million (White, 1994: 493). During Mill's administrative posting in the Naga Hills, he had collected excellent material culture specimens and carefully sent them to the Pitt Rivers Museum. Based on the collection of J.P. Mills and that of J.H. Hutton, Balfour developed a specific corner in the museum devoted exclusively to Naga artifacts. Mills contributed more than two thousand objects for the Pitts River Museum, out of which 89 were collected during his visit to Chittagong Hill Tracts (Mey, 2009:23).

According to Mills (1953:5), museums across the globe are highly indebted to amateur collectors. As an amateur collector, it was not easy for Mills to collect the valuable objects from the people of an alien culture, where he was administratively posted. However, he could overcome this hurdle due to his elaborate friend circle. Mills mentioned that the number and variety of material objects you are likely to see is directly related to the size of the circle of friends and acquaintances. Usually, people of a community keep most of their possessions in a very natural manner in their houses instead of exposing them to outsiders. To go indoors and access such possessions, one must be a friend of the owner or maybe with the person with whom you are approaching. Usually, amateur collectors of museum objects rarely label their specimens collected. Mills, along with Hutton, was very particular in this case, who meticulously labeled every specimen they had collected for museum display (Hobson, 1996:4).

As an ethnographic photographer

J.P. Mills was an extraordinary photographer. More precisely, he may be called an ethnographic photographer due to his unique skill of capturing momentous ethnographic photographs. Mills captured a significant amount of black and white photographs of the tribal groups and their material culture during his service in North-east India. His photographs documented a way of life of the people that had vanished long back (Hobson, 2005:10). Mills monumental monographs on the Nagas consist of numerous photographs of the people, their dress and ornaments, house type, implements, tattoos, rituals and festivals, and many more aspects of their material culture. He preferred to take long tours of his administrative regions and loved visiting the houses of the natives. Because of his friendly relationships with the many local inhabitants, he was always welcomed into their homes. This has allowed him to capture photographs even of their rare material culture, which would never be available to a stranger (Hobson, 1996:4).

Henry Balfour was one of the first curators to realise the significant value of still photographs in museums to study tribal people and their material culture (Hobson, 1996:4). Balfour always encouraged the researchers and collectors to capture still images along with the collection of objects as much as possible. In her book *World on a Glass Plate* (1981), Elizabeth Edwards mentioned that the value of still photographs lies in their preservation of moments in time. They can be referred to again and again for the information, perhaps now lost, about the details of a particular group of people and their culture, showing how objects were made and used, the environment of the people who made them, the relationships between the sexes and age groups, their use of space (as cited by Hobson, 1996:5).

As a close friend of Balfour, J.P. Mills was highly influenced by him to capture still photographs of the material culture specimens he had collected, particularly for Pitts River Museum. Twenty-four photo albums and two boxes containing loose photographs, captured by J.P. Mills, along with negatives, are still preserved in the library of School of Oriental and African Studies (SOAS) Archives, University of London. These still photographs lucidly depict the life ways of the Naga people, which disappeared long before. The photos primarily include the daily life activities of the Nagas, their festival, and rituals, material culture, including dress and ornaments. Mills had even taken photographs associated with head-hunting of the Nagas, which now become obsolete; however, when Mills documented such photographs, head-hunting was a part of the culture of many Naga tribes (Hobson, 1996:5). In many cases, Mills had taken photographs of the Naga material culture along with its original owner or, in some cases, with his friends. These photographs are now digitally preserved at SOAS digital archives and are accessed by browsing: http: // digital. soas. ac. uk /LOAA 005302 / 00001.

Conclusion

J.P. Mills was a great illustration of an anthropologist in the form of an administrator. At a very early age, he was compelled to live far away from his home, in the isolated areas of North-east India, after joining the Indian Civil Service. However, he fully utilized his long thirty-year stay in the Naga Hills by engaging himself in studying the culture of the uncontacted tribal groups. Mills considered anthropology as his hobby, and in pursuing his hobby, he had made many significant anthropological contributions. He considered himself privileged for his Indian Civil Service because of which he could carry out his anthropological research as a resident, without any time limit and with multiple choices of informants. His hobby even helped him to administer the tribal groups in many critical situations. Mills was a versatile person who had collected a considerable amount of Naga material culture specimens and captured many ethnographic photographs. J.P. Mills will always be remembered for his tireless efforts to document the Naga cultures, which changed with time.

Mills had to pay a heavy price for spending a long period of his life in the hills of North-east India during his service. He used to go on long tours and had to spend nights in tents. This has caused him to suffer frequently from malaria and other tropical diseases. Deadly malaria had not only affected Mills, but even his elder daughter Philippa also died of malaria at the tender age of fifteen. After he retired from the School of Oriental and African Studies (SOAS) in 1954, Mills suffered many health complications and succumbed to heart disease on 12th May 1960.

References

Edwards, E. 1981. *World on a Glass Plate*. Pitt Rivers Museum, University of Oxford.

Haimendorf, CV. 1960. Obituary: James Philip Mills, C.S.I., C.I.E. 1890-1960, *The Geographical Journal*, 126, 3: 380-381.

Hobson, G. 1995. Introduction In J.P. Mills: *The Pangsha Letters: An Expedition to Rescue Slaves in the Naga Hills*. The Pitt Rivers Museum, University of Oxford.

Hobson, G. 1996. *J.P. Mills Photographic Collection: A Descriptive Catalogue of the J.P. Mills Photographic Collection in the Library of School of Oriental and African Studies*. Retrieved on 10th November 2021 from https://digital.soas.ac.uk/AA00000033/00001.

Hobson, G. 2009. Foreword In Mey Wolfgang: *J.P. Mills, and the Chittagong Hill Tracts, 1926/27, Tour Dairy, Reports, and Photographs*. Retrieved on 15th November 2021 from https://crossasia-repository.ub.uni-heidelberg.de/548/. DOI: 10.11588/xarep.00000548

Jhala, AD. 2019. *An Endangered History: Indigeneity, Religion, and Politics on the Borders of India, Burma, and Bangladesh*. New Delhi, Oxford University Press.

Mey, Wolfgang, 2009. *J.P. Mills and the Chittagong Hill Tracts, 1926/27, Tour Dairy, Reports and Photographs*. Retrieved on 15th November 2021 from https://crossasia-repository.ub.uni-heidelberg.de/548/.DOI: 10.11588/xarep.00000548

Mills, JP. 1922. *The Lotha Nagas*. London, MacMillan and Co. Ltd.

Mills, JP. 1926. Among the head-hunters of the Naga Hills. *Sphere*, February.

Mills, JP. 1926. Certain aspects of Naga culture, *The Journal of the Royal Anthropological Institute of Great Britain and Ireland*, 56: 27-36.

Mills, JP. 1926. Folk stories in Lotha Naga. *Journal and the proceeding of the Asiatic Society of Bengal,* New Series 22: 235-318.

Mills, JP. 1926. *The Ao Nagas*. London, MacMillan and Co. Ltd.

Mills, JP. 1935. The effects of rituals upon industries and arts in the Naga Hills, *Man*, 35: 132-135.

Mills, JP. 1935. The Naga head-hunters of Assam. *Journal of the Royal Central Asian Society*, 22,3: 418-428.

Mills, JP. 1937. *The Rengma Nagas*. London, MacMillan and Co. Ltd.

Mills, JP. 1938. A Lotha Naga 'Apotia' Death. *Journal of the Indian Anthropological Institute*. 1: 23-27.

Mills, JP. 1952. The Mishmis of the Lohit Valley, Assam. *The Journal of the Royal Anthropological Institute of Great Britain and Ireland*, 82,1: 1–12. https://doi.org/10.2307/2844036

Mills JP. 1953. Anthropology as a hobby, *The Journal of the Royal Anthropological Institute of Great Britain and Ireland*. 83, 1: 1-8.

Mills, JP., and Mukhopadhyay, S. 1987. *Folk Stories in Lhota Naga*. New Delhi, Gyan Publishing House.

Mills JP. 1995. *The Pangsha Letters: An Expedition to Rescue Slaves in the Naga Hills*. The Pitt Rivers Museum, University of Oxford.

Rizvi, BR. 2003. J.P. Mills and the North East In T.B. Subba and G.C. Ghosh (Eds.): *The Anthropology of North-East India*, New Delhi, Orient Longman Pvt. Ltd.

Vidyarthi, LP. 1978. *Rise of Anthropology in India,* Vol.1. Delhi, Concept Publishing Company.

White, C. 1994. Museums and art galleries. In H. Brain (Ed.): *The History of the University of Oxford,* Vol. VIII, New York, Oxford University Press.

Chapter – 2

Dr. Biraja Sankar Guha

Nabakumar Duary

A hundred years of celebration of the teaching of Anthropology in India is a very auspicious occasion. In this context, the name of Dr. Biraja Sankar Guha is very significant and relevant. Dr. Guha was founder Director of the Anthropological Survey of India. Dr. Guha devoted his entire life to institutionalising Anthropology and its development. He is remembered all over the world for his academic brilliance, pioneering anthropological studies, and administrative capabilities. Dr. Guha was born on 15 August 1884 in a respectable, renowned, and distinguished Kayastha family in the then Shillong, capital of Assam. His nickname was Makhan. Biraja Sankar was the second child among ten children of *Dharmaprana-Ratnagarbha* Srimati, Khirodabala (Ghosh), and Rai Bahadur Abhayshankar Guha, a renowned civilian of Assam. His ancestral house is named '*Guha Lodge*' located at Pan Bazar in Guwahati. During the mid-seventeenth century, Guha's forefathers came from Daulatpur in Khulna district of East Pakistan to Assam and their surname was Guha Majumder. Dr. Guha married Labanyaprabha (Das) in December 1920 and after her sudden sad demise he married Uma (Bose) on 28th May 1931 and they have four children namely, Aloke Sankar, Bhaskar Sankar, Rupal Sankar, and Alta (Ahmed).

II

The intellectual excellence of Biraja Sankar was marked since his childhood. He secured the first position in the *Praveshika*

Examination in 1908 at Cotton Collegiate School in Gauhati. In 1910, he passed IA from City College, Calcutta in the first division. In 1912, he passed BA with honours in Philosophy from Presidency College, Calcutta. He passed a Post-Graduation degree in Mental and Moral Philosophy from the University of Calcutta in 1915. Thereafter, he started teaching Sociology and Philosophy in Cotton College, Guwahati as well as in Bangabasi College, Calcutta from 1915 to 1916. The names of his principal teachers were Dr. A.N. Mukherjee and Sri Brajendra Nath Seal, a renowned Indian humanist philosopher of Bengal. He also had the opportunity to the association of Sir Asutosh Mookerjee, Sir Jagadish Chandra Bose, Sri Ramaprasad Chanda, Sri Prasanta Chandra Mahalanabis, Sri Suniti Kumar Chatterjee, and many other stalwarts of that time. At that time, he gradually became interested in indigenous people and archaeology. In 1917, he did anthropological fieldwork for the first time on the Khasis of Meghalaya under the Government of Bengal Research Scholarship. In 1920, he worked with Professor R. B. Dixon of Harvard University under the prestigious Hamenway Fellowship. Later he did a Master's degree with distinction in Anthropology from Harvard University. He was the 14th recipient of a Ph.D. in Anthropology in the year 1924 from Harvard University for his research on '*The Racial Basis of the Caste System of India*' under Professor Dixon. He was awarded the Winthrop Scholarship from the same university in 1925.

III

The scholastic aptitude of Dr. Guha earned several fellowships from India and abroad. Like two years of research fellow in anthropology in India; he carried out an ethnological investigation on behalf of the American Bureau of Ethnology during the summer of 1921. He studied foreign languages like Germany and French. He was a Research Associate in the Natural History Museum, Boston and New York; Museum of Anthropology, Colorado, and Bureau of Ethnology of the Smithsonian Institute, Washington in 1922-24 and carried out field investigations in Red Indian Reservations of Colorado and New Mexico. Harvard University provided him with a Teaching

Assistant in Anthropology from 1923-24. In 1924, Dr. Guha read a paper in the Anthropology Section of the American Association for the Advancement of Science by special invitation. Harvard University awarded him the Winthrop Scholarship in 1925.

IV

Dr. B.S. Guha is considered to be the first person trained in professional physical anthropology in India. In 1926, he joined the Anthropology Department (Estd.1920), the University of Calcutta as a lecturer. Then he was permanently appointed as an Anthropologist and Sectional in-Charge of the Anthropological Section of the Zoological Survey of India in June 1927 by the then Director Dr. Seymour Sewell. During 1926-27, he was entrusted by the Government to do an anthropological investigation of the elimination of practices of human sacrifice in the Naga Hill region near the Burma border. Dr. Guha served as Anthropologist in the Census Commission of India on deputation (1930-33). During that time, he reached up the pinnacle of worldwide fame with the results of the 1931 Census for scientific measurements and observations. In his concept of Indian Races, he classified the Indian population into six major racial types, namely Negrito, Proto-Australoid, Mongoloid, Mediterranean, Western Brachycephalic, and Nordic. Dr. B.R. Ambedkar, the father of the Indian Constitution once wrote – Guha's explanation of racial classification in India is more authentic than Risley's work.

V

Dr. Guha's vision was to establish a separate anthropological institution of excellence. He proposed to the Government of India on December 30th, 1944 to fulfill his vision. He was supported by Dr. Seymour Sewell and then retired Director of Zoological Survey of India, Dr. Nelson Annandale. To protect valuable collections from the attack of the Second World War, the Zoological Survey of India was shifted from Calcutta to Varanasi at Kaizer Cassel, 64 Cantonment on the bank of river Baruna on 11th May 1942. The Anthropological Survey of India was established on 1st December 1945, as a separate entity from the Zoological Survey of India, in the same building with only 6 employees. A separate library was set up with 1039 books. Here he developed a friendship with Sarvapalli Radhakrishnan, the then Vice-Chancellor of Banaras Hindu University. On 13 April 1944, he delivered a radio talk on *Culture Contact* which was broadcast by All India Radio, Lucknow.

On 1st August 1946, he was appointed as the Director of Anthropological Survey of India with an additional assignment of Anthropological Advisor to the Government. Dr. Verrier Elwin was appointed Deputy Director on 17th October 1946. In January 1948, the Anthropological Survey of India was renamed as Department of Anthropology. In May 1948, the office was transferred to the Indian Museum Building, Calcutta. In the wake of interdisciplinary work, several sections, such as Morphology, Human Biology, Osteology, Psychology, Cultural Anthropology, Physical Anthropology, Ancient Human skeletal remains Repository, Radiology, Bio-Chemistry, Linguistics, Statistics, Photography, Cinematography and sound section were started. Additionally, an independent printing press was established in 1950 and began publishing Bi-annual Bulletin in 1952.

His endeavour resulted in appointing the first Travelling Fellow and Foreign Fellows like Professor Lidio Cipriani from Italy in 1950, Dr. Chi Nakane a Japanese Scholar, and Dr. E.C. Buchi, from Zurich University, joined Department of Anthropology on invitation from Dr. Guha. They contributed substantially to imparting training of fieldwork and laboratory work to young physical and cultural anthropology scholars for three years. He organized a multidisciplinary research team number of times; as team members work in different aspects of a particular society. He started such a kind of multidisciplinary study among the Abors during 1948-1952. Dr. Guha had done fieldwork amongst the American Indians and Red Kaffier. He had also studied various indigenous tribal groups like Khasi, Jaunswar Bawar, Garo, Riang, Kaipeng, Uchai, Rankhol as well as different tribal groups in North-Eastern India and Andaman and the Nicobar Islands. Concerned by the refugee problems in Bengal, Dr. Guha worked on a project titled Social tension among East Bengal Refugees with Professor Gardner Murphy of UNESCO in1952.

Dr. Guha opened the first Sub-Station of the Department of Anthropology in two rooms of the Cellular Jail at Port Blair in

December 1951. The Sub-Station in North-eastern Frontier Area was opened at Shillong in May 1953. To portray the cultural heritage of India Dr. Guha collected ethnographic artifacts from people, particularly the tribes, and arranged to preserve and display them for the public in a meaningful way through museums. His collections as collections made during his tenure in Anthropological Survey of India/ Department of Anthropology from 1945-1954 from areas like the then Abor Hills (present Upper and Lower Siang districts of Arunachal Pradesh), Jaunsar-Bawar of Western Himalaya, erstwhile Travancore-Cochin States (present-day Kerala State), Andaman and Nicobar Islands and some other states of India.

Dr. Guha established the Ethnographic Museum at Calcutta in 1952. The Port Blair museum started with the rare exclusive artifacts of the Onges. In all, he collected 744 artifacts of 31 types. One such artifact was 'Wooden effigy of the Khalash of Hindukush' which is worth mentioning. Perceiving the importance of music in the lives of the tribals, he documented it on a double-sided gramophone disc. He also made two silent documentary films – *Abor of NEFA* and *Abor Dance*.

Dr. B.S. Guha collaborated with the Archaeological Survey of India on the excavation of the megalithic monuments at Sampur, Mound, and Maski of the Hyderabad state during 1950-1951. He emphasised upon research and study of prehistoric, proto-historic, and ancient human skeletal remains to unfold the mystery of racial heritage and biological relationship of the contemporary population of India. He made untiring efforts for procuring ancient and contemporary human skeletal remains and under his able guidance, the Anthropological Survey of India emerged as a custodian of this important biological heritage of our country. A notable collection of human remains of his time in from the Mohenjo-Daro, Harappa, Nal, Bayana, Makran, Sialk, Taxila, and other such areas. He was instrumental in collecting samples of ancient human skeletal remains from the Chalcolithic to Historical era, from India and neighbouring countries. From this repository, he scientifically tried to understand the complexities of the ethnic composition of the people of India.

Dr. Guha's publications provide a testimony of his vast knowledge and varied interest and some of them are a landmark in the history of anthropological research. He had great contributions in the progress of Anthropological Research in India, in Anthropological Problems, Racial Ethnology, Affinities, Stone age, Indus valley civilization, Aboriginal population, Tribal welfare, nation-building to Nationality and various others aspects.

VI

Dr. B.S. Guha was the President of the anthropology section of the Indian Science Congress twice - in 1928 and 1938. He was closely associated with the Asiatic Society. He became the council member and Anthropological Secretary and first Indian Honorary General Secretary from 1931 to 1942. He received Annandale Gold Medal from the Asiatic Society for his fundamental works in Anthropology. He became a trustee of the Bose Research Institute, Calcutta in 1931. From 1934 to 1939, he became a Fellow of the Royal Anthropological Institute; Treasurer of the National Institute of Science. He became a permanent member of the Council of the International Congress of Anthropology and a member of the research committee for the Standardization of Anthropological Methods of the International Congress of Anthropology. He was also the founder member and Honorary Secretary of the Indian Anthropological Institute in Calcutta. He was the Vice-president of Adimjati Sevak Sangh in Delhi and was attached with many other professional bodies in India and abroad. He was attached as an Editor and Executive member of several journals and bulletins in India and abroad namely *Bulletin of the Department of Anthropology, Bulletin of the Bihar Tribal Research Institute, Mankind Quarterly, Homo, Journal of the Indian Anthropological Institute,* and *The Anthropologists*. He took a special interest in creating separate departments for Anthropology at Delhi University and Gauhati University.

Other than anthropological work, Dr. Guha would also visit the house of famous Bengali writer Rajsekhar Basu (Parasuram) at 14, Parshibagan Lane, Calcutta for *adda* i.e. rendezvous. There were many famous people gathered over there in *adda* were eminent historian Acharya Jadunath Sarkar, writers Prabhat Kumar Mukhopadhyay, Sarat Chandra Chattopadhyay, prominent archaeologist Rakhaldas

Bandyopadhyay, Professor of linguistics Suniti Kumar Chattopadhyay, artist Purnachandra Ghosh, Pulinchandra Kundu, and others. This association indicates the intellectual position and interaction level of Dr. Guha. Sometimes he earned ideas through the typical constructive *adda.*

VII

Dr. B.S. Guha retired from the post of Director of the Department of Anthropology on 31st July 1954. After his retirement, he was actively engaged in anthropological research under the government of India's Retired Scientist Scheme. Dr. Guha took over as the Director of Bihar Tribal Research Institute at Ranchi. Dr. Guha was the ex-officio advisor of the Indian Government in Tribal Welfare. On 20th October 1961, when Dr. Guha was returning from Calcutta to Ranchi after a meeting of the Anthropology Advisory Committee, he met with a tragic train accident near Ghatsila and died on spot. The news of his untimely death spread widely across the nation through print media and radio. The Anthropological fraternity deeply mourned the great loss of a towering Anthropological personality. The condolence meeting was held at Rammohan Hall in Calcutta, on 5th November 1961. Obituaries were published in several reputed national and international anthropological journals. Some of the opinions about Dr. Guha are worth mentioning –

Dr. D.K. Sen wrote - *His death removes one of the chief architects of Indian anthropology.*

N.K. Bose wrote - *By his death, the society has thus lost a distinguished fellow and an outstanding scientist.*

Sri Kanaklal Barua, the famous historian wrote - *Guha is a scholar of international repute.*

Verrier Elwin and C.S. Coon had written - *Dr. B.S. Guha as an architect of 20th Century Indian Anthropology.*

VIII

The year 1994 was observed by the Anthropological Survey of India as the Birth Centenary Celebration of Dr. Biraja Sankar Guha (1884-1961), the founder Director of this Survey. The occasion was celebrated through several academic exercises like exhibitions, seminars, and memorial lectures on B.S. Guha and publication of books. The Asiatic Society, Calcutta, brought out a publication *The Asiatic Society and Anthropological Studies in India* in 1994. A book *Anthropology of B.S. Guha* was published by the Anthropological Survey of India in 1996. A Lecture Hall was named after him in the Dehradun office of the Anthropological Survey of India. A silver medal is awarded in memory of Dr. B.S. Guha by the Department of Anthropology, Guwahati University, Assam. The Indian Anthropological Society and Anthropology Department of Visva-Bharati jointly organized a National Conference and seminar on the occasion of the Birth Centenary Celebration of Dr. B. S. Guha from 10-12 December 1994 at Shantiniketan, Birbhum. A one-day seminar on B.S. Guha was organized by the Asiatic Society and the Indian Anthropological Society titled *Biraja Sankar Guha: His Contributions towards Development of Multidimensional Approach in Indian Anthropology* on 29th March 2017.

125th Birth Anniversary of Dr. B.S. Guha was celebrated by the Indian Anthropological Society, Kolkata on 15th August 2019. Dr. Nabakumar Duary, made a documentary titled *Untiring Mind: Life and Anthropological Journey of Dr. B. S. Guha* on his 125th Birth Anniversary and celebration of the centenary year of teaching in anthropology in India (Duary 2019: 177-179). This film was released on 14th October 2019 by Professor Sarit K. Choudhuri, former Director of Indira Gandhi Rashtriya Manav Sangralaya, Professor Barun Mukhopadhyay, and Professor Vijoy S. Sahay in Vivekananda Auditorium of Vinoba Bhave University, Hazaribag, Jharkhand on the occasion of 49th Annual Conference of the Indian Anthropological Society.

An unexplored tale in Indian Anthropology is like that in 1936, Lithuanian traveler and Anthropologist Antanas Paskevicius Poska submitted his Ph. D. thesis to the Calcutta University under Dr. B.S. Guha. The title of the thesis was – *Physical Affinities of Shin Speaking People of the Western Himalayas*. On 28th November 2014, Poska was conferred honorary D. Litt. (Posthumously) by Sri Keshari Nath Tripathi, the then Governor of West Bengal and Chancellor of the University of Calcutta; Sri Pranab Mukherjee, the then President of

India, was also present at the occasion. The certificate of D. Litt. was received by Poska's daughter Laimute Poskaite Antanas Poska in the University Convocation of 2014 (Duary, 2019:211-214).

IX

Dr. Biraja Shankar Guha had dedicated his entire life to the development of Anthropology. His anthropological researches were multidimensional; practically cover both depth and magnitude. Recognition for his works and appreciation of his zeal, about anthropology, have been made by scholars, both from India and abroad. He was, perhaps, the only personality with whose sole endeavour the Anthropological Survey of India was established. It is not merely the foundation of an institute, but he also made all efforts for proper organization of research activities. As an academician, Dr. Guha executed his research thinking in a well-planned and organized manner with the help of a group of scholars. The intellectual journey of Dr. Guha is indeed remarkable. As an academician, Dr. Guha will be remembered in the world of Anthropology for his pioneering research and establishment of the world's largest anthropological research institute. Indian Anthropology cannot afford to forget Dr. Biraja Sankar Guha.

Acknowledgement

I express my sincere gratitude to Dr. Jayata Kumar Sarkar, former Director in Charge of the Anthropological Survey of India for his suggestions to write this chapter and also grateful to Alta Ahmed, daughter, and Shri Rabindra Sankar Guha, nephew of Dr. B.S. Guha for giving time for taking interview on Br. B.S. Guha during April-May, 2017.

References

Barua, Kanaklal 1973. *Studies in the Early History of Assam*, pp.318. Assam Sahitya Sabha, Jorhat-Gauhati, Assam.

Basu, Rajsekhar. 1992. *Parasuramer Galpa Samagra*, pp.15, M.C. Sarkar and Sons Private Limited, Calcutta (First publication 1969).

Bhattacharya, RK and Sarkar Jayanta 1996. *Anthropology of B.S.Guha*, Edited volume, Anthropological Survey of India, Kolkata.

Bose, NK.1962 (1961). *Year Book of The Asiatic Society*, IV:150.

Das Gupta, BK.2007. Biraja Sankar Guha, *Anthropological Perspectives*, Creative Data Centre, Kolkata.

Duary, Nabakumar 2019. Untiring mind: A documentary film on Dr. B.S. Guha, *South Asian Anthropologist*, 19, 2:177-179.

Duary, Nabakumar 2019. Poska, and Biraja Sankar Guha: An unexplored tale in Indian Anthropology, *Anthropos India*, 5, 2:211-214.

Duary, Nabakumar 2019. *Untiring mind: Biraja Sankar Guha - Life and contribution in Anthropology,* Documentary, Memorywala Production, Kolkata.

Elwin, Verrier 1948. The Anthropological Survey of India, Part-I, History and Recent Development, *Man*, 78 -79: 68-69.

Elwin, Verrier 1951. Dr. B. S. Guha, *Illustrated Weekly of India*, 25 November 1951.

Elwin, Verrier 1948. Department of Anthropology, Government of India, *American Anthropologist*, N.S.50:576-581.

Ghosh, RR.1993. Biraja Sankar Guha, *Biographical Memories of Fellows of The Indian National Science Academy*, Vol.17, pp.1-8. Indian National Science Academy, New Delhi.

Institute for Research 1948. *World Biography-Biographical Encyclopedia of the World* Biography International Biographical Encyclopedia-1945, 3rd Edition.

Kundu, KK. 1994. Ananya Biraja Sankar, *Desh* (Bengali magazine), Year 61, No. 24 Calcutta (24th September 1994, pp. 41-50).

Majumdar, DN.1953. India, Pakistan and Ceylon, *International Directory of Anthropological Institutions,* Edited by William L.Thomas, Jr and Anna M. Pikelis, Wenner-Gren Foundation for Anthropological Research, Incorporated, New York.

Sen, DK.1962. Biraja Sankar Guha 1894-1961, *Eastern Anthropologist,* 15, 2 : 170-171.

Sen, Dharani 1974. Proceeding of the Seminar on *Indian Anthropology Today,* Department of Anthropology, Calcutta University, Calcutta.

Syamchaudhuri, NK., and Ray Shyamal Kumar 1973. The growth of faculty of Anthropology in the University of Calcutta, *Bulletin of the Anthropological Survey of India*, XXII, 1and2: 1-85.

The Asiatic Society 1994. *The Asiatic Society and Anthropological Studies in India.* This publication is dedicated to the memory of Biraja Sankar Guha on the occasion of his Birth Centenary, The Asiatic Society, Kolkata.

Zoological Survey of India 2016. *Souvenir,* Zoological Survey of India Hundred Years Celebration-1916-2016, Kolkata.

Chapter – 3

Contribution of Prof. Kshitish Prasad Chattopadhyay to Anthropology in India

Sumahan Bandyopadhyay

Works and contributions of Kshitish Prasad Chattopadhyay to the anthropology in India in its constructive period should be evaluated in the perspective of a discipline in connection with the social relevance and identity of its own suited to a soil where it was then newly planted as an academic subject. This evaluative is particularly warrants since we know that Professor Chattopadhyay had training at the University of Cambridge under the guidance of W.H.R. Rivers. Though he followed his illustrious teacher to a certain extent, yet we can well discern that he carved a niche for himself through his anthropological studies which were quite different from that of his master. He was very much a nationalist anthropologist in the sense that he consciously attempted to use his anthropological understanding to the nation-building and in solving the burning problems the country was facing (Chattopadhyay, 2000; Guha, 2020). The terms of praise as Sarkar used for him as '...pioneering, path-breaking Anthropologist, a dedicated educationist and a courageous defender of Civil Liberties...' seem quite justified when we try to analyze his life and works (Sarkar, 2000). In the following discussion, I shall attempt to map his intellectual journey along with political activism with an unfailing eagerness to know the cardinal points of his contributions to anthropology. Endeavour is also made to see whether his contribution was only academic or its implications rest far beyond. Moreover, we should know how his anthropological approach was connected with colonial forms of knowledge and its creations. Therefore, the present paper is not just a biographical sketch, rather it is a modest to evaluate the life and works of a *dramatis personae* of Indian Anthropology, Professor Kshitish Prasad Chattopadhyay.

Family background and education

Kshitish Prasad was born on 15 December 1898 in Kolkata to an illustrious family of Bengal having lineages with two great renaissance personalities – Pandit Iswar Chandra Vidyasagar on the maternal side and Raja Rammohan Roy on father's side. His father Jamini Mohan Chattopadhyay was the great-grandson of Chandrajyoti Devi who was a granddaughter of Rammohan Roy. Motimala Chattopadhyay, mother of Kshitish Prasad was the granddaughter of Iswar Chandra Vidyasagar. Kshitish stood seventh in the Matriculation examination in 1913 and stood first in the I.Sc. Examination (nowadays equivalent to Higher Secondary) in Science stream in 1915. He was indeed a brilliant student and got first-class in Physics from Presidency College in 1917 (Sengupta and Basu,1960). Kshitish did not have any plan initially to study anthropology when he went to Cambridge in 1919. His goal was to study Physics under J.J. Thompson, the Nobel laureate physicist who discovered the first sub-atomic particle electron. In Cambridge, Subhas Chandra Bose, Dilip Kumar Roy, and Kshitish Prasad were close friends. During this time, Kshitish was drawn to anthropology under the influence of W.H.R. Rivers. It was a curious case that made this change in Kshitish. W.H.R. Rivers was a Praelector of Natural Science Studies at St. John's College, Cambridge at that time. In this role, Rivers used to meet the students freely and to hold informal and formal talks before them. It may be conjectured that Kshitish came in contact with Rivers in any of such interactions and was moved by the personality of Rivers. He was quite amiable and kind-hearted man. Moreover, Rivers had a socialist-leaning. He was being slated for a Labour candidature in British Parliament and could have been a member of the parliament not passed away untimely. All these factors might have some influence on the choice of anthropology in Cambridge and his later life as an academician and activist.

Kshitish won Anthony Wilkins Fellowship to do research in Anthropology after getting a postgraduate degree from Cambridge University in 1922. When he was planning to work on the Newar of Nepal, but he could not start as his fellowship was withdrawn. It is held that he was denied the fellowship for his sympathies for the Indian seamen in London and suspected communist leanings (Guha, 2020; Sarkar, 2000). He planned to carry out his research on the Newar of Nepal. But the colonial British government did not permit him to go there since he was suspected to have communist connections. However, he wrote about this incidence that the Nepal Government refused to give him necessary permission (Chattopadhyay, 1935). He participated in Congress-led Civil Disobedience movement and was on good terms with Mahatma Gandhi, at the same time C.R. Das preferred him very much and Subhas Chandra Bose was his friend. He had also shown his close comradeship with the leftist groups as well. He accepted the post of President of Pradeshik Krishak Sabha and also organized people's relief committee campaigns. Later he was elected as an independent member of the assembly with support from the left.

After his return from London, he was appointed as a lecturer in the newly established department of anthropology in the University of Calcutta at the behest of the then Vice-Chancellor Ashutosh Mukhopadhyay in 1923. But he had to give up the university job in 1924 to join the post of Education Officer at the Calcutta Municipal Corporation at the insistence of 'Deshbandhu' Chittaranjan Das who was the Mayor of CMC at that time. 'Deshbandhu' was looking for an efficient officer in this post who could bring real change to improve the condition of education in the city. Kshitish Prasad did not disappoint him. When he took charge as the first Education Officer of the CMC, there were only 3 primary schools in the civic body. He raised the number of schools to 232 with an enrollment of 50,000 students in 1935 when he left the organization (Sengupta and Basu, 1960).

After leaving Calcutta Municipal Corporation, he returned to the department of anthropology at the University of Calcutta and worked there till his retirement in 1962. This period was academically more active years for Kshitish Prasad Chattopadhyay. He has also the distinction of being the first Professor of Anthropology in the University of Calcutta in 1937 (Beteille, 1994).

Explorations in kinship and social organization

Professor Chattopadhyay was trained in the tradition of British social Anthropology under the direct guidance of W.H.R. Rivers. It was a fact that he did some works in the kinship and social organization following that tradition. But, he was also keen on utilising his anthropological skill and understanding for the development of the country and mitigating the social problems faced by the nation. One of these problems was related to education which was a thrust area of his study. His works on kinship and education are always referred to as his contributions and several scholars have concentrated on these works only to assess Professor Chattopadhyay (Chattopadhyay, 2000). However, there are some other fields in which Professor Chattopadhyay's contributions deserve mention. He was by training and orientation positivist and he had great reliance on the quantitative data. His empirical surveys can be taken as contributory works in this regard. Besides this, he worked on rituals and religion. He studied the Santal community. His works on caste and social organization based on secondary sources are mention-worthy, too.

Kshitish Prasad's study of Newar culture was one of his early works which shows the potential of this budding anthropologist (Chattopadhyay,1923). The study was done as part of his dissertation work in Cambridge. Although his plan of an ethnographic study on the Newar in Nepal was never realized, yet his ethnological study on this community continued to influence the subsequent researches done by other scholars on these people (Nepali, 1965). Some of his conclusions or observations based on the scrutiny of the secondary sources were proved valuable in the later study with particular reference to the weaving apparatus of the Newar people or the non-use of the plough in Nepal valley.

Kshitish Prasad Chattopadhyay published substantially on kinship and social organization (Chattopadhyay, 1921, 1922, 1927,

1939, 1941, 1957, 1962). Bhattacharyay (2000), while writing on the contribution of K. P. Chattopadhyay to the kinship studies has remarked that the latter believed in Robin Fox's words which state what nude is to art and logic is to philosophy, so is the relationship between anthropology and kinship. Bhattacharyay (2000) mentioned that K. P. Chattopadhyay published at least ten valuable papers on kinship between 1921 and 1962. The first of his publications on kinship was brought out in *Man in India* when he was a student in the United Kingdom (Chattopadhyay, 1921). The paper discussed some Malayalam kinship terms. His second paper published in the following year dealt with the practice of levirate and its reflection in the kin term (Chattopadhyay, 1922). This paper also gives us a clue of his following Rivers' kinship theories which he states at the beginning of the paper. In the 'Lecture I' of his book *Kinship and Social Organization* (1914), Rivers says that a close connection exists between 'methods of denoting relationship or kinship and forms of social organization, including those based on different varieties of the institution of marriage' (Rivers:1914:1). This statement made by Rivers is important for understanding Kshitish Prasad's intellectual genealogy. However, he acknowledged Rivers' guidance. In the paper, he showed that the junior levirate has been widely practiced in North India and the terminological system indicates the difference between husband's younger and elder brother, whereas no such difference exists in the case of husband's younger or elder sister or wife's younger or elder sister or brother. Citing references from the ancient texts, he went on to show the prevalence of junior levirate among many of the castes and tribes of northern India including Bengal and Odisha. However, this custom is strikingly absent in southern India and the kin terms do not show any such distinctions. Not only the kin terms but the functions or pattern of behaviour associated with the term are also indicative of the existence of a particular kinship system – this was also a thesis of Rivers. Following this hint, Chattopadhyay has shown the differential attitudes between a woman and her husband's elder and younger brothers. To study the 'history of social institutions,' he also advanced his searches on the historical rulers like Satakarnis and Sungas (Chattopadhyay, 1927). The paper on Sunga and Satakarni was remarkable not only for its contributions to the understanding of the relationship between a kin term and social organization as he came to infer that the rule of succession was the principal factor determining the use of metronymic in the case of the Satbahanas. The paper's importance lies in its unique methodological approach of combining textual, archaeological, and genealogical data in interpreting the social history of the past Indian society. This anthropological findings shed significant light in understanding the history as well. The marriage institution and rules regulating marital exchanges were considered by Rivers as an important entry point for understanding social organization (Rivers, 1914). Khsitish Prasad studied marriage concerning succession and polyandry apart from levirate (Chattopadhyay, 1939, 1957).

It will not be out of place to present a very brief note on the development of kinship studies in his times (Fox, 1967). K P Chattopadhyay was trained mainly by Rivers and was conceived to have followed diffusionism. But we must agree that the schools and concepts have some internal connections among themselves. The concepts and theories developed by Morgan happened to be the starting points for many of the studies undertaken by Rivers. Morgan's study of the classificatory system of kin terms has been staples of many studies that followed including that of Chattopadhyay's, although he did not hesitate to point out the lacunae in Morgan's understanding of kinship. Morgan also talked about the descent. Malinowski added a functional attribute and some psychological tinge in the kinship studies. For Evans-Pritchard, lineage has an important place. However, Levi-Strauss took the matter from consanguinity to affinity and stressed the importance of marital exchange in building the kinship network in society. Therefore, we may say that the basic issues were kin terms, locality, and descent, unilineal descent group, bi-lateral and double descent, cognatic descent, exogamy, direct exchange, restricted exchange (Fox, *ibid*). Kinship and marriage have been intricately related since the common areas of research are concerned. Thus, marriage types, polyandry, forms of marriage, matrilineality, matrilocality have been the common areas of investigations for the anthropologists interested in one area or the other (Deliege, 2011). Therefore, it was quite natural for Chattopadhyay to embark on the studies of levirate, polyandry, and kinship system of the Khasis simultaneously because of the intersecting conceptual and empirical domains. At a mature stage of his academic career, he wrote a paper on the terms of kinship and social relationship in an edited volume in the memory of D.N. Majumdar (Chattopadhyay,1962; Madan and Sarana,1962). This paper brings before us a synoptic note of Chattopadhyay approach to kinship studies. He preferred the term 'kinship equation' to 'kinship identity'. He formulated several equations to explain how kinship terms are related to their functions and reveal the nature of social relationships. One such equation T = f (l, s) states that Kin term (T) is related to the functions (f) of the family (l) and social groups (s). He used this equation for the first time in his Sunga and Satakarni paper (Chattopadhyay, 1927). In this equation, 's' is a lumping of 'c' (clan) and 't' (tribe). He has come out with a formula that he called the 'law of disappearance of kinship correspondence'. This penchant for nomothetic formulation shows the positivist bent of mind of the scholar. Secondly, this paper also presents the influence of the structural-functionalist approach as he tries to show the correspondence between functions of a kin term and its location in the social relationship. Therefore, it cannot be blatantly said that he was a diffusionist or he did social history much like his mentor Dr. Rivers. However, he was not dismissive of the role of cultural contacts and their effect on the kinship system. This could be taken as the third importance of this paper. Fourthly, we find that he has referred to the ancient texts in constructing the kinship system of the past to throw light on the ancient social organization and its evolutionary stages. This may be considered as socio-historical so far as his approach is concerned. Fifthly, we also see in this paper that he differed from Rivers and Morgan in some of his postulates. Similar observations have also been forwarded by other scholars who analyzed his works in different contexts (Chattopadhyay, 2000).

His paper '*History of Indian Social Organization*' which he originally presented in the world Anthropology Congress (International Congress of Anthropological and Ethnological Sciences) in July 1934 was a review based on secondary sources. He tried to follow a social-historical approach to construct the historical development of caste organization in India. In the paper, he made the following conclusion on the stages of evolution of the social organization in India. For the East and South, the stages were as he wrote:

'(i) An immigration of one or more cultural people, laying stress on the household exogamy, and not on paternity, leading to a growth of the matrilineal society of different types under different conditions, with anomalous kin marriage.

(ii) Interaction of matrilineal-people from different areas leading to further changes.

(iii) Immigration of a patrilineal people leading to cross-cousin marriage, along with mother right – but giving an appearance of father-right in case of patrilocal residence, and elsewhere imparting strongly patrilineal traditions.

(iv) A final cultural domination by a patrilineal people. In North India, the first three stages seem to have been followed by another patrilineal immigration leading to the definite intermixture of races.' (1935:394)

According to him, the earliest stage was represented by fisher folk – then iron working in eastern India and copper working in the western and northern part. The third stage was represented by some tribes and partly by Sungas and Satakarnis who tended to break the barriers of incest. The fourth stage was represented by pastoral Vedic people (immigrants) who gave rise to Brahmanic culture (Chattopadhyay, 1935). This is an important observation in the sense that it threw light on the cultures preceding the Vedic one and the nature of the social organization in these cultures. It also establishes the pluricultural foundation of Indian social organization at its inception and the fact that it is still on the flow.

Chattopadhyay studied three festival rituals, namely Manda, Chadak, and Dharma (Chattopadhyay, 1934, 1935a, 1943). He was of opinion that these worships were closely connected, 'identical in many respects and have a common origin.' (1935a:406) He described the Charak rituals as observed in Kolkata and suburbs based on his observation, interviews of the informants from different parts of Kolkata, Tarakeshwar, Birsinha of Medinipur (presently in Paschim Medinipur District). According to him, the main idea behind this festival is resurrection. His paper on Dharma worship is a very exhaustive discussion on the topic. He dealt with a large corpus of textual works on the Dharma worship that flourished during the medieval period in Bengal and several *Mangal Kavyas* known as *Dharmamangal* were written eulogizing this deity. This theme of Chadak returns in another study on the observance of Chadak festivals by the Santals at three places, namely Brindaban village in Santal Paraganas, Mayurbhanj, and Ranchi (Chattopadhyay, 1963). This has been a clear example of the exposition in diffusionism. He concluded that this festival was diffused to the Santals from the Hindus by stating the mechanism at work: '....diffusion of a religious cult is that initiative for it rests on individuals ... not acting in concert as a social group' (Chattopadhyay, 1963:333).

Apart from the Santal and the Khasi, he studied another tribe named Korku. The Korkus living in central India was visited by several times by Professor Chattopadhyay for social and physical anthropological investigations. On one hand, he enquired into their funeral customs (Chattopadhyay, 1943b), on the other he took the anthropometric measurements of these people to determine their racial affinity (Chattopadhyay, 1952). Professor Chattopadhyay also studied material culture traits like Bengal basketry and came to an interesting revelation that unlike standard basketry techniques simulating weaving, the Bengal coiled basketry is characterized by a technique akin to carpentry (Chattopadhyay, 1943a).

Studies on education and its problems

One of the life-long engagements of Professor Chattopadhyay was his studies on education, education policy, problems of education. He was not just complacent in discussing these issues theoretically. He was actively engaged in improving the condition of education especially for the underprivileged sections of society. It has been already mentioned that he worked as the Education Officer in the Calcutta Corporation. As an anthropologist, he conducted many surveys on education (Chattopadhyay *et.al.*, 1954; Chattopadhyay and Bose, 1962).

Chattopadhyay's article on tribal education (Chattopadhyay, 1953) dealt with different aspects of education from a pragmatic point of view. It discussed how education can be imparted for the tribals.

He envisaged a detailed syllabus from Grade I to Grade IV for the tribal students. Here he discussed what could be the contents of the textbooks, medium of instruction, script, method of teaching. He also discussed types of schools required for these students. For him, training of the teachers should get a priority. He emphasized the need for the central and the regional committees on education. Professor Chattopadhyay was of opinion that the textbooks for the tribal students should incorporate relevant details of their culture. His view was that the teaching of the tribal students should be through their language. The teaching of regional language could be made after the first four years of primary education. It was suggested by him that the method of teaching should be directed towards using as many as words that occur frequently in their day-to-day life, to be collected for the primers at the lowest grade. He collected such vocabularies for the Bengalee children and published a primer in 1933. According to him, syllabic drills and spelling drills must occupy an important place in primary teaching. His pedagogical suggestion was to start teaching with a couple of letters, then a syllable followed by a whole word accompanying a picture. Providing appropriate schooling infrastructure in forest or interior areas appeared to him a challenge. He calculated that for a density of 300 people per square mile population, there would be a little more than one hundred children. In that case, the target should be to bring 2/3 of these students to two-teacher schools, in a much smaller population provision of at least one-teacher school should be made. With the declaration of the universal primary literacy campaign in India, this might appear irrelevant, but one cannot deny the depth at which Professor Chattopadhyay attempted to address the issue from an applied anthropological perspective. He considered that the training of teachers must be a priority area for tribal education. He suggested that the main thing would be 'to equip the teachers with a working knowledge of the language of the area where he is to work and also the socio-historical approach to teaching' (Chattopadhyay, 1953:10). He talked about demonstration lessons for the teachers by a team of pedagogues who would be visiting in nature. As Education Officer in Calcutta Corporation, he organized such training programmes for the teachers in 1926.

His two more surveys on the state of higher education brought to the fore the results having great significance for the planning education for the country (Chattopadhyay et.al. 1954; Chattopadhyay and Bose, 1962). The survey on the undergraduate students was founded upon a noble motive to understand what the students needed most so that the university could plan accordingly to address their problems. Among many things, this study revealed that 43 percent of the students studied suffered from malnutrition and disease. It recommended subsidized food for these students in the canteen premonishing the idea of a mid-day meal much before. Another interesting solution it offered was on the kind of accommodation that would suit best to the requirements of the students. The study on how guardians plan education for their wards was more like a comprehensive survey on the socio-economic background of the students of the University of Calcutta during 1950. It not only highlighted the guardians' preferences for the future career for their sons but also the conditions of living, family income, etc. were reported in the survey.

Survey and study on the Santals

Professor K.P. Chattopadhyay did ethnographic studies on three tribes, namely Khasi, Korku, and Santal. Among these works, his study on the Santals occupies a prominent place. The most important of his publications on the Santals was a report on the socio-economic condition of this tribal community (Chattopadhyay, 1947). It was a report on the Santals in Northern and Western Bengal based on the survey at six places, namely Malda, Balurghat, Birbhum, Bankura, Midnapore, and Jhargram conducted during 1945-46. The study was commissioned by the Government of Bengal. The Special Officers were instructed to send the list of Santal villages to Professor Chattopadhyay who requested Professor P.C. Mahalanabis, the then Director of Indian Statistical Institute to draw the random samples for the study. Accordingly, 69 villages were selected out of 4552 Santal villages. The inquiry was originated from a letter to the Department of Anthropology sent by the government to seek a report on the survival of the Parganait system among the Santals. Professor Chattopadhyay informed the government that an anthropological investigation was required to know the actual situation. There was no study on the socio-economic status of the Santal after McAlpin's survey done in 1909. But it can be added that McAlpin's survey was not based on the scientific methodology that was followed in Chattopadhyay's survey. Though the inquiry of the state of the Parganait system was one of the objectives of the study, yet the survey was not confined only to this point. It collected data on the occupation, nature, and amount of land holding, cattle, indebtedness, grain *gola,* literacy, and village officials of the Santals in the studied areas. Based on this study, he came up with some observations and recommendations. He was of opinion that the Parganait system was not equally followed or organized everywhere. It was of recent origin at some places like Malda. In Midnapore, this system was though present yet it was not much prominent. He also reported that the village officials were not present in their full traditional body in all the villages under study. This has an impact on their observance of rituals and festivals which were not held at some villages in the last year or so as his study revealed. He recommended a quasi-government status for the Parganait of the Santals. This official would look after the traditional affairs and petty village-level disputes and customary issues. Therefore, a kind of sanction to the customary laws of the tribal people was suggested by him. Today, we come across some tribal boards constituted by the members of their community in West Bengal. The boards are not the same as suggested by Professor Chattopadhyay, however, these institutions reflect his idea of self-management and philosophy of self-governance for the tribal people. Even, concerning the use of tribal language in their education, his views still possess relevance when he advocates the use of their language as the medium of instruction.

The need to emphasise the education of the tribal people was further supported by the findings of his report on the Santals. In Midnapore, the literacy rate was about 1.0 percent, in some other places it was further less.

His Santal report is important on another ground which is related to the officials engaged in the tribal affairs. His comment on the nature of their cadre still deserves scrutiny because it still needs some administrative reforms. He pointed out the necessity of

Social Anthropological training for the officials engaged in the administration in tribal areas. Not only this time, but he has also recommended the importance and necessity of anthropological training for administrators. In the early years of anthropological teaching in the country, such reiterations of the importance of anthropology carry special significance for the newly founded discipline. It can also be added that he wished to employ anthropological knowledge to understand the particular social and economic problems of the country. He probably thought that the importance of the subject must be propagated before the administration if we attempt to stake more demands for anthropology to the government. He utilized his contacts with the people who are in administration or politics to that effect. His other studies, more survey type in nature can prove this point better. The studies on the famine, rehabilitation, jute labour, undergraduate students, planning of the guardians were directed to understand the present and to assist better planning for the future.

Professor Chattopadhyay surveyed the jute labourers in 1945 at the request of Chatkal Mazdoor Union with the funds and technical assistance from the Indian Statistical Institute (ISI). He again undertook another survey in 1948-49 on the socio-economic condition of the jute labour (1952) with the necessary funds and technical assistance from ISI. A special feature of this survey was the use of the genealogical method in the collection of some social data, particularly on the non-resident dependents. The study was done on the jute factory workers living in Jagatdal police station to the north of Kolkata. 2 percent of the samples were drawn from a total of about thirty-eight thousand workers. The study shows that the majority of the Jagatdal mill workers came from Bihar (43.85%) and Uttar Pradesh (35. 73 %). The Hindus constitute almost three-fourth of these labourers. He determined 8 different types of family units including individuals without following the terminological classifications of the family into simple or nuclear, joint, or extended types. This type of classification helps to understand the situations of the migrant labourers better. For example, there were 209 units out of 840 total units, having persons with families at home but living here alone, either cooking for self or messing with one or more unrelated persons or eating in a restaurant.

Again, there were 220 units with a person living with a wife and one or more children, which can be well classified as 'simple family', the term Chattopadhyay is preferred to 'nuclear family' which fits well to the standard terminology for a family in anthropology. But, no such classification was possible in the former case cited here.

Social and political activism

Kshitish Prasad Chattopadhyay was socially and politically a very conscious person. His activism was not superficial in this regard. We have already known that his doctoral scholarship was denied on the ground of his sympathies for the Indian seamen and their political activities. In later years of his life, he had always rallied for the protection of rights for the people and justice. Kshitish babu (*babu* being the honorific for the Bengali gentleman) was the Working President of the Civil Liberties Committee (CLC) formed sometime in the 1940s in Bengal. Its functions were carried out from his Palm Avenue residence in Kolkata. People used to refer to this organization as the '*Kshitish babuder* committee' (the committee run by Kshitish *babu* and others; Dutta, 2000). Kshitish Prasad Chattopadhyay's historic role in the civil liberties movement can be remembered for its relevance even today. The committee had members from different political backgrounds. It included Advocate Atul Gupta as its President, among the other members there were congressmen as well as communists among whom persons like Jyoti Basu (who later became Chief Minister of West Bengal), Professor Hirendranath Mukhopadhyay, noted journalist Vivekananda Mukhopadhyay, Professor Habibullah, writer Manik Bandyopadhyay, Phani Sett were the members. The ideological foundation of the organization as transpired through a public declaration was clear from the following statement:

'From the history of the national movement, we have drawn the lesson that freedom means freedom of the people, the freedom to campaign and to organise, the freedom to speak and write, the freedom to live as a healthy and civilized human being…' (Datta, 2000:23)

For a newly independent state, it was a challenge to protect the civil rights which appeared to be bulldozed in the post-colonial state that had yet to have come out of the colonial vices. Professor

Chattopadhyay probably foresighted the danger of the abuses of civil rights in free India. In 'One Year of Freedom' published by the CLC in 1948, a clarion call to the citizens was heard: 'From your local Civil Liberties Committee, stand up against all repression and attempts to curtail civil liberties. Demand repeal of the Security Act and withdrawal of ordinance rule, insist on your Democratic Rights.' (*Ibid*, 31) History has repeated many times in Independent India since the morning of the early years of the country won freedom showed the days of the future. And here lies the relevance of activism in which Professor K.P. Chattopadhyay was deeply involved.

Another aspect of Professor Chattopadhyay's social concern was his work for the educational upliftment of the people. He was not content only with academic surveys and research on education but wanted to do something in the practical field. It has already been mentioned that he worked as Education Officer in Calcutta Corporation. In this capacity, firstly, he increased the number of primary schools in the city from 3 to more than 232. Secondly, he knew that poverty spawned illiteracy to a large extent, thus he concentrated in the bustee and similar enclaves mostly inhabited by the downtrodden people. Thirdly, he started training the teachers to ensure quality education. Fourthly, he wrote primers to suit the needs of the students. And most importantly he advocated free and compulsory universal literacy in the 1930s much before the adoption of a policy for universal literacy in India. His anthropological career was somehow connected with this mission. He visited primary schools in European countries when he attended the first World Anthropology Congress held in London in 1934. The experience he gained through this exposure was utilized in his drafting of the proposal of a universal literacy programme for the Calcutta Corporation. Thus, it can be said that it is important to know social and political engagements to understand his academic inclinations.

Hutton (1963), in his information-rich obituary note on K. P. Chattopadhyay, gave succinctly how professor Chattopadhyay was actively associated with different organizations. He was treasurer in the People's Relief Committee. He was also an independent member of the State Legislative Assembly. He was active in the Civil Disobedience movement and courted imprisonment once for participating in the national freedom movement. During the riots in Kolkata, he built up a 'Peace Corps' to mitigate the fuming violence in 1946.

Honours and awards

Professor Chattopadhyay was the President of the Anthropology and Archaeology Section of the Indian Science Congress in 1931. He became a Fellow of the Indian National Science Academy in 1951. In the next year (1952), he was elected Vice-President of the Council of International Congress of Anthropology. He was the first President of the Indian Anthropological Society registered in 1958. He served on the Advisory Board of Cultural Research Institute of Government of West Bengal. He was a consultant at the UNESCO Resource Centre. Sanskrit College, (Kolkata), Ecole Française d'Extreme Orient (Paris), Learned Society of Arts Prehistorique (Paris) made him Honorary Fellow. He became Vice-President of the Learned Society of Arts Prehistorique, too. He had great acumen in Sanskrit. He was honoured with the *Sarvabhauma* award by Calcutta Pundit Samaj.

Conclusion

While discussing the genesis of colonial forms of knowledge in India, Cohn (1996) mentioned that the emergence of 'science' disciplines like ethnology played an important role in shaping the colonial forms of knowledge in India. However, this knowledge was further reshaped by a section of Indian scholars trained in western education but grounded in oriental realities. Professor K. P. Chattopadhyay belonged to this class of intellectuals who faced the transitional turbulations generated by the polarities of colonialism and nationalism. His intellectual location is well characterized by a kind of 'Oriental Empiricism' as theorized by Ludden (1993). Ludden (1993:273) mentions about this situation developed under the influence of colonialism in the following words:

'It is also embedded rhetorically and institutionally in political culture, revitalized by re-invocation in national histories that show South Asian peoples struggling for freedom and progress in their own terms'.

It was a fact that the concatenation of ideas gave rise to hybridization that came through the translation of conceptual categories by the agency of a new class of professional practitioners in the newly founded departments in Indian universities (Chatterjee, 1995). Professor Chattopadhyay represented that agency that acted as the harbinger of a new disciplinary practice that attempted to lay its foundation on scientific ground. Thus, he also personified the modernity of anthropology in India, which seemed more meaningful because he was the Head of the first anthropology department in the country.

In the light of the foregoing discussion on the academic landscape during the time of colonial rule, it is presumably an onerous task for a person to steer through an emerging department. The features of his academic and activist self are marked in the intellectual outputs Professor Chattopadhyay has left. He was a follower of the holistic, positivist, empiricist, tradition of anthropology and himself carried out studies in social-cultural, physical, and archaeological anthropology. Theoretically speaking, he had lineage in British Anthropology of Rivers, but he was never confined to the diffusionist, social-historical approach of anthropology. Therefore, it is difficult to specify a linear academic trajectory for him. He wanted to utilise the applied benefits of anthropological knowledge and put it to the welfare of the nation. We notice a shift in his study in the later years from theoretically oriented studies on kinship and social organization to the applied as well as survey type of works. He might have thought that a true balance between applied and theoretical works would ensure a better future for the discipline. Wherever he got an opportunity for the application of anthropological knowledge, he made a plea for the professional expansion of the discipline. He could have done more researches in anthropology as he was capable of, but his role in building up the discipline should be judged side by side in order to understand his contributions in the right perspective.

References

Beteille, A., 1994. Introduction. In *Essays in Social Anthropology:* Kshitish Prasad Chattopadhyay, pp vii – xii, Calcutta: K. P. Bagchi and Co.

Chatterjee, P. (Ed.). 1995. *Texts of Power – Emerging Disciplines in Colonial Bengal.* Minneapolis: University of Minnesota Press.

Chattopadhyay, G. (Ed.) 2000. *Life and Times of an Indian Anthropologist: K.P. Chattopadhyay.* Calcutta: The Asiatic Society.

------- 1921. Some Malayalam kinship terms. *Man in India* 1, 1:53-55.

------- 1922. Levirate and kinship in India. *Man* 22 (March): 36-41.

------- 1923. An essay on the history of Newar culture. *Journal and Proceedings of the Asiatic Society of Bengal.* N.S. XIX: 465-560.

------- 1927. Social organization of Satkarnis and Sungas. *Journal of the Asiatic Society of Bengal.* N.S. 23:503-554.

------- 1935. History of Indian social organization. *Journal of the Royal Asiatic Society of Bengal* 1: 377-395.

------- 1935a. The Chadak festival in Bengal. *Journal of the Royal Asiatic Society of Bengal Letters* 1: 397-406.

------- 1939. Satkarni succession and marriage rules. *Journal of the Asiatic Society of Bengal Letter* 5:317-339.

------- 1941. Khasi kinship and social organization. *University of Calcutta Anthropological Papers,* New Series 6:1-39.

------- 1943. Dharma worship. *Journal of the Royal Asiatic Society of Bengal Letters* VIII: 99-135.

------- 1943a. Bengal coiled basketry. *Journal of the Royal Asiatic Society of Bengal* IX: 39-42.

------- 1943b. Korku funeral customs and memorial posts. *Journal of the Royal Asiatic Society of Bengal Letters* IX: 201-209.

------- 1947. *Report on the Santals in Bengal.* Calcutta: Calcutta University.

------- 1949. Changes in Santal economy. *Man in India* 29, 2: 71-75

------- 1952. *A Socio-Economic Survey of Jute Labour.* Calcutta: Department of Social Work, Calcutta University.

------- 1952a. Korku physical type and racial affinities. *Journal of the Asiatic Society Science* XVIII, 1: 23-34.

------- 1953. Tribal education. *Man in India* 33,1: 1-18.

------- 1957. On polyandry. *Journal of the Asiatic Society of Bengal.* Science. 22:163-191.

------- 1962. On terms of kinship and social relationships. In T.N. Madan and Gopala Sarana (Eds.) *Indian Anthropology*, pp. 339-351. Bombay: Asia Publishing House.

------- 1963. Diffusion of a religious cult. In Bala Ratnam (Ed.), *Anthropology on the March*, pp. 325-333. Madras: The Book Centre.

------- 1994. *Essays in Social Anthropology.* Calcutta: K. P. Bagchi and Company

Chattopadhyay, KP. and Ray G., 1947. *Municipal Labour in Calcutta*. Calcutta: Calcutta University.

Chattopadhyay, KP. and Bose PK., 1962. *How Far Guardians Plan Education.* Calcutta: Calcutta University.

Chattopadhyay, KP., Bose PK. and Chatterjee, A., 1954. *Undergraduate Students in Calcutta: How they live and work – A survey.* Calcutta: Calcutta University.

Cohn, BS. 1996. *Colonialism and Its Forms of Knowledge – The British in India.* Princeton: Princeton University Press.

Dasgupta, (Eds.) S. 2019. Kshitish Prasad Chattopadhyay (1897-1963). In *Doyens of Indian Anthropology*, Amitabha Sarkar and Samira Dasgupta, pp. 26-30. Delhi: Agam Kala Prakashan.

Deliege, R., 2011. *Anthropology of the Family and Kinship.* New Delhi: PHI Learning.

Dutta, N. 2000. K.P. Chattopadhyay and civil liberties in the infant state. In G. Chattopadhyay, *Life and Times of an Indian Anthropologist: K.P. Chattopadhyay,* (Ed.), pp. 18-33. Calcutta: The Asiatic Society.

Fox, R. 1967. *Kinship and Marriage.* Harmondsworth: Penguin.

Guha, A. 2020. Physics to anthropology: The journey of a nationalist scholar. *Frontier*, June 14, 2020.

Hutton, JH. 1963. K. P. Chattopadhyay: 1898-1963. *Man* 63: 155-156.

Ludden, D. 1993. Oriental empiricism: transformation of colonial knowledge. In *Orientalism and the Postcolonial Predicament: Perspectives on South Asia*, C.A. Breckenridge and Peter van der Veer (Eds.), pp. 250-278. Philadelphia: University of Pennsylvania Press.

Mondal, SR. 2012. Contributions of Prof. Kshitish Prasad Chattopadhyaya to Indian Anthropology. *South Asian Anthropologist* 12, 1: 71-75.

Nepali, GS. 1965. *The Newars – An Ethno – Sociological Study of a Himalayan Community.* Bombay: United Asia Publishing.

Ray, SK. 1974. Kshitish Prasad Chattopadhyay (1897 – 1963). In *Bibliographies of Eminent Indian Anthropologists*, pp. 45-55. Calcutta: Anthropological Survey of India.

Rivers, WHR., 1914. *Kinship and Social Organization.* London: Constable and Co. Ltd.

Sengupta, SC. and Basu, A. (Eds.) 1960. Kshitish Prasad Chattopadhyay. *Sansad Bangali Charitabhidhan,* pp.109-110. Calcutta: Sahitya Sansad.

Chapter - 4

Dr. Achyut Kumar Mitra: A Tribute

Prasanta Kumar Chattopadhyay

Not a day passes when I do not reverentially remember my teacher Achyut Kumar Mitra (D.Sc.). It all began on 16th July 1961, when as an M.Sc. (Previous) Anthropology student at Delhi University I asked him if I could speak to him in Bengali. His instant reply, 'Yes, of course,' still rings in my ear. The intimate relationship in the *Guru-Shishya Parampara* that started that day ended with his untimely demise on 14th July 1970. However, my intellectual relationship continues.

In the summer of 1963, I was vacationing in Calcutta after my M.Sc. final examinations. He wrote to me an inland letter asking me not to waste time but to join him in his village, Jejur, in Hooghly district to work on Bengalee cultivators. He had the notion that the 'angle atd' in the palms change with age and wanted me to work on it. I could not have asked for more.

After I reached Jejur, he asked one of his share-croppers, to take me around the village and help me collect palm prints and anthropomorphic measurements of Duleys and Bagdis, two schedule caste groups of West Bengal. After each day's work, Dr. Mitra would discuss till late evening the anthropological significance of the physical features of the people I visited. I must confess that this helped me later when I started my teaching and research career in Forensic Science.

After two weeks of work, sometimes wading through knee-deep water and muddy *kutcha* roads, in Jejur and some surrounding villages,

I had to stop as I could not get more subjects. I analyzed the palm prints and gave him a working draft of the paper. The paper was finalized to his satisfaction after several rounds of writing and re-writing. At this stage, to my amazement, Dr. Mitra deleted his name from the authorship but instead suggested that I acknowledge him and my other teachers. He typed the final draft of the paper himself and personally handed it over to Dr. B.K. Chatterjee of the Asiatic Society of Bengal, saying 'Bajra this is my student's paper. Try to publish it in the current issue of your Journal.' That is how I had my first paper, '*Mainline index distribution and angle atd among the Bengalee Cultivators*' published in the *Journal of the Asiatic Society of Bengal* in 1964.

Another life-changing incident occurred in 1962. After listening to a lecture by Dr. R. Ruggles Gates F.R.S., Professor of Genetics, University of Cambridge, U.K. in our Department I discussed with Dr. Mitra my interpretations of the Genetics of *Hypertrichosis Pinnae Auris* (hairy ear rims). He immediately stood up and said don't utter a word more and discuss with anybody else. Write down whatever you told me and send it to Professor J.B.S. Haldane, F.R.S. immediately. I followed his advice. I was very scared and nervous. I felt that Professor Haldane was so towering a scientist of international repute that he may not even care to read my note. I left for Mussoorie to work on the Tibetans.

Within a few days, I received a telegram from my eldest brother Professor Paresnath Chattopadhyay, who was with the Delhi School of Economics, asking me to return to Delhi as soon as possible, as Professor Haldane had accepted my views. Professor Haldane, besides accepting my views on the subject, wanted me to send all the data I had collected to him for publication in his journal, the *Journal of Genetics*. The paper, '*Inheritance of Hairy Ear Rims*', was published in the Journal in 1964 and brought me recognition from scientists all over the world including Professors E.L. Tatum, U.S.A. and Bernado A. Houssay of Argentina, both Nobel Laureates and Dr. Hans Gruneberg of the Galton Laboratory, London. Dr. Mitra was very happy when he saw Professor Haldane's letter and a few months later the published paper. I have highlighted these details leading to the publication of the papers just to indicate how caring and supportive he was of his students. Many teachers in his position would not have been able to shun the temptation of having their name as an author thereby depriving the student of the richly deserved credit.

Born on 31st March 1903 in Calcutta, Dr. Achyut Kumar Mitra passed his Matriculation examination from Kidderpore Academy and joined the Intermediate Course in Science in St. Xavier's College, Calcutta. He had to discontinue his studies abruptly because he participated in the Non-Cooperation Movement for which he was jailed for some time. He came under the influence of the great leader Netaji Subhash Chandra Bose and became actively involved in the freedom movement. Subsequently, he joined the *Jatiyo Vidyapeeth* (which became a part of Jadavpur University later) from where he did his Bachelor's and Master's degrees. He studied Chemistry, Indology, Archaeology and learned Pali, Prakrit, and Sanskrit.

Dr. Mitra joined as Curator to set up the Museum at Khiching, Mayurbhanj, Orissa where he worked till 1929. Later he joined the Zoological Survey of India (Anthropology Section). In 1934, he went abroad for higher studies first to Italy, and thereafter to Germany as an Alexander von Humboldt Fellow to work in the Department of Anthropology, Munich University. He worked with Professor Theodore Mollison, a very renowned name in Morphological Anthropology. After obtaining the D.Sc. Degree (the first Indian to do so from Munich University) he returned to India just before the Second World War and rejoined the Zoological Survey of India. When the Anthropological Survey of India (AnSI) was established with Dr. B.S. Guha, the Doyen of Indian Anthropology as its Director, joined it as an Assistant Anthropologist and rose to the position of Deputy Director (he was Director In-charge of the Survey for some time).

On his superannuation from the Anthropological Survey of India in 1959, he moved to Delhi to join the Department of Anthropology, the University of Delhi as a Reader in Physical Anthropology. He played a very important role in updating the teaching curriculum and gave tremendous impetus to the study of Morphological Anthropology, Primatology, Prehistoric Archaeology, Human Physiology, and Anatomy. While being involved with teaching and research in anthropology, he also studied French and passed the degree course in

Italian from Delhi University. In March 1970, he joined the prestigious Indian Institute of Advanced Studies (IIAS), Shimla as a Fellow.

He often mentioned that Netaji inspired him to study Anthropology. While at the AnSI he worked under the guidance of Dr. B.S. Guha. He played a very important role in setting up the Anthropology Section of the Indian Museum, Calcutta, and in the excavations at Sarnath while he was posted at Benaras. He ably supported Professor P.C. Biswas in updating the teaching curriculum, organising the various laboratories and the museum thereby helping in building the Department of Anthropology, the University of Delhi to an institute of world fame.

As a researcher, he was very meticulous in the planning and execution of his projects. He worked in the scorching summer heat in the villages of Delhi doing anthropometric measurements on the Jats, Ahir, Gujjar, and the Rajputs in search of their origin. He continued, as an extension of this, to work on the anthropometry of the Kashmiri workers in Shimla. He was the President of the Anthropology Section of the Indian Science Congress, at Hyderabad in January 1967.

He was a voracious reader and had a very good collection of books. His command over several Indian and foreign languages such as Bengali, Hindi, Sanskrit, Pali, Prakrit, English, French, Italian, and German helped him read literature, archaeology, history, geography, and anthropology and communicate with his peers and teaching students. He was closely associated with a galaxy of outstanding anthropologists, archaeologists, and historians such as Dr. Henry Field (U.S.A.), Professors Lidio Cipriani and Mario Cappieri (Italy), Professors Fleischaker and Emil Breitinger (Germany), Sir Mortimer Wheeler, and Sir John Marshal (U.K.), Dr. Kalidas Nag, Professors Nihar Ranjan Roy, Nirmal Kumar Bose to name only a few.

I rue very much that the manuscript of his translation of the famous book *Lehrbuch Der Anthropologie* by Rudolf Martin and K. Saller was lost forever when he died. He would read from the original in German and dictate it to me in English. I would write from morning to evening in his Model Town residence and pass it to him before leaving.

The great teacher breathed his last on 14th July 1970 in Jejur. We lost a great teacher and researcher, a wonderful human being, and a selfless mentor, friend, philosopher, and guide to his students, something which is a rarity today.

Acknowledgements

I have no words to thank Dr. P. Dash Sharma, Dr. Nabakumar Duary, and Dr. Mitra's children Aparna, Amit, Aparajita, and Abhijeet. I would not have been able to write this paper without their help and support.

A few important publications of Dr. A.K. Mitra

1941-1942. Blood group distribution of the Bengalis and their comparison with other Indian races and castes. *Indian Culture*, 8,2-3: 197-217.

1942. Dravidian and Mon-Khmer speakers or Australoids? A study in variation. *Indian Culture*, 8: 329-368.

1952. Physical Anthropology of the Muslims of Bengal. *Bulletin of the Department of Anthropology*, Govt. of India. I,2: 79-104.

1956. The Riangs of Tripura. *Bulletin of the Department of Anthropology,* Govt. of India. 5, 2:21-120.

1961. Progress of Anthropology in India since 1938, Part I (co-authored with Dr. B.S. Guha). *The Mankind Quarterly*, Edinburgh. pp.107-120.

1962. Progress of Anthropology in India since 1938, Part II (co-authored with Dr. B.S. Guha). *The Mankind Quarterly*, Edinburgh. p. 200.

1962. Note on a tour of the Andaman and Nicobar Islands. *Bulletin of the Anthropological Survey of India.* 9, 1:1-11.

1963. Indian anthropology gets into stride, in Bala Ratnam (ed). *Indian Anthropology on the March,* pp. 3-7. Social Science Association Publication, Madras: The Book Centre.

1963. The Aryan problem in Indian Anthropology. In Bala Ratnam (Ed): *Indian Anthropology on the March*, pp. 116-122, Madras.

1965. Racial stratification in the caste hierarchy of Bengal, *Anthropologist,* 2:47-63.

1966. Inheritance of the a-b ridge count in human palms, (with PK Chattopadhyay, P. Dash Sharma, A. Bardhan), *Humangentik,* 2, 1, 25-27.

1967. *The authors of the food-producing revolution and some agricultural populations of North-West India*, Presidential address, Section Anthropology and Archaeology, Proc. of 54th Indian Science Congress Association,

Hyderabad, Part 2, pp. 165-181. Also appeared in *Journal of Indian Anthropological Society*, 2, 2: 131-143.

1968. Inheritance of the palmar main lines D, C, B, and A: A study of 53 Bengalee families. *Proc. Symp. on Dermatoglyphics*, pp 113-122. Delhi; University of Delhi.

1969. Rajput origin of the Tomars of Delhi. (with B.R.Ghosh) *Anthropologist.* (Special Volume) : 181-195.

1969. *The Andamanese and the Negrito Problem,* Miami: Field Research Project, Occasional Paper No. 5.

Chapter – 5

Dr. Sasanka Sekhar Sarkar: The Doyen of Indian Anthropology

Sovanjan Sarkar

At the outset, let me proclaim unhesitatingly that I am literally in the horns of a dilemma to write about the Doyen of Indian Physical Anthropology, Dr. Sasanka Sekhar Sarkar, because of a couple of reasons. On one side, he resides in the mind and soul of many Anthropologists in India and outside, and also took a chair at the highest position in anthropology across the sub-disciplines. Here, I do not want to say 'highest position' in terms of academic position (because he never became a full 'Professor'), but what I meant is, 'at the highest point of intellectuality'. The anthropology fraternity of India and abroad would not be going to exonerate me if I fail to do justice to provide an apt portrayal of his life and work. Secondly, I proudly feel that I am one of the most fortunate persons, who has the responsibility to carry the baton that he unknowingly gave me to pass on to the future students of anthropology, as his grandson. Here again, I feel insecure from the attack of my family members of my earlier generation, if I miss mentioning any imperative information regarding their father and father-in-law. However, expecting those affectionate scolding, I am taking this opportunity to fold my hands (what my father and my teachers taught me, that '*if you fold your hands in front of anybody, most of your problems will be solved*') in front of the readers and trying to open the curtain, behind which, some unknown scenes (not for all readers, though) of my grandfather would be exhibited.

Birthplace and childhood

If you board a Laxmikantapur (24-Parganas South) bound train from Sealdah south railway station, after about an hour of journey, the train will arrive at a station named '*Baharu*'. From that station, a village, named '*Moydah*', is located just 2 km. away. On the 30th day of March 1908, Sasanka Sekhar Sarkar was born as the eldest son in a very respectable family. His father Nanda Kumar Sarkar was a non-professional Ayurvedic doctor, while by profession, he worked with Indian Railways. His mother, Manimala Sarkar, was a real homemaker. Dr. Sarkar had three younger brothers and two younger sisters. He spent his childhood days in the village with his parents and siblings. He had his early schooling in 'Moydah High School', situated at a walkable distance from his home. Later, he had been admitted to 'Chetla Boys School' in Kolkata (erstwhile Calcutta), as his father started residing initially in the Majherhat area and later in Kasba, a place near Ballygunge railway station. Due to weak financial conditions, he used to walk from his residence at Majherhat to school at Chetla. However, he kept regular contact with the village and the villagers where he spent his childhood. I do not have any information regarding his attachment with any sports and other recreational activities, because of the absence of a key informant, who could have thrown some light on this matter. However, I heard that he used to play football, sometimes. We had our small pond in the village, where he used to swim while taking bath. The fact of the matter is, we all had familiarity with that pond till 2019 before the house along with the pond has been sold due to lack of maintenance. The house was devoid of electricity. The kerosene lamp (*lanthan*) was the principal and only source of light. The house was mud-built with a thatched roof. However, later, Dr. Sarkar made it brick-built as he had a plan to spend his last life in his village. Bringing drinking water from a tube well near a Kali temple, cutting fuel wood, making broomsticks from the leaves of the coconut tree, fishing in his pond were some of his regular duties. He was an expert in fishing through the fishing net (cast net; *khepla jal*) and sometimes he demonstrated the techniques of fishing to his students. The above information has been gathered from my grandmother and my father, who used to tell me many stories about him.

Adulthood and family life

After leaving school, he earned his graduation and post-graduation degrees in Anthropology from the University of Calcutta. At the age of 19 years, in 1927, he got married to Renuka Sarkar (nee Bose) when he was a student. They had four sons and 5 daughters. Most of them were born in Kolkata, except his youngest son and daughter, who were born in the village *Moydah*. Nevertheless, they spent their life overwhelmingly in Kolkata. He took a rented house in Ballygunge Station Road, due to the scarcity of space in the house at Kasba. Finally, he shifted to another rented house in Jamir Lane (Address: 16/2B Jamir Lane, Calcutta – 700019; which is also situated near Ballygunge Station and Kasba, where he breathed his last on 9th March 1969.

Personal life

The information I am furnishing in this part of the article was again gathered from his wife and his children, specifically my deceased father, my fourth aunt, and my uncle. 'Early to rise and early to bed' – was his principal liking of daily life. He used to get up early in the morning. He was never a very foodie person and was almost vegetarian; his lunch and dinner time were generally 12:30 pm and 9 pm, respectively, when he used to stay at home. However, flexibility in the schedule was noticed due to academic discussions with other academicians. One example can be mentioned here, that Professor Sudhir Ranjan Das, renowned Archaeologist, and a next-door neighbour, used to come to his home very frequently during the evening for academic discussions and on those days, he used to take dinner at a later time. Smoking cigars was his only addiction. Wearing white shirts and trousers was his topmost choice. He had a dignified, somber, and statuesque personality. He never used to talk too much unnecessarily and always remained busy with his research in his small study and no one was allowed to make noises or even talk in a louder voice when he is at home. He was unquestionably punctual regarding time. On the contrary, he had some peculiar behaviour of idiosyncratic nature. While eating, mixing all the cooked vegetables with rice was one of his unique practices. Secondly, as per information gathered from his post-graduate students, Professor Ranjan Gupta (Professor (retired) of the Indian Statistical Institute) and Professor Buddhadeb Chaudhuri (Ambedkar Chair Professor (retired), Department of Anthropology, Calcutta University), he frequently used to utter the word '*sekene*' ('in that case', in Bengali) while speaking in Bengali. He didn't have a favourable opinion towards the people who migrated from Bangladesh (East Bengal) during the independence. I do not know the reason as my key informants failed to throw any light on the matter. However, being a woman from such a family, my mother didn't face any predicament after her marriage with his third son, Shyaman Kumar Sarkar, my father.

His commitment towards research sometimes made him fairly reluctant about domestic affairs. He seldom paid attention to family-related matters. However, his concern about his students will always be remembered. While doing fieldwork with his students, he used to carry the breakfast for the students to the field area from the field camp. He used to inspect every room of the students in field camp during the night. These small incidences not only portray his enormous affection towards his students but also unravel a soft person behind a hard and firm personality. He had also some different views towards life. He didn't allow any of his children to study Anthropology. He thought that if any of his children truly do have potentials, s(he) won't be recognized in his/her career in anthropology. He realized that his view and thinking towards the scope of the subject is at least 50 years ahead of his time and thus, the potentials of his children might have been misunderstood under his name. He possessed an opposite view of '*Gharana in classical music*', where the artists carry the tradition of one particular type of subject generation after generation. As I mentioned earlier, he had a soft mind inside a hardcover, he used to send letters to his sons and daughters when he stayed in different countries of the world to give importance to the growing and upcoming generation. He also engaged my father to click pictures during his fieldwork in different parts of West Bengal and other parts of eastern India. Furthermore, he gave charge to his second daughter (Mekhala Basu Mazumder) to clean the skulls (used to come from village Moydah and Contai of undivided Medinipur District) to be sent to Delhi and to put in the Department of Anthropology, Calcutta University.

Life was never smooth for my grandfather all the time. The most shocking accident happened to his life when he lost his eldest son 'Kajal'. At 11 years of age, he passed away after suffering from typhoid. He didn't believe his son's death, and while going to the cremation ground, he stopped the persons, carrying Kajal, thrice and checked if there is still life in him. Another shocking incidence happened in his life when his sister returned to him with her newborn son after the death of her husband. Since return, she stayed with other members of my grandfather's family. Later, she was attached to a high school, as a teacher of Bengali.

Academics and research

In the following paragraphs, I shall try to present a snapshot of the academics and research of Dr. S. S. Sarkar. I admit that I can't show his research endeavour in detail because it would have been another separate article. To ease my job, I shall subdivide the topics on which he put his valuable touch in pursuing several topics of research and to enrich the future generation researchers in anthropology.

Before I begin, it should be mentioned that he could think much ahead of his time. In the late 1950s and early 1960s, he thought of the immense importance and necessity of interdisciplinary research in human welfare. His research and publications were also indicative of the same fact.

Ethnography

His first article appeared in the Indian Historical Quarterly, in the year 1933, an ethnography of a tribal community, namely, Malpaharia. In the same year, another article on the ethnography of Malers and Malpaharias was published in the *Current Science*. Finally, in 1938, the book titled '*Malers of Rajmahal Hills*' was published by the Book Company Ltd., of Calcutta. This research was considered to be a skillfully conducted ethnography and widely referred by the anthropologists and ethnographers of India and abroad.

Demography and migration

In 1943-44, he wrote an article on plural and multiple births and their effect on demographic features which was published in '*Transactions of the Bose Research Institute*'. The article specifically highlighted the frequency of twins in India. Again in 1944, in '*Man in India*', he wrote on different demographic aspects of the Malers. In 1953, he showed the migration of the Negrito Racial Strain to the Andaman Islands. He opined that this migration took place in the primitive Jarawa rafts by hops through intervening islands during low tide. In 1958, he did a landmark study on different demographic aspects of the tribal populations of West Bengal. Further, in 1960, he initiated a study on clan demography of an Abor village and settlements of Onges of Andaman Islands. His research on the Negrito Racial strain in India was and is still recognized throughout India with huge appreciation.

Palaeoanthropology and archaeology

Dr. Sarkar did extensive fieldwork in Harappa and Mahenjodaro of Indus Civilization sites, during 1930-31, under the general supervision of Sir Robert Eric Mortimer Wheeler. From different strata of the sites, many burials were found with the help of which he did extensive research on disposal of the dead bodies, which was published in *Science and Culture* in 1937. In the same year, he also wrote notes on *Pithecanthropus erectus* and a skull found in Eyassi of East Africa. Next year, he wrote another research note on *Sinanthropus pekinensis* in *Science and Culture*. Based on an excavation in Taxila between 1913 and 1934, a report has been published by him along with B. S. Guha and H. K. Bose, on human remains. In 1960, his in-depth craniometric research on the human remains of Brahmagiri, including megaliths and infant skeleton, found an autochthonous Australoid and Scytho-Iranian stocks in the remains.

Blood group study

The all-embracing and elaborate study on the blood group system in India put him on the top of Everest of anthropological research, for which he was awarded the prestigious '*Griffiths Memorial prize*' in 1938, by the University of Calcutta. He started his journey on blood group study among the Santals of Santal Pargana area of the then Bihar (now Jharkhand), Bagdi population of South 24-Parganas of West Bengal, and Oraons in 1936-37. Later, in 1937-38, he got the opportunity to work with E. W. E. MacFarlane and conducted extensive fieldwork on blood groups, and published the landmark article in the *American Journal of Physical Anthropology* on blood group distributions in India in 1941. Blood group distribution among the Angami Nagas put his name in '*Nature*' for the second time in 1940 for correspondence. Before that, in 1936, he wrote a correspondence on Negrito Racial Strain in India, published in '*Nature*'. Since then he continued to work on blood groups among different ethnic population groups throughout India to see the change in allele frequencies of the ABO blood group system. In 1959-60, he reported much important information on the ABO blood group system among the Kotas of Nilgiri hills, Kadars of Kerala, and three ethnic groups, viz. Khond, Santal, Juang of Orissa (Odisha).

Genetics and twin study

Another area where Dr. Sarkar has contributed substantially was genetics, with special reference to twin study and population genetics. It is needless to mention that genetics about the ABO blood group system was also included under this domain of research. He started his research in genetics with the blood group system in 1936 with the polymorphism of the ABO blood group among the Santals of Santal Parganas. In 1937, he worked on genetic polymorphism among the Eastern Himalayan population groups and aborigines of Bihar. Of course, association with E. W. E. MacFarlane gave him the golden opportunity to collect blood group data from a huge number of ethnic groups in India, and later, he established an East-West trend in the frequency of genotypes of ABO blood groups in India. In 1941, he rightly pointed out the necessity of eugenic research in Bengal. I already mentioned earlier that, he had a unique intelligence to think way ahead of his time. Thinking of the study of eugenics in the early 1940s is one such example. He clearly explained the methods, scope, and utility of eugenics in public health in this article. Since 1942, he devoted himself to genetic research of varied aspects. He did extensive research on twins about their finger dermatoglyphic features, nails, and phalanges, birth interval, the inheritance pattern of different traits, and other parameters. Other than twin studies, among the Car Nicobarese, he studied the genetics of neurofibromatosis in 1951. He is in the pages of '*Lancet*' for his research on hairy pinnae, a Y-linked trait. In 1963, he studied the inheritance pattern of hairy pinnae among Bengali females. Although he noticed some hair on some of the girls' pinnae, those were devoid of the medulla. Further, in 1964, along with famous geneticist Curt Stern, he reported the problems of inheritance patterns of hairy pinnae. Afterward, he published many articles on Y-linkage with special reference to hairy pinnae. In 1967, among the Baigas of Madhya Pradesh and Kayasthas of West Bengal, he studied the inbreeding pattern of marriage. Earlier in 1956-57, he also worked on haemophilia, a rare X-linked recessive trait, among different populations of India.

Dermatoglyphics and forensic anthropology

Apart from twin genetics and other domain of genetic aspects like X- and Y-linked inheritance patterns, Dr. Sarkar did notable research in the field of dermatoglyphics and forensic sciences. Starting from 1934-35 with the skeletal remains found in a Malers' cemetery, he continued his research in forensic anthropology for a couple of decades. The feature of ape-like line in the human hand was published in *Calcutta Police journal* in 1953. The fingerprint study among the aborigines of Orissa showed a close relationship between the Juang and Sabara population groups. Dermatoglyphic variation among the Malers and other population groups were also considered milestone studies done by him during the late 1960s. One of the most important contributions of Dr. Sarkar in the practical field of forensic anthropology happened in 1956, which was popularly known as the '*Belarani Murder Case*'. Belarani, a housewife, was brutally murdered by her husband and her body was cut into pieces. Her left foot (a body piece covered in newspaper and found in a sac) was somewhat different in shape. The tracing print of her foot along with the prints of the foot of her father and uncle were sent to Dr. Sarkar in the Department of Anthropology, Calcutta University for verification by Calcutta Police, with a query, whether those prints belonged to the same family. Dr. Sarkar, after thorough research, opined affirmatively and depending on his opinion the identification of the victim was ascertained. Another contribution he made where he helped in identifying a criminal with the presence of a big toe, which the criminal lost during a robbery and murder. Thus, Dr. Sarkar's contribution was not restricted only to academics, but also, his intelligence was equally appreciated in the domain of applied anthropological arena.

Anthropometry, variation, and evolution

Dr. Sarkar's interests in anthropometry and population variation were noticed since the beginning of his research career. In 1938, he proposed a classification of the nasal elevation index. Later in the same year after comparing several anthropometric measurements, he differentiated the head forms and some other body features between the Santals and Malers of Rajmahal Hills. Further, he compared his data set with larger data on anthropometrics collected earlier from a population of Sumatra. Again, variation in digits of hand was also attempted by him between population groups. In the year 1954, he published the landmark book, '*The Aboriginal Races of India*', where ethnic variation in head shape among the tribal populations of India was examined. The populations of undivided India were classified into different groups based principally on head shape, while other characters were also considered as well. This particular research on population variation in India was hugely recognized throughout the world, and for decades, this classification is included in the undergraduate and postgraduate syllabi of Anthropology in many Universities and Institutions of many countries. Again, in 1955, he studied the prevalence of brachycephaly among different population groups of India. He had substantially contributed to the evolutionary aspects of hormones, dermatoglyphic traits, human hair, and genetic aspects of the blood group. '*A Laboratory Manual of Somatology*', a book by Dr. Sarkar, was undoubtedly the first attempt to make the students understand the practical knowledge on anthropometry on the living individuals.

Some more domains

Dr. Sarkar has also done some work on growth studies. Back in 1936, he worked on anthropological aspects of physical growth, and much later during the end of his life, in 1968, he started work on growth, maturation, and development with special reference to menarcheal variation between populations. He also did some social cultural and material culture studies among different population groups of India, like Malers, Nicobarese, Santals, Oraons, and some other tribal populations. In 1968, he delivered '*Bijoy Chandra Memorial lectures*' on mating system and marriage, where he showed the misconception of population problems, which was initially thought to be the result of marriage systems. 'Human welfare' was always his dictum of research. He rightly pointed out the necessity of inter-disciplinary research to formulate sex education for the young and preparation and counseling of marriage. Again, it is evident from his Presidential Address of the Indian Science Congress in 1951, where he showed certain findings of human biology relevant to social welfare like breast cancer and sexuality. He also revealed that human biologists may contribute in the domains of marriage law, differential fertility, demography, and other such areas about human welfare.

Popular and Bengali articles

He wrote many popular articles throughout his career, of which, '*The Orient and Europe*', '*Racial composition of Indian Tribes*', '*The Jarawa of the Andaman Islands*' are worth mentioning. However, the list of articles is huge and is truly difficult to present in a nutshell. In addition, he wrote many articles in Bengali which were published in leading Bengali newspapers and magazines. In a very simple and easy language, he described the factors responsible for birth and sex determination in an article '*Janmo Rahasya*'. Again, in '*Jauna Paribartan*' he discussed the possibilities of sex change in an individual. '*Jamajer kotha*', '*Banghshanukrom O Jamaj*' and '*Jora Jamaj*' were three beautiful articles where he eloquently elaborated on the genetics of twins. From his extensive fieldwork in the Rajmahal hill area, he narrated many aspects of the life of '*Malers*' and '*Saorias*' in his Bengali articles. '*Rajmahaler Pahari Jati*', '*Rajmahaler Aar Ekti Pahari Jati*', '*Rajmahaler Paharia Dharma*' are some of them. Later, during the middle of the 1950s, he wrote some Bengali articles on applied anthropology, of which, '*Folito Nribidya*' and '*Folito Nritatwa*' were noteworthy. He wrote a book named '*Lokgatha*' based on popular myths of different tribal communities. This book was specially written for children. Interestingly, when he left the job of the Anthropological Survey of India (AnSI), the publication of Bengali articles in magazines helped him in earning some wages to cope with the hard economic situations.

Affiliations and achievements

At the beginning of his career, he joined Bose Research laboratory and became the Research Fellow in 1935. In 1938, he won the 'Griffith Memorial Prize' of the University of Calcutta and in the same year, he was awarded the prestigious 'Humboldt Scholarship' by Berlin University and he took the opportunity to work under the able supervision of Eugene Fischer at the 'Kaiser Wilhelm Institute of Anthropology' in Berlin. On his return, he joined the Anthropological Survey of India as Anthropologist. Unfortunately, he was compelled to resign from his job due to some unavoidable weird situations. Even, he refused the request of Prof. Nirmal K. Bose to rejoin AnSI. His daring personality never allowed him to make a compromise with any unethical issues, neither did he bow down in front of an odd situation faced in his lifetime. His research ethics forced him to contradict his own opinions in different aspects of research, e.g. Indo-Aryan stock, Negrito strain, etc. Simultaneously, his moral value constrained him to refuse the requests of authority to rejoin his job. When he left the job of AnSI, there were no earning members in his family to feed 11 of them. Dr. Sarkar was the first D. Sc. in Anthropology (1948) under the University of Calcutta. In 1951, he was elected as a Fellow of the National Institute of Science (presently INSA) and in the same year, he presided over the 'Anthropology and Archaeology Section' of the Indian Science Congress, where he delivered a milestone talk on '*The place of Human Biology in Anthropology and its utility in the service of the Nation*' as the presidential address. This lecture was overwhelmingly recognized by the scientists and policymakers at that time and paved the inclusion of human biology in anthropological research. Lastly, in 1957, he joined as a Lecturer in the Department of Anthropology, the University of Calcutta on request of Professor K. P. Chattopadhyay, a renowned anthropologist. Later he became the Reader of the Department and continued his service till his demise in 1969. Dr. Sarkar was attached with many Universities of India in different capacities and remained members of many scientific bodies, among them the National Institute of Sciences in India, the Asiatic Society of Calcutta, The Indian Anthropological Society, Calcutta, the International Association of Human Biologists of Paris, France and Society for the study in Human Biology, London. In fact, '*The Indian Anthropological Society*' is the brainchild of Dr. Sarkar, who took initiative to revive the '*Anthropological Club*' (formed under the Presidentship of Sir Asutosh Mookherjee, the then Vice-Chancellor, Calcutta University). The club stopped functioning after a few years. In 1958, the Indian Anthropological Society was born and registered, and Dr. Sarkar became the first General Secretary of the society.

Last life

Famous Bengali poet Madhusudan Dutta wrote a line in one of his well-known poems '*Janmabhumir Proti*', which reads, '*Jonmile morite hobe, amar ke kotha kobe*', meaning: '*When you have taken birth, you will die one day, no one in this world is immortal*'. Dr. Sarkar had suffered from many shocks, including the death of his eldest son at the age of 11 years. He also had a tough time when he resigned from AnSI, which put the entire family in hand to mouth situation. However, he received all sorts of support from many of his students, namely, Prof. Amulya Ratan Banerjee, Professor Ajit K. Ray, and another student Kamal Agarwal. Many such incidences, though didn't diminish the mental strength of my grandfather, however, those might be some of the reasons behind his health-related issues. He was suffering from hypertension and mild heart-related problems and used to take a blood thinner. He got operated for hydrocele late in his life. The morning of 9th March 1969 was absolutely fine for all. He went to the Department as per the schedule and returned home at the usual time. After dinner, he used to take medicine regularly. Unfortunately, he failed to find the medicine himself (as my grandmother had gone to her eldest daughter's home in Barrackpore, North 24-Parganas). His daughters and son, who were present at that time at home, also remained unsuccessful to find the same. He slept for a while and suddenly woke up with some irritations. My uncle called the doctor but meanwhile, my grandfather had fallen on the floor due to a massive cerebral stroke. '*Doctor it's acid*' was the last statement he made when the doctor arrived and minutes after, he breathed his last on the lap of my aunt (Mridula Basu). Professor S. R. Das and his wife Madam Amiya Das arrived immediately after hearing the shocking news. The relatives started coming to his place as and when they received the dreadful news. On the next day, innumerable people came to his Jamir Lane residence to see him for the last time. His students arrived one by one and assisted his children in all the last rites. He loved his birthplace, '*Moydah*', like anything and had planned to spend his last life in that village. Unfortunately, his dream remained unfulfilled due to his untimely demise at the age of 61 years.

Dr. Sasanka Sekhar Sarkar might have gone to the heavenly abode, but unquestionably he put his insignia in the domain of anthropology. He would be remembered by the fraternity of Anthropology for his versatility, audaciousness, and his ability to glean information from each topic he had touched.

He was very much reluctant about savings and building assets. He didn't make any nominee for his bank account and for this reason, after his sudden untimely demise, a succession had to be made to withdraw the money from the provident fund and others. The then Vice-Chancellor of Calcutta University had arranged a family pension of Rs. 100.00 per month for his wife. His last book, titled '*Ancient Races of Deccan*' was published in 1972 by Munshiram Manoharlal, as a result of an untiring effort made by his youngest brother Sri Haribishnu Sarkar.

Acknowledgements

One could easily understand that this article is the outcome of certain information that I could gather from many persons for years, even decades. Some of my key informants are no more in this world. I gathered much important information from his children late Syamal Kumar Sarkar (my father), Kalyan Kumar Sarkar (my uncle), and my aunts, late Mrs. Manjula Ghosh, Mrs. Mridula Basu, and Mrs. Mekhala Basu Mazumder, on his attitude towards life and other family-related matters. I came to very close contact with many of his students. The names of Prof. Amulya Ratan Banerjee, late Papia Bhattacharjee (Banerjee), and late Prof. Amitabha Basu should come first. Dr. (Mrs.) Bhattacharjee was thought to be one of his daughters. They affectionately shared enormous information with me when I started my career in Anthropology. I also gratefully acknowledge late Prof. Manish Chakravartti, Prof. Bhubon Mohan Das, Prof. Aloke Kumar Ghosh, and Prof. Tulika Sen, Dr. Rekha Rani Ghosh, and Dr.(Mrs) Jaya Chaudhuri (all have left us forever) for sharing information as and when we met in several academic programmes. I was also enriched by Professors Buddhadeb Chaudhuri and Ranjan Gupta for sharing some interesting stories about my grandfather. Last but not the least, I must mention the name of late Smt. Renuka Sarkar (wife of Dr. S. S. Sarkar). She had a '*Thakumar Jhuli*' ('*Grandma's bag*') for her grandson in a real sense. Very frequently she narrated many happenings of her husband's life in her way in a storytelling manner, which I would remember throughout my life. I would stop my pen here begging mercy from those persons, whose names are not included here inadvertently.

I take this opportunity to pay homage to my grandfather, Dr. Sasanka Sekhar Sarkar, the doyen of Indian Anthropology.

Endnote

- A substantial portion of Dr. Sarkar's articles written in Bengali has been taken from '*Bengali Writings of S. S. Sarkar*' by Rekha Rani Ghosh. *Journal of the Indian Anthropological Society*. 1998. 33: 303-306.
- 'My Master, Dr. Sasanka Sekhar Sarkar: Personal Reminiscences' by M. R. Chakravartti. *Journal of the Indian Anthropological Society*. 1998. 33: 139-143.

- A small portion has been taken from the 'Introduction' of the compilation '*Physical Anthropology and its Extending Horizons*', pp. 1-16. Edited by, A. Basu, AK Ghosh, SK Biswas, R. Ghosh. 1971. Orient Longman, India.

Chapter – 6

Prof. Madhab Chandra Goswami and Anthropology in North-east India

Upala Barua

The years 1947 and 1948 are important dates for Anthropology in North-east India as teaching and researches in Anthropology had begun a new journey right after Indian independence. With the commencement of the Intermediate level Department at Cotton College in 1947 under Calcutta University, the seed of Anthropology was enthusiastically planted at the initiative of Assam's first Chief Minister Late G.N. Bordoloi and Prof K.P. Chattopadhyay, the then Head Department of Anthropology, Calcutta University. The following year, Gauhati University was created, and Anthropology was given a prominent place in the region's academic curricula. While Prof M.N. Saloi, a practicing lawyer with a Master's in Anthropology from Calcutta University, was heading the Department of Anthropology at Cotton College; Prof. M.C. Goswami, also trained under noted Anthropologist Prof. K.P. Chattopadhayaya, Calcutta University, was put in charge of the Anthropology Department in the Gauhati University.

The life story of Prof. M.C. Goswami reveals a story of grit a young scholar from a rural respectable family to pursue and achieve academic excellence overcoming extreme pecuniary constraints. Born to late Baladev Goswami and late Kamala Priya Devi, on 1st October 1918, at Bihampur Xatra, near Nalbari Assam, Prof Madhab Chandra Goswami, through his penetrating observation, deep scholarly insights, perseverance, and the staunch support from his elder brothers (who could not pursue higher education due to economic hardships) had not only completed his graduation and post-graduate education with high grades but also have successfully shaped the future of Anthropology, then a lesser-known, but very important discipline so far as North-east India or the erstwhile Assam is concerned (*Source:* MCG family, 1971).

Throughout his academic career, he has been a constant achiever. Beginning with his matriculation with distinctions in 1935 from Chamata Higher Secondary School, Nalbari, Assam, he secured the First Division in Intermediate Arts from Cotton College, with a State Scholarship in the year 1937. In 1939, Prof. Goswami received his BA degree with Hons. in Sanskrit from Cotton College, then part of the University of Calcutta. For economic reasons, he then worked as a secondary school teacher for a while and also qualified for the BT (now called the B.Ed.) examination in 1944. His life as a secondary school teacher brought him closer to his tribal pupils, which in itself was a turning point in his future career. His brief teaching experiences in Sivasagar made him aware of the tribal way of life of the Miri (Mishing) and Deori tribes of eastern (or upper Assam). First-hand knowledge of the socio-economic conditions of the colourful yet unsophisticated tribesmen and close touch with their children inspired him to offer anthropology as a subject for his post-graduate studies.

At this new phase, he had been greatly encouraged by the great scholar Sri Krishna Kanta Handique to study Anthropology which was a new academic university discipline study till then in India. In 1947, he passed the MA examination in Anthropology from the University College of Science and Technology of the University of Calcutta and was the recipient of the University Gold Medal and SC Mitra Gold Medal in Anthropology for being placed in the first division and first in the order of merit. His specialization was social and cultural anthropology and he had been trained in the techniques of field investigation by late Professor Tarak Chandra Das, of the University of Calcutta in 1946 among the Hos of Bihar. The newly created Gauhati University appointed him as a lecturer to initiate an undergraduate Anthropology Department in 1948. Here, he continued as the Lecturer in Charge of the UG Department till 1956, the year of opening of the post-graduate course in Anthropology when he was promoted as a Reader. In the meantime, he left for Cambridge in 1952, London to study in the Department of Archaeology and Anthropology under Prof Meyer Fortes and Dr. E J Lindgen. During this period, he had presented a short but succinctly written paper entitled Structure of An Assamese Village in the year 1953. In 1954, he was awarded M.Litt. from Cambridge University for his dissertation on '*Mongoloids and Their Contribution to the Growth and development of Assamese Culture*'. On his return, he relentlessly continued to develop the Anthropology Department at the University of Gauhati in a holistic way. He had genuinely encouraged the growth and development in all the major branches of Anthropology viz, physical (or biological), social and cultural, and prehistoric (or archaeological) anthropology. He became a Professor in 1962 at Gauhati University, and in 1972 he was acknowledged as a UGC Senior Professor. Prof Goswami was elected as the President of the Section of Anthropology and Archaeology in 1969 while he served as the Co-Chairperson of the Post-Plenary Session of the 10th International Congress of Anthropological and Ethnological Sciences which was held in Lucknow in the year 1978.

During his long tenure spanning three decades (from 1948-1978), at the helm of the Anthropology Department as the Head, Prof Goswami had built up a rich ethnological museum covering all the three major branches mentioned earlier, as an aid in teaching and research in Anthropology in entire North-east India. This rich museum boasts of specimens collected by him from different ethnic groups of Assam, Nagaland, Manipur, Mizoram, Meghalaya, and Arunachal Pradesh (erstwhile NEFA). Needless to mention here that the Assam in the period immediately after Indian Independence included all these different states (except Manipur and Tripura) of today within a single administrative frame. He conducted ethnographic field investigations among different tribal communities like the Karbi, the Garo, the Rabha, the Adi, the Boro-Kacharis, the Khasi, the Lalung (Tiwa), the Dafla (the Nishi or Nyshi); Dimasa Kachari, and many other non-tribal communities of this vast region. After his retirement, he became in1979 a Visiting Professor at Utkal University. He was offered

Visiting Professorship in 5 other Universities but could not join. When he was the Project Co-ordinator of Law Research Institute (LRI), Gauhati High Court during 1980-1987, a series of reports, (sponsored by NEC and LRI), on the customary laws of many different tribes across the entire North-east India were published under his supervision. These include tribal communities like the Garos, the Wancho, the Mizo, the Tankhul, the Aos, the Pati Rabhas, the Riangs, the Apatanis, the Angamis, the Tripuris, the Chakmas, and the Dimasa. In 1999, he was conferred upon RP Chanda Gold Medal for his contribution to Anthropological Studies in North-east India. Prof. Goswami breathed his last on 28th July 2002.

He had more than 30 scientific papers to his credit and 14 scholars had qualified for Ph.D. under his supervision. These scholars have successfully carried forwarded the spirit of ethnographic and archaeological anthropological researches in different universities and institutes of the region. He had co-authored two books *The Social Institutions of the Garos of Meghalaya* (jointly with Dr. DN Majumdar) and *The People of Arunachal Pradesh* (Jointly with Prof. P.B. Das).

His research papers and contributions to the anthropology of the region could be discussed into two distinct but interrelated aspects. While he had contributed towards the social, cultural, economic, political, and religious lives of the myriad communities of the region with the encyclopaedic vision of a true ethnographer; he, in missionary zeal, had also successfully initiated and directed the trend of prehistoric (and later historic) archaeological research in North-east India during the post-Independence period. At times, his ethnographic fieldwork revealed the probable existence of an archaeological site. On the other hand, he could relate ethnographic information with prehistoric and historic processes.

The themes of his academic writings on social and cultural anthropology are varied and range from the social structure of Assamese villages to the Garo Matrilineal Matrix or Mother's Brother in Paite Society; from labour organizations among the Thanga fishermen of Manipur to the bell-metal workers of Sarthebari or the role of *Samadi* (youth dormitory) in a changing Lalung society; from shamanism at the Kamakhya temple to the magico-religious uses of neolithic celts among many different ethnic groups across North-east India. He had also contributed his views on 'Corporations and Social Classification by D. E. Brown, along with many other distinguished anthropologists [*Source:* Current Anthropology, Vol. 15, No. 1 (Mar. 1974), pp. 29-52]. This is only a partial list. His contribution to the archaeological anthropology of the region is immense, covering explorations and excavations of neolithic times in the hilly areas like Garo Hills and the then N.C. Hills of Assam, the metal ages (Iron Age), and finally the early historic site of Ambari. And it is almost impossible to touch upon his every work within this limited space. Therefore, an attempt has been made to touch upon his core ideas or concepts and how he had developed or used these concepts to understand the diverse yet germane socio-cultural issues and illuminate different processes that are in operation in North-east India even today.

Theoretical orientations and his contributions

Start from margin a direct student of Prof Meyer Fortes and Dr. E J Lindgen, was a fervent follower of the British School of Social Anthropology. This is apparent in his brief communication entitled '*The Social Structure of an Assamese Village*' (1953). His field research in upper and lower Assam villages immediately after World War II led him to see the society of the plains people of Assam, which differs from that of the region's hill tribes, as an extension or 'section' of the Indo-Aryan civilization of Northern India. In this context, he used the word social structure to refer to 'the web of links existing between individuals and groups of individuals in the same village and within a larger area.' He has also observed that these relationships in an Assamese village are governed by the (i) the ties within the elementary or the joint family; (ii) the wider kinship relations by blood and marriage; (iii) the caste group; (iv) the organization of the *khel* (section, division) and (v) the *satra* (monastery) institution of with the village prayer hall (*nam-ghar*) as its replica in each village. Assamese society is characterized by the *khel* organization and the institution of *satra*. A *khel* generally consists of persons belonging to different castes yet the *khel* system does not disturb the 'traditional caste rules of separate eating and endogamous marriage'. Members of a *khel* retain unity by following the leadership of its 'acknowledged leaders'.

In the aforesaid paper, he (1953) had limited his focus on the *khel* organization and the institution of *satra*, which are the hallmarks of Assamese society. A *khel* generally consists of persons belonging to different castes yet the *khel* system does not disturb the 'traditional caste rules of separate eating and endogamous marriage.' However, unlike caste, a *khel* group is characterized by the twin processes of fission and fusion. Meanwhile, members of a *khel* retain unity by following the leadership of its 'acknowledged leaders.' As regards the institution of *satra*, the authority of the *satradhikar* (pontiff) is undisputed among his disciples. To be able to take part in the ritual life of the community's socio-religious gatherings, the people following the Vaishnavite sect of Hinduism, have to undergo an initiation rite, before or after marriage. In all social relationships, there is a sense of brotherhood among the disciples of the same preceptor. However, the tie is much closer amongst persons initiated by the same preceptor at the same time and place. Known as *Hari-bhakat* (devotees of God) to each other, they consider themselves as siblings and follow exogamous rules. Such bonds of spiritual brotherhood, extend over at least three generations, overriding caste barriers. In his observation, the occurrence of illegitimate sex relations disturbs the equilibrium in the social structure of an Assamese village to a great extent. To rectify the irregularity, the perpetrators must invite all fellow members of the *khel* group, including members of the extended family (*bangah*), to participate in purificatory rituals.

While presenting a functional study of the factors and forces responsible for the bell metal craft in Sarthebari-a village inhabited by three different castes, viz., Kalita, Keot Koch, and a few Muslim families, Prof. Goswami (1973) revealed and made certain pertinent comments on the nature of the caste system, like the absence of a marked *jajmani* relationship, and the weak link between caste and occupational segregation in Assamese society. He notes that the ecology of a locality, covering its physical, geographical, and socio-cultural aspects, lies at the root of the rise or decline of a particular craft in that area. On the contrary, he has illustrated that, in Assam, the caste structure has no major role to play in this regard. A craft is generally open to any caste and is not necessarily hereditary. People in an agricultural community generally adopt crafts such as bell metal, gold and silver smithy, blacksmiths, carpenters, and weavers of Assam are at heart cultivators. They take up a trade prescribed by the hierarchical caste organization only when they find no cultivable land in their vicinity, either as cultivating landowners or as sharecroppers (*Ibid*). Sarthebari, being located in a low-lying area, is ravaged by floods every year, and paddy cultivation is possible only to a limited extent. Because a large area was unfit for cultivation, the villagers had no option but to adopt artisan crafts. Most of them have taken up bell metal craft as some of their forefathers were trained in the craft. The article also dealt with the problems and hardships faced by these craftsmen along with the altered ecological setup – population growth, the spread of education, urbanization, growth of land transport, and easily available means of earning a living that has induced the upcoming generations to give up their traditional trade that demands heavy physical strain. Thus, in his characteristic lucid style, he had not only dealt with the particular craft in a particular locality but also illuminated the nature of the caste system and occupational patterns in rural Assamese society.

In the introduction to *Social Institutions of the Garo of Meghalaya* (Goswami and Majumdar,1972) which he had jointly authored with his student, Dhirendra Narayan Majumdar, who also happens to be an eminent anthropologist of the region himself, bears testimony of his inclination towards structural functionalism and functionalism. In this Introduction, they had discussed how they had adapted the theories of A.R. Radcliffe-Brown, B. Malinowski, and Leach. (*Ibid*: 1-10) while analyzing the social institutions of the Garo tribe. His interest in functionalist analysis and Garo matrilineal institutions through his intimate connection with the Garo society since 1948, also got expressed in one of his essays written in 1992 wherein he dealt with the 'matrix of relationships' that exists among the Garos, particularly among those who follow traditional religion and practice shifting cultivation. By applying the functionalistic approach, (which according to him was the surest way for structural analysis) Prof

Goswami, demonstrates that the *maharl-machong* (matrilineage-matriclan) syndrome of the Garo lie at the center of the web of relationships 'between and among the matrilineal social institutions like inheriting daughter, (*nokna),* resident son in law (*nokrom)*, head of the property owing mahari (*aking*-nokma), permanent bond between a husband and wife (akim;) mother-in-law marriage, replacement of spouses, step-daughter step-father marriage, groom capture, etc., satisfy the functional needs of matriliny as observed under normal situations.

However, in his discussions on different ethnic communities of NE India and the processes operating in the inter-community relations, it appears that he had looked towards the concepts like 'Tribe-caste-peasants' continua; anthropology of 'great and little traditions' and the process of Sanskritization to a certain extent without going into or referring to these concepts in details. Thus, his writings appear to leave clues for future scholars to take up serious studies on these lines. With his strong academic background in Sanskrit as well as his deep knowledge of the socio-cultural lives of the different tribal and non-tribal people of the region, he could understand the intricacies of the interaction between the great and little traditions. He was a pioneer in evolving an anthropological perspective towards understanding the ethnic groups and processes of myriad communities of North-east India. While doing so, he had referred to (or used the concepts of Sanskritization) the processes of Sanskritization (Goswami, 1969) and Hinduization. He had also discussed at length about the new dimensions of peasant and neo-peasants without much referring to the works of Redfield or Firth. In his opinion, a social group in North-east India is either a caste, a religious entity, or a tribe. According to him, in North-east India, 'the emotional attachment to a group name' arising out of a tradition of being originated from the common ancestors is the defining feature of a tribal identity rather than the use of a common tongue or occupying the same territory. This he illustrated with cases from the different sections of the Rabha tribe. He does not attempt to define tribes as such but does say that a tribe preserves its identity until it is drawn and incorporated into the 'broader framework of the social organization of the soil' [meaning caste system]. As a tribe integrates into larger Indian society, it loses its former tribal identity, but it keeps it for a time before recasting itself as a caste unit. The cases of Deuri, Miri, the Chutiya, the Ahoms, the Rabha, the Kachari, and the Dimasas are examples. This process of integrating tribal units into nuclear Indian culture [meaning caste system] involves several stages that vary from place to place and from time to time. Despite the long-drawn-out process, the outcomes are truly ground-breaking. According to him, there are multiple interrelated stages of transition from highland to a peasant economy and society along with associated folkways. (Goswami,1971) The intervening stages, according to him, are semi-highland and semi-peasant stages. This has been illustrated here in a sequence:

Highland society → Semi-highland society → Semi-peasant society → Peasant society

In the highland stage, there was very little or no contact of the tribal communities with the outside world. Such isolation continued till around the 1920s. Among the tribesmen themselves, three distinct sets of tribal settlers may be categorized: viz *paharua,* the highlanders; *tarua* or *datival* (boundary line residents), the foothill dwellers, and the *thalua* that, the plains settlers or the settled agriculturists of the riverine areas. In his opinion, the tribal folk or the highlanders first adopted the techniques of settled agriculture from the people living in the plains through the hill to plains migration. Later on, very gradually they started absorbing the rituals associated with plough cultivation. The transitional phase when a tribe comes out of isolation and began adopting the peasant way though not fully merging itself into peasantry could be called neo-peasants. The neo-peasants combine the characteristics of both tribes and peasants. (Goswami, 2004). In another paper (Goswami, 1992) he expresses the same point much more clearly: some of the high land-dwelling Tibetans came to be known as Bhutia, who in turn became recognized as Bodo or Kachari [now a Scheduled Tribe living in the plains] and in course of time was recognized a Koch [now recognized as the Other Backward Class and are in the first rung in the caste-hierarchy] and still later as Saru Kalita (a caste group). Similarly, the Adi group of communities living in the higher altitudes became Mishings, Chutia or Deuri, of the plains, some of whom have lost their tribal identity due to the influence of the Satra or Monastery organization of Assam and progressively got merged in the 'none-too-rigid caste hierarchy of the Brahmaputra Valley' (Goswami, 1992). In this paper, he had also feared that some of the constitutional provisions for the welfare of the tribal or backward communities have fuelled the rise of ethnic identity movements with separatist tendencies for achieving political ends hampering the regional and national solidarity. During his times, maybe it was quite natural for him to conclude that the neo-peasant groups of North-east India are in the process of losing their tribal identities and are on the way to establishing themselves as castes (Goswami, 2004; 1992). Now, it is high time for contemporary anthropologists to carry out research to assess the patterns of such changes that are continually occurring in the ethnic scenario since his times.

Due to the combined forces of natural population growth, coupled with the mass migration of immigrants from undivided Bengal, migration of Tea Garden labourers hailing from such places like Bihar, Orissa, central India, Prof. Goswami (1971) had discerned a reversed process of upward or rather inward migration by the permanently settled tribesmen into the hilly region. This is how inter-ethnic and inter-community conflict came to be initiated in the region mainly for the ownership of cultivable land. This is how inter-ethnic and intra-ethnic tensions have appeared on the scene, particularly on the borderlines between the hills and the plains of the Brahmaputra valley.

At the same time, he also mentioned that throughout history, the hill tribes have been coming down occasionally to the foothills through *duars* or the gateways and meeting places for the transaction of essential items that ultimately grew as marketplaces *(haat)*. Ceremonial friendly relations (*mita* or *kurma*) thus developed between many a hilly tribesman and the plains dwellers were in actuality, precursors of close contact between communities. He observed that that the tribesmen regularly visiting the marketplaces were attracted by the rich cultural contents of river valley civilizations having 'high prestige value'. This led many of them to settle in some intermediate locations from where they could sustain trade relations between their congeners, the highlanders, and their clients of the plains. (Goswami, 1971) many of whom eagerly waited for an expected visit of the *mitta* or *kurma* i.e. ceremonial friend. The smooth and ever-expanding trade relations strengthened by ceremonial friendship bonds encouraged some of the highlanders to settle permanently in the plains areas. The rapid economic prosperity of these exploratory settlers tempted other venturous highlanders to gather the courage to follow it. They too began settling in either in 'no man's land or earmarked for such colonisers by the administration.' The glaring instances of such cases include the Nyishi (Dafla) settlement near Charduarr; Bhutia Basti to the north of Jalah among others. Incidentally, he also mentioned that the Chutiyas, the Barahis the Mishings Deuris, the Turungs, the Aitonia, the Tai Phakes, the Singphos the Khamtis, the Monpas, the Tai Ahoms, the Dimasas, the Kacharis the Lalungs the Rabhas, were once highlanders at some points of history. (Ibid)

His paper on Shamanism at Kamakhya, (Goswami, 1975) the primordial temple complex of Goddess worship that celebrated the Goddess-power, brings out many important aspects related to shamanistic socio-religious practices/ dances observable not only in the Kamakhya but also among many ethnic communities of the region. He notes that within the lower (western) districts of Assam, particularly in many peasant villages, shamanistic centres have grown up that are in actuality are offshoots of the place of its origin at Kamakhya. In these areas, the shamans are generally male persons, and except for a few Brahmin shamans in the past, are mostly from lower castes. In these areas, the serpent Goddess Manasa is also being worshipped.

According to him, the traditional dictionary definition of the shaman as a wizard-priest or as 'a person who has direct communication with supernatural beings through dreams, visions, or spirit possession' (Lowie, 1947, cf Goswami, 1975) does not fully encompass the native Assamese terminology, *deodha* 'the echo of the divine.' or *jaki.* (the possessed one'). Ordinary human beings can act and behave in ways that local faiths attribute to a visible manifestation of a particular deity when specially chosen by that deity. Possession by a deity results in a temporary loss of civil status for two months [Shrawana and Bhadra] corresponding to the period between16 July and 17 September during the rainy season when the agricultural activities keep the peasants tied to their villages. Incidentally, during these two months, the peasants and the neo-peasants remain busy in their plough cultivation and are unable to visit the Kamakhya temple for any emergency. Moreover, during these times they are afflicted with various tropical diseases like cholera, smallpox, etc over and above there is the constant fear of being bitten by poisonous snakes. Therefore, they are forced to visit the local shamans at their residences.

Along with a plethora of spiritual and sociological causes like belief in fate and fatalism, recurring family problems, a lack of readily available medical services, and barrenness in women, Prof. Goswami had specifically mentioned that the growth and dissemination of the widespread Eka Sarania sect of Vaishnavism[1] among the rural masses of Assam contributed toward the convictions about the efficacy of the shamanistic prescriptions. Due to their religious proscription on idolatry, the Vaishnavite disciples are unable to visit proscribed to visit the Shakta[2] temples, of which the temple of Goddess Kamakhya, in Guwahati city, happens to be the primordial site. He explains that most of the shamans are the vehicles of recognized deities, the majority of which have a standing temple at Kamakhya. However, the shamans have their *Thapana* or Altar for the presiding deity, in their respective residences, which any interested devotee can attend without being publicly reprimanded. A visit to the Kamakhya temple site by followers of this sect, on the other hand, is frowned upon by the general public. The *Thapana* has no image, and veneration for it elicits no negative emotions in devotees of this group. Moreover, all other peasants can easily consult the shamans at the village temple.

Prof Goswami has noted two major types of shamans in Assam. In his view, the shamanistic dancers are popular in the lower Assam [western] districts, where the Bodo group of tribes like the Rabha, the Koch, the Karbi the Lalung, or the Tiwa belong to the first category represented by the shamanistic women *Kherai* dancers of the Bodo people. The other centre of shamanism in Assam could be observed among the Tai people of upper [eastern] Assam wherein the priestly classes, like the Deodha, Bailung and Mohan are notable for their oracular and shamanistic forecasts. He had mentioned also the Lai Haroba festival of the Meitei of Manipur where the Maibi or the shamaness is possessed by the presiding deity of the festival. Thus, the diverse ethnocultural composition of the people of Assam provided a very fertile ground for the growth and luxurious flourish of the shaman dancers. The human vehicles of these deities, known as *ghora* or *jaki*, rise above the hierarchical restraints of socio-cultural behaviour during the period of possession by transcending the established caste order. Most of these human vehicles are from lower castes. While women are not allowed to become *ghora* or *jaki* at or any local units connected with Kamakhya temple; many tribal communities are still practicing shamanistic dances where the chief shamanistic medium happens to be a woman. He further notes that the neo-peasant groups of Assam represented by those highlanders who in the prehistoric and historic periods gradually migrated to the plain's areas in search of better and more fertile arable lands are now devout clientele of the shamans of Kamakhya. The tribal highlanders very rarely come to visit these shamans at Kamakhya.

His central theme of gradual, phase-wise migration of isolated tribal economies based on shifting cultivation leading to their transformations and amalgamation into peasant society of the valleys or plains on their adoption of the techniques of wet paddy or plough cultivation also finds its way in his assessment of the role of Samadi or youth dormitory in the changing society of the Lalung (Tiwa) tribe. In this regard, he hypothesizes that a bachelors' dormitory or its prototype is a must in a shifting economy. With a gradual shift from this neolithic type of economy pervading their socio-economic and ritual life to a peasant economy, the dormitory organization finds itself in a disarray until its disappearance in a pure peasant economy that co-exists with an urban-oriented industrial economy.

He had discussed three phases of an economic pattern of the Lalung society from the intensive study of four villages. Shifting cultivation was the main economic activity of the Hill Lalung villages where the Samadi organization was fully functioning at the time of his field visits. The subsistence mode of the border dwelling and Lalungs living on foothills showed a combination of both shifting cultivation and wet cultivation where the Samadi organization was also quite active. However, the youth dormitory gradually declined in the economy of subsistence of the Lalung society from completely shifting cultivation of the hill Lalung; the combination of shifting cultivation and wet cultivation of the border or foothill dwelling Lalungs and the wet cultivation practiced by the migrant Lalung in the plain's areas. It identifies the relevance of the bachelor's dormitory (Samadi) in a humming economy and among villagers who combine shifting with wet cultivation while focusing its absence in the peasant economy of the plains Lalungs. He had also explored the hypothesis that the bachelor's dormitory or its prototype is a must in a shifting economy based on data collected from four typical Lalung villages representing different phases. He thus believed that the bachelor's dormitory is pivotally connected with shifting cultivation. It identifies the relevance of the bachelor's dormitory in a *jhumming* economy and among villagers who combine shifting with wet cultivation while focusing its absence in the peasant economy of the plains Lalungs. An attempt had been made by him to test a hypothesis that the bachelor's dormitory or its prototype is a must in a shifting economy based on data collected from four typical Lalung villages.

Prof Goswami's idea of a self-reliant shifting economy approaches 'a Neolithic type of economy'. The use of this phrase, 'Neolithic type of economy' reveals not only his profound prehistoric cultures in this region, besides understanding the ethnographic scenario of his times but also connects his pioneering contributions in the field of archaeological exploration and excavations uncovering prehistoric cultures and river valley civilizations in North-east India. This leads us to discuss his contributions to the archaeological anthropology of the region presently.

After the establishment of the Gauhati University in 1948, the first university in the entire North-eastern India, where facilities for systematic studies and research in anthropology and prehistoric archaeology were provided under the guidance of Prof. M.C. Goswami, who took a keen interest in organizing systematic field investigations in different parts of North-east India. As a result, a large number of Stone Age artifacts from various parts of the regions were collected the most of which came from the Garo Hills, where he uncovered a particularly rich Stone Age site at Chitra Abri near Rengsanggiri village (Goswami and Bhagabati, 1959a). [Sharma: 1980) In 1960, MC Goswami collected some neoliths from the houses of some Dimasa persons, near Maibong in North Cachar hills (now Dima Hasao). He also visited a place called Deojali Parbat in North Cachar Hills where a large number of neoliths happened to be unearthed by the workmen engaged in the construction of a road. Based on these reports, a stratified Neolithic site was discovered and subsequently excavated at Daojali Hading in the North Cachar Hills district of Assam.

Excavation of the Daojali Hading site, situated on a crest of a hill, took place between 1961 and 1963. To evaluate the stratigraphic sequence and culture contents of the site, a test pit (trench A) measuring 3.50 x 0.75 m was dug in 1961 at the already disturbed area of the site (Goswami and Sharma, 1962; 63-66). In 1963, four regular trenches (B, C, D, and E) were excavated in the undisturbed area of the site, each measuring 3.50 metres square. Only trench B reveals a regular sequence of both natural and cultural deposits. The top layers were eroded in the rest, either fully destroying the cultural levels or exposing them on the surface (Goswami and Sharma, 1963: 45 - 47). On the technological ground, the stone implements of Daojali Hading may be classified into Flake tool, edge ground tools, and fully ground tools. It suggests that the neolithic people of Daojali Hading prepared and utilized a very limited quantity of flake tools. The majority (96%) of the edged tools at Daojali Hading are shaped initially by chipping and then finished by grinding either fully or partly. This group of tools could be classified into three well-defined types, viz., triangular celt with the flat and thin body; quadrangular celt with flat sides and faces; shouldered celt showing two varieties - the crude or curvilinear variety; and the square cut rectilinear ones. On the whole, the stone industry of Daojali Hading suggests a neolithic type of economy.

Continued work on this site by T.C. Sharma revealed in later excavations that the most important archaeological find at Daojali Hading is the pottery showing cord-marked designs predominantly of grey colour. Around 95 percent of potteries are of the cord-marked type but it was not possible to reconstruct the shapes of the pottery vessels as the potsherds were very much fragmented. The fabric is rough and porous and is hand-made by a coil building method or process. The final shape of the pots is achieved by beating the walls of the vessels with a beater that is either wrapped in a cord or thread or roughened by engraving designs on the blade of the beater.

Prof Goswami had made a significant collection of Stone Age antiquities from different parts of Garo hills [of present-day Meghalaya] during his numerous ethnographic field trips which helped in illuminating the archaeological potentialities of the region. (Sharma,1980). Sharma (Sharma, 1966: 187) classified the collection of Prof. Goswami and noted the presence of hand axes, choppers, scrapers, flakes, and blades cores (Sharma, 1966: 187). From 1966, systematic investigations were conducted in the Rongram, Ganol, and Simsang valleys in the Garo Hills by Prof. Goswami and Prof T.C. Sharma resulting in the discovery of several Stone Age sites in the central Garo Hills area among which the sites at Rongram, Waram Thebrongiri, Selbalgiri, and Mishimagiri are found to be very rich in their culture-contents and stratified in nature. (Sharma, 1980). Moreover, a report of a collection of 18 neolithic celts from the Kameng district of Arunachal Pradesh was made by Prof. Goswami and his pupils (1972, 29-35). These tools included shouldered celts in addition to trapezoidal, triangular, and splayed axes.

While gathering or exploring for neolithic tool-types all over Assam, he and his team had come across varying degrees of unscientific and queer notions about the metaphysical properties of the celts of diverse description. A predominant idea among the rural mass-tribal or non-tribal closely associated with the celt is about its medicinal values and super-human properties. Such semi-divine or divine qualities as a cure from its wrongly assumed source of origin, the lightning, which phenomenon is overwhelmingly supernatural to the unsophisticated and unenlightened rural folk. (Goswami, 1961)

In this way, Prof. Goswami was instrumental in conducting scientific exploration, excavation of various prehistoric archaeological sites in a region which is strategically located in the region between South Asia and South East Asia. He had mentioned it in connection with the then ethnographic scenario of the region. Studies by his junior contemporaries like T.C. Sharma and others have revealed close affinity between the cord-marked pottery, quadrangular adze, shouldered celt, or the ground and polished stone tools of North-east India (particularly from) Daojali Hading and Garo Hills with the

Hoabinhian axes of Southeast Asia. Sharma observes that 'based on this evidence we are inclined to believe that in the post-palaeolithic period the Hoabinhian tradition entered into northeast India from Southeast Asia'. When the ground and polished stone tools are analyzed, it becomes evident that there is an unmistakable influence of South East Asian Neolithic tradition over the Garo Hills. The presence of a large number of shouldered celts in the Garo Hills is clear evidence of such cultural affinities.

Professor Goswami's contribution towards archaeological anthropology is not limited to pre-neolithic and neolithic phases only. It was under his directorship that the roots of Brahmaputra valley civilization began to be unfolded at the famed Ambari excavations. The Ambari Archaeological site situated in the heart of the Guwahati city in Kamrup District of Assam was accidentally discovered while digging the foundation for the building of the Reserve Bank of India in 1969. The Department of Anthropology, Gauhati University, under the supervision of Prof M.C. Goswami in collaboration with the State Department of Archaeology, carried out salvage digging at Ambari which is located on the bank of an old channel of the Brahmaputra, the present course of the river being 1 km. to the south. According to the Archaeological Survey of India, 'the excavated trenches showed five layers (from the top downwards) :

- (i) dark grey earth (30 cm.) mixed with the debris of modern industrial activity;
- (ii) light brown earth (25 cm.), containing sculptures, brick fragments, pottery, etc.;
- (iii) compact brown earth (50 cm.), containing bricks, large quantities of pottery, pebbles, hearths, etc.;
- (iv) brownish-grey earth mixed with rubble and pottery (30 cm.); and
- (v) dark-grey earth (partly exposed), containing brickbats, pottery, etc. Subsoil water-. the level was reached at a depth of about 1-82 m. below the present surface: At no point was the natural soil exposed.

During salvage operations, over forty stone sculptures were obtained from the second layer including images of Vishnu, Surya, Nandi, Durga, and Agni besides *lingas* (phallic symbol of the god

Shiva) and yonis (the vulva, especially as a symbol of divine procreative energy conventionally represented by a circular stone) of various sizes. Stylistically, they may be assigned to ninth-tenth century A.D. Besides, structures of stone and brick and a brick-paved drain, with side walls of dressed stone blocks and partly dressed stone cover-slab were also unearthed. Adjacent to the structure, to its North-west, was a burnt earth patch indicating its probable use as a fireplace.

The pottery, mostly wheel made, could be grouped into five classes based on surface colour: (i) kaolin white; (ii) buff; (iii) red; (iv) grey, and (v) dark grey to black. Almost all of these are made on the wheel. Besides, a fragment of Chinese Celadon Ware and sherds of local glazed ware, showing green, silver, cream, and red surface colours were also found. Among other finds, mention may be made of a cornucopia-shaped lamp-stand (pl. IIIC), beads and bangles variously of terracotta and glass, terracotta figurines (pl. IV), a terracotta seal showing a human head (?), an iron arrow-head, a few rings of copper and iron and a small copper coin minted by the East India Company. After this first excavation in 1970 under the supervision of Prof Goswami, the Ambari site has been excavated at different points of time by different excavators till 2007-2008. However, in the present context, only the work accomplished by Prof Goswami and his team is mentioned.

The occupation of Ambari was initially has been made into two distinct cultural periods ranging from c. 7th to 12th c. AD and 13th to 17th c. AD respectively. (Lal, 1971: 3-4). However, the age of the human habitation activities at the site has been determined to be that of the Sunga-Kushana period, that is 2nd century BC or 1st century BC to 3rd century AD. (Roy, 1977). Before Ambari excavation, the literary history of Assam could be traced only up to the 6th century AD. It may be mentioned here that the excavation at Ambari was conducted with two major objectives. First, it was intended to establish an archaeological sequence so that in the long run, it might mutually support the available literary evidence. Thus, it was hoped that the hidden ruins unearthed at Ambari will ultimately illuminate the dark patches or the gaps in the existing knowledge about the most ancient period of Assam's history. The city of Guwahati mentioned as Pragjyotishpura in the Mahabharata stands on a large number of temples and other archaeological ruins. However, the fact remains that, even after almost half a century of Ambari excavations, the antiquity of the major portion of these ruins has not been completely unveiled and determined.

In the preceding paragraphs, it becomes more and more clear that Prof. Goswami had accomplished a great task of complementing ethnographic researches with archaeological explorations. Very often, it was during his field trips to tribal areas, be it in the North Cachar Hills (the present Dima Hasao District) of Assam or Garo Hills in Meghalaya, new archaeological sites were discovered, located, and were available for future researchers. Besides, prehistoric archaeological researches into the neolithic and pre-neolithic cultural roots of the region, he headed the excavation at Ambari that pushed back the timeline provided by the literary-historical materials. His deep penetrating observations and insights gathered through intimate life-long field researches among the tribal and peasant communities, their interactions with their geo-cultural settings, their migration patterns besides the tenacious interrelations between economy, social organization, religion, and polity (as a true structural-functionalist) are revealed in every article he wrote.

In sum, Prof Goswami's central theme of understanding the multi-ethnic processes and situation of the North-eastern region of India happens to be is a gradual, phase-wise migration of isolated tribal economies based on shifting cultivation that leads to their transformations and amalgamation into peasant society of the valleys or the plains through their adoption of the techniques of wet paddy or plough cultivation. Only after the adoption of plough cultivation, these communities, termed as Neo-peasants by him, very slowly are drawn into the fold of Hinduism. This very theme is visible in most of his academic writings. As already mentioned, his writings offer plenty of avenues for taking up new research or to open up constructive academic debates/ discussions on many diverse yet pertinent issues of the region at large.

Professor Goswami is undoubtedly the first anthropologist of India during the post-Independence period who had successfully played the roles of a teacher-mentor, ethnographer, theoretician and an archaeologist, to carry forward the messages of a holistic science of humanity in understanding the complex processes that are operating in this frontier region of India.

References

Bhattacharyya, NN. 1974. *History of the Sakta Religion,* Munshiram Manoharlal Publishers. New Delhi.

Budhi Singh Ch and Goswami, MC.1970. Tenure and allocation of phoompham among the Thanga fishermen of Manipur. *Man in India.* 50, 4: 379-389.

Goswami, MC 1961. A note on the magico-medicinal uses of celts in Assam. *Journal of University of Gauhati,* 12, 2: 17-24.

Goswami, MC, Das RC, and Sharma HC. 1972. A typological study of some prehistoric tools from the Kameng district, NEFA (Arunachal) *Journal of the Assam Science Society* 15, 1: 29-35.

Goswami, MC and Roy SK, 1972. A report or selected potsherds from Ambari, Assam, *Bulletin of Department of Anthropology, Gauhati University,*1: 22-27.

Goswami, MC and Roy SK, 1976. An introductory note on the pottery of Assam with special reference to Ambari excavations. *Bulletin of Department of Anthropology, Gauhati University:* 6: 1-19.

Goswami, MC and Roy SK, 1979. A short note on a Tangsa hoe. *Bulletin of Department of Anthropology, Gauhati University*, 4: 71-73.

Goswami, MC and Sharma TC, 1962. A brief report on the investigation into the prehistoric archaeology of North Cachar Hills, Assam, *Journal of the University of Gauhati,* 13, 2: 63-66.

Goswami, MC and Sharma TC, 1963. Further report on the investigation into the prehistoric Archaeology of North Cachar Hills, Assam, *Journal of University of Gauhati,* 14, 2: 45-47.

Goswami, MC, 1971. *Tribe, peasant-caste relation in North-east India*, Presidential Address, 58th Indian Science Congress, Section of Anthropology and Archaeology, pp. 1-18.

Goswami, MC, 1973. Bell-metal workers of Sarthebari, Assam, *Bulletin of Department of Anthropology, Gauhati University*, 2: 1-12.

Goswami, MC, 1994. Garo matrilineal matrix. *Journal of the Indian Anthropological Society* 29, 1 and 2: 187-194.

Goswami, MC, 2004. Peasants and neo peasants in North-east India: Their new dimensions in Shakuntala Devi (Ed:: *Introduction to Social Anthropology,* Raj Publications.

Goswami, MC, and Singh Ch B. 1973. Ethnic and spatial framework of organizations of Thanga fishermen of Manipur; *Bulletin of Department of Anthropology, Gauhati University,* 2: 62-91.

Goswami, MC, and Kamkhenthang H. 1972. Mother's brother in Paite Society, *Man in India* 52, 1: 21-38.

Goswami, MC, and Singh Ch. Budhi, 1974. Labour organizations of Thanga fishermen. *Eastern Anthropologist*, 27, 1: 35-43.

Goswami, MC, and Singh Ch. Budhi, 1971. Symbolic attitudes of the fisher-folk of Thanga toward a dug-out canoe. *Journal of the Assam Science Society* 14, 2: 117-123.

Goswami, MC, and Bhagabati AC. 1959a. A typological study of shouldered Celts from Rengchangiri (Garo Hills). *Journal of University of Gauhati*, 10, 2: 105-122.

Goswami, MC, and Bhagabati AC. 1959b. A preliminary report on the collection of neolithic tool types from Western Assam. *Man in India*. 39, 4: 312-324.

Goswami, MC, 1992. Peoples and cultures of North-east India. *Bulletin of Department of Anthropology, Gauhati University*, 6: 1-8.

Goswami, MC,1972. A report on an iron celt bar from Garo Hills. *Bulletin of Department of Anthropology, Gauhati University*, 1: 97-98.

Goswami, MC, 1972. A report on an iron Celt bar from North Cachar Hills, Assam. *Bulletin of Department of Anthropology, Gauhati University*, 1: 99-100.

Goswami, MC,1975. Shamans and shamanism at Kamakhyadham. *Bulletin of Department of Anthropology, Gauhati University*. 4: 1-12.

Goswami, MC. 1954. The social structure of an Assamese village. *Man*, 54: 27-28.

Goswami, MC. 1960. An annual shamanistic dance (*Deodha Nach*) at Kamakhya, Assam. *Journal of the University of Gauhati (Science)* 11, 2: 37-58.

Goswami, MC. 1967. Tribe-peasant relationship in Assam. In R.Mitra and B.Das (Eds): *A Common Perspective for North-east India*, pp. 72-80 Calcutta.

Lal, BB. 1971. *Indian Archaeology 1968-69- A Review*. Archaeological Survey of India, Calcutta.

Mahanta, D and Goswami M.C, 1973. Ritual and secular role of a Duania Monastery. *Bulletin of Department of Anthropology, Gauhati University*, 2: 32-40.

Roy, SK. 1977. *A Study of Ceramics from Neolithic to Medieval Period of Assam: An Ethno-archaeological Approach*; Unpublished Ph.D. Thesis, Department of Anthropology, Gauhati University.

Sharma, TC. 1980. Prehistoric archaeology in North-Eastern India, in T.C. Sharma and D.N. Majumdar (Eds): *Eastern Himalayas-A Study on Anthropology and Tribalism*. pp. 102-135, Cosmo Publications, New Delhi.

Notes

1. The Vaishnavite faith Ekasarana Dharma (literally: Shelter-in-One religion) is a neo-Vaishnavite religion spread by Srimanta Sankardeva in Assam between the 15th and 16th centuries. It rejects Vedic ritualism in favour of devotion (*bhakti*) to Krishna expressed through congregational listening (*sravan*) and singing his name and deeds (kirtan). Historically, it has been

opposed to the caste system and, in particular, animal sacrifices, which are prominent in other sects of Hinduism, particularly Saktism. It was known for its egalitarianism and posed a severe challenge to Brahminical Hinduism, converting people of all castes, ethnicities, and religions (including Islam).

2. Sakta/ Saktism (or shakta/ shaktism) : a form of religion among the Hindus. Those who worship the supreme deity exclusively as a Female Principle are called sakta. They conceive their Great Goddess as the personification of primordial energy and the source of all divine and cosmic evolution. (Bhattacharyya, 1974, 1)

A note from the author:

With great honour, I recall meeting this doyen of Anthropology of NE India, many a time, since around 1968 -69, when the excavations at Ambari were going on and I was a student of 4th or 5th standard. Ambari excavation was one of the few other reasons or rather attractions that led me to take up Anthropology, a completely new subject quite unfamiliar with the school syllabus. Although I never had the opportunity of being his direct student, during my post-graduate days, I often used to visit him, at the High Court when he was the Director of Law Research Institute, while on my way to the Gauhati University. He would often narrate his experiences, in RIA or explain about structural-functionalism of Radcliffe-Brown lending me some of the books from his collections. We were in touch till I joined Cotton College and I fondly remember the occasions of visiting him at his residence with my senior colleague, Dr. Lanu Devi, who was one of his Ph.D. scholars. With Dr. Chandana Sarma, my junior colleague at Cotton University, I often shared each other's anecdotes of MCG and his family. I humbly pay my deep respects to the memory of Professor M. C. Goswami, the leading figure of Anthropology in North-east India and beyond.

I am thankful to Sri Ranjan Goswami, Chief Manager, Oil India Ltd, the son of Prof. M.C Goswami; noted anthropologist Prof. Birinchi. K.Medhi, Dr. Wooma Sankar Dev Nath, former Librarian, Krishna Kanta Handique Library, Gauhati University; Prof Dwipen Bezbaruah; Prof Sukanya Sharma; Dr. Queenbala Marak and Dr. Gitanjali Himanka for their help and support in providing rare materials and significant insights.

Chapter – 7

Prof. Prabodh Kumar Bhowmick: A Glimpse of the Journey towards Tribal Development

Pradip K. Bhowmick

Early life

Prof. Probodh Kumar Bhowmick (1926 – 2003) was born in the British colonial era, in an affluent Mahisya (landholding class) in Amdabad a remote village under the Nandigram Police Station of erstwhile Midnapur District (at present Purbo Medinipur after bifurcation of the district in 2002). A look into his total life activities indicates that his coming to the limelight of the academic sphere was not silver lined rather there were varied troubles with which he had in continuous contention. In course of time, he could identify himself as an international personality especially in the domain of the application of anthropological knowledge.

His childhood was filled with too many affections and love from his family members especially from his three beloved grandmothers living together in a healthy well to do family. He completed his school education from a village school named, Kolagachia Jagadish Vidyapith, four miles away from his house. So, from a tender age, he had to stay in a school hostel. From his early days, he witnessed many evils done by the local policemen influenced by the British administrators as his family was engaged in the Swadeshi movement. Frequently their house was burnt, material goods were destroyed, women and children had to be transferred to safe places for protection and security as their target was to arrest the male members of the Bhowmicks family. In the year 1942, he actively participated in the 'Quit India' movement. As a result, Bhowmick was arrested and sent to jail in Contai Police Station of erstwhile Midnapur district when he was a student of class-VIII. Due to his tender age, he was identified as a Third-Class prisoner and stayed with other blue colour criminals. The national leaders marked as First-Class Prisoners confined in the same prison loved this little boy and took care of him. There is no denying the fact that his academic interest was unconditionally entangled with national politics over his life starting from a very early age. He was tuned with the national ideas and ethos inculcated in his philosophy of life and works. He appeared in his final Board Examinations during the time of his imprisonment and achieved great success.

His college education started at Bangabasi College with Anthropology (Honours). He took admission to Calcutta University and completed his master's. After that, he joined his alma mater as a lecturer. A new door was opened when he got Prof. Nirmal Kumar Bose as his guide, philosopher, and well-wisher. Bhowmick was a real disciple of his teacher and was influenced by Bose's ideas, thoughts, and philosophy of life and work. Close interaction with Prof. Bose helped him to explore his eternal zeal to become a field anthropologist. The mission and vision of Bose were followed by his devoted scholar, Bhowmick. He was an Indian anthropologist in all academic senses and cultural implications. He dressed in *Dhoti* and *Punjabi* with a *Chador* made of Khadi. His attires that symbolized his world-views attracted his colleagues and contemporaries. Even the foreigners admired his attires as a cultural presentation of the link between his life and work.

The singular motto of his life was simple living with high thinking. He always preferred to stay at Bidisha his *Manas Kanya* away from the comforts of his home at Lake-Town, Kolkata. His only mission was to live and work for the underprivileged ethnic communities for whom he spent many valuable years of his life, even sometimes neglecting the duties and responsibilities towards his family, namely Mrs. Latika Bhowmick (his wife, is an outstanding person who supported not only emotionally but also economically this unassuming extraordinary person), Mr. Pradip K. Bhowmick, Former Associate Professor, Rural Development Centre, IIT Kharagpur, Mrs. Samita Manna, Former Vice-Chancellor, Sidho Kanho Birsha University, and Former Professor, Department of Sociology, Kalyani University, Miss Sarita Bhowmick, Senior Research Fellow in the Anthropological Survey of India, and Mr. Pratim Bhowmick, Ex-Chief General Manager (Geology), ONGC. But unfortunately, Lt. Sarita Bhowmick (1956 – 1982) met with a premature fateful end because of a car accident while she was on the way to a National Conference in Anthropology held at Bidisha.

According to Prof. M. Afsaruddin, from Dhaka University, P. K. Bhowmicks's contribution to the field of social science was so vast that it can hardly be matched. His sincerity towards the well-being and development of the ethnic communities was so immense that the subcontinent had lost not only an extraordinary anthropologist or social scientist but also an eminent political thinker and an astonishing human being who but come once in every hundred years. I will never forget his cordiality, kindness, and warmth for his family, friends, disciples, students, or to his subordinates.

Academic career

Dr. Bhowmich joined as a Lecturer at the Department of Anthropology, Bangabasi College, Calcutta in 1952 and remained there till 1962. A new paradigm of his career started when he joined as a teacher at Calcutta University. He was then a young courageous scholar. He got his Ph.D. degree in 1961. His famous ethnographic work '*The Lodhas of West Bengal*' (1963) was the monograph of his Doctoral Dissertation. He took up the identity issue of the Lodha tribe inhabiting in the remote forest – adjacent villages of the western part of West Bengal. During his time the Lodhas was known as a criminal tribe. His views on the Lodha tribe did not end with the fulfillment of his academic degree, but on the other hand as a social engineer. Through proper planning, he tried to rehabilitate them, and Bidisha, as Samaj Sevak Sangha (1960) was established in Narayangarh locally known as Daharpur (erstwhile in Midnapur district now Paschim Midinipur), where he was the son of the soil. He got blessings from the then Prime Minister Pandit Jawaharlal Nehru and Chief Minister Dr. Bidhan Chandra Roy for fulfilling his mission. His energy and spirit engaged him to do continuous work. Till today every house of the district recalls Bhowmicks name as a great son of the district, who did welfare work for the downtrodden people. He was a very affectionate person especially for the people of his region. If someone faced any distressed situation and wanted to seek help, at once he tried his best to do something for him. His positive interest showed them a new light for their survival. The Adivasis or the tribal communities of the district addressed him as Probodh Babu and claimed him as their Man. His long and intimate association with the Lodhas earned the name *Lodha Bhowmick* for him – a name he enjoyed and relished.

During his time there were no proper transportation and communication facilities in the district. Most of the time bus service was not available. As a result, he had to travel from one area to another on foot. Untiring works and energetic efforts helped him to understand the community, culture, and society of that region. Gradually, through his research and close interaction with the local people, he became the most resourceful person in the district. His *'Socio-cultural Profile of Frontier Bengal'* (1976) was the smoldering example of his novel work dealing with the socio-cultural history of the frontier region. His research works were mainly based on in-depth fieldwork stemming from participant observations, case studies, and free-floating interviews. In his study, he gave much importance to social history. Historical events played significant roles to shape and reshape the cultural specificities of the groups in different historical epochs. Without knowledge history, the present condition of any group – ethnic or rural or urban- their culture, and nature of interactions and finally the assimilations of traditions – little or great – the holistic understanding of society and culture could hardly be possible. Bhowmick recorded all valuable sources of information of folk songs, folk tales, folk rituals, and rights of different marginalized groups with their socio-cultural canopy which made him a real anthropologist of that region.

He was a good ethnographer as well as an ethnologist and an Indologist. All his published articles and books were real examples of what type of man he was. In general, anthropology is a holistic study of society and culture. He followed it strictly. Though he was an oriental anthropologist, his ethnographic works were very much influenced by the works of Boas (1948), Malinowski (1922, 1935), Rivers (1914), and Radcliffe – Brown (1923). To conduct his ethnographic study during the time of his fieldwork he spent a prolonged period with the respondents and followed their everyday life activities closely. He mainly prepared the combined approach of *emic* and *etic* to understand the tribal culture and society, as a whole. It needs passion, devotion, and perseverance. Bhowmick had all those qualities to internalise their problems within him. His philanthropic attitude highlighted their problems and with a humanitarian welfare approach immediately, he extended his hands and tried to do something for them. Consequently, the tribal welfare officer of the district was informed and he also engaged himself to verify whether their names were listed in the SC or ST categories, and accordingly different positive suggestions were also rendered to them.

He did his other excellent ethnographic works on the Chenchus of Andhra Pradesh in the year 1979. This work was published in the form of a book entitled '*Chenchus of the Forest and Plateaux*', 1992, and received an International award from Germany. In this work, he tried to establish the interrelationship between ecology, culture, and humanity. He focused on the human rights of the community and called upon anthropologists to work for the service of man. It was another example of his challenging endeavour. In this way, he was the author of many books and articles. In the mid-20th century, he wore the caps of glory. There are sixty such Thrice Born field workers from different fields of social sciences, who completed their doctoral dissertation from Calcutta University under the guidance of Professor Bhowmick. Bhowmicks vastness of knowledge and versatile work of friction often created jealousy among his contemporaries. Perhaps this reaction helped him to become a giant scholar in his field. Both his friends and foes admit that he was an institution, not merely an anthropologist.

Prof. Bhowmick was a profound scholar, a social researcher, and a great social architect who had developed his institute namely, The Institute of Social Research and Applied Anthropology (1974), at Bidisa, Narayangarh, now at Paschim Midinipur near Kharagpur. It is a social laboratory of Applied and Action Anthropology. This Institute was blessed and glorified by his guide Prof. Nirmal Kumar Bose and the presence of many great scholars of anthropology of our country and abroad. A few names were mentioned who were just like pearls in the world of anthropology and whose direct co-operation and academic help made the Institute most vibrant and important. Prof. Sol Tax, an American anthropologist coined the term action anthropology in 1951. According to Tax (1958), 'Action Anthropology adopted a Clinical or Experimental method of study'. His presence at Bidisa in 1978 contributed a lot to the development of the Institute at that time. Erwin Deutscher, Department of Sociology, Akron University, USA, Prof. M. Afsuruddin, Department of Sociology, Dhaka University, Prof. A. Choudhury, Department of Anthropology, Dhaka University, Prof. G. Saran, Department of Anthropology, Lucknow University, Prof. B. Saraswati, UNESCO Professor, Prof. Harsha N. Mukherjee, Department of Sociology, Tennessee Tech University, USA, Mr. R.K. Gupta, Inspector – General of Police of West Bengal, Prof L.P. Vidyarthi, Department of Anthropology, Ranchi University, Prof. Sachidananda, Department of Sociology, Patna University, and Director, A.N. Sinha Institute, Prof. S.N. Ratha, Department of Anthropology, Sambalpur University and many stalwart social scientists, young researchers, and administrators extended their co-operative hands to Prof. Bhowmick to develop his Institute. After that Prof. Vijay S. Sahay, Department of Anthropology, Allahabad University, Prof. R.M. Sarkar, Professor, Editor of Man in India, Prof. A.K. Danda, Former Director, Anthropological Survey of India, Prof. V. K. Srivastav, Former Director, Anthropological Survey of India, Dr. M.K. Raha, Former Joint Director, Anthropological Survey of India and many renowned personalities from different Universities and Institutes of India and beyond and members of different Commissions of Union Government were always with him. Many of his students are now Vice-Chancellors or Directors or holding topmost positions of this country who had visited Bidisa. To them Bidisa, the Institute of Professor P.K. Bhowmick was not merely a hub of intellectual worth but a pilgrimage.

He was not a doyen anthropologist by like an ascetic he was engaged in practicing austerities throughout his life. He maintained good social relations not only with his fraternities in academics but also continued well-connected dealings with a good number of administrators, civil servants, and different Government officials working for tribal development in the State as well as in various departments of the Government of India. He had that charismatic power. He established cordial social relations with his students also. During his days in Calcutta University maintaining some sort of distance from the students was a common practice but he was exceptional in establishing a new type of relation with the knowledge-seekers and encouraged the students to become free, open, and frank in academic exchanges. Even in his classroom teaching, he made both-way interactions, and at the end of the lecture, he encouraged his students to raise questions. His teaching was interactive with a blending of theoretical knowledge and his unparallel vast field experiences. In this way, he used to create a lively situation in his classroom. For this reason, students were also much close with him and they shared their problems with him.

After superannuation in 1994, he has been a visiting Professor of Anthropology at the Department of Social Anthropology, S. V. University, Tirupati, Andhra Pradesh. He was attached to the Indian Institute of Social Welfare and Business Management, Calcutta, and the Indian Institute of Technology, Kharagpur as a Guest Lecturer. He has been a member of the Asiatic Society, Indian Science Congress Association, Institute of Social Research and Applied Anthropology, and the Indian Anthropological Association, among others He had also delivered illuminating speeches at Kalyani University, Kalyani and Vidyasagar University, Midnapur. He also acted as an Inspector and Lecturer at the International School of Dravidian Linguistics, Trivandrum. He became a member of the U.G.C. He has also participated at the World Congresses of Applied Anthropology in Amsterdam, Edinburgh, Italy, and West Germany. He set up the Nandigram Sitananda College, the Medinipur Sanskriti Parishad, and the Medinipur Itihas Parishad.

Bidisa experiment- Centre for applied and action anthropological institute

Bidisa experiment is popularly known to many as an experiment of development for the Lodhas, who was designated as a Criminal Tribe till the revocation of the concerned Act in 1952. It is a joint venture of the two registered Societies, namely, The Samaj Sevak Sangha (SSS) established in 1960, and The Institute of Social Research and Applied Anthropology established in 1974. Prof P.K. Bhowmick is the founder member of both these Organizations which are located at the site Bidisa, a name coined from a work by the ancient Indian poet Kalidas. Bidisa means diffusing light i.e., causing enculturation in an area of prevailed darkness. In course of time, Bidisa earned the blessings and cooperation of many eminent people and organizations both at home and abroad. Since, its progress from an initial stand of welfare through involvement, Bidisa had faced many difficulties and constraints from time to time. Having achieved success, it is now a burning light that attracts the attention of people from far and wide.

Bidisa complex is situated in a village named Bagabhera, under the Narayangarh Police Station of Midinipur district, West Bengal. It is about 20 km south of Kharagpur Railway Junction of the South Eastern Railway. The place is well connected with a metal road (O.T. Road) on one side the Narayangarh Railway station on the other. One also finds other tribals here like the Santhals, The Koras, and the Mahalis in different degrees of concentration and interspersed with the local castes, thus, constituting a mosaic of ethnic complexity. These groups have a distinct economy and cultural life but their interlaced within a strong ecological fabric and are overshadowed by a dominant democratic political setup. The complex has about 40 acres of land on which can be found thatched cottages, three-storeyed pucca buildings, numerous trees, and patches of cultivable land. Fish abound in tanks and orchards of various kinds provide an alternative for people traditionally lacking technology. On this island, one finds an atmosphere that is an amalgam of the traditional and the modern. Pre-historical tools co-exist with a well-disciplined ashram life and attract the attention of visitors.

Prof. Bhowmick had the advantage of researching the Lodhas under the guidance of Late Prof. N.K. Bose in the earlier 1950s. Many aspects of Lodha's life were highlighted through research. The problem had thus to be tackled in three ways:

1. On humanitarian grounds – to bring the Lodhas back on the accepted course of life with a new identity.
2. To change the mentality and outlook of the administration associated with the development of the Lodha's as also of their neighbours who often attempt to exploit them, and
3. Finally, to set up a model of a micro growth Centre for the experiment.

The then Superintendent of Police, Medinipur, and the District Magistrate and collector evinced take keen interest with the Tribal welfare officers at the Local and State Level. At this time the State Home Police department and the Tribal Welfare Department appeared on the scene and made some attempts at rehabilitating the Lodhas. Late Prof. P.K. Sen, through the Harijan Sevak Sangha and the Bharat Sevasram Sangha, came forward and espoused the cause of the Lodhas. But all this effort made only a marginal dent in the problems of the Lodhas. The district administration then requested Prof. P.K. Bhowmick to take an interest in Lodha's rehabilitation work with an allotment of Rs. 1500 per family for 369 families at Daharpur a village near Bidisa. This slowly brought about changes among the Lodhas who reacted accordingly.

Thus, a new effort is been made at Daharpur through a subcommittee of the Samaj Sevak Sangha constituted of three government officials (one of the State level, one at the district level, and one at the Block level) along with two social scientists. At every stage, detailed discussions were carried out and budgetary provisions were made for the fruitful implementation of the projects. The Lodhas, in general, showed little enthusiasm, and response in the beginning. More emphasis was laid on the purchase of land, as the group of people lived in an agrarian enclave and the idea was to imbue them with knowledge of agriculture. One community hut was constructed to accommodate the homeless and the young staff among them. Radio was provided and worked in the form of mat-making, weaving, and tailoring to convert their free /leisure time into gainful employment.

A few thatched residential huts were also provided to those who wanted their residences. With the involvement of social workers, the night school programme was facilitated. A model agricultural firm by way of a kitchen garden was also provided so that it could be emulated by the local people. The arrangement was also made to raise a flower garden to introduce the Lodhas to the beauty of nature and the finer things in life; a cooperative spirit slowly began to emerge. The local tribes like the Mundas and the Santhals were allowed to participate to avoid inter-group hostility. Provisions were made to supply plants and seedlings to the people of their locality when they wanted them and they were also urged to grow and tend them themselves.

An awakening was thus ushered in gradually, a multi-purpose cooperative society was organized with all Lodhas and as its members, consequently, local political, leaders and others with a vested interest began to be concerned. In the habit of making the Lodhas steal for them or employing them as domestic servants at a chip rate, they did not like the idea of the Lodha's being educated or established on a sound economic footing. A section of the Lodha's joined hand with these schemes but outwardly showed an ambivalent attitude to this type of social work. Some of the Lodha's sold the goats, bullocks, and even the corrugated iron sheets provided for the construction of their huts by the government. They also began to lease out the land given to them by the government for the rehabilitation schemes, naturally, all this created problems for the social workers and the organisers and the entire project came to be faced with severe problems.

At present, welfare programmes are being implemented by the government officials in collaboration with gram panchayat functionaries, local leadership, and the Institute of Social Research and Applied Anthropology and Samaj Sevak Sangha situated at Bidisha under Narayangarh block, Paschim Medinipur are actively involved in carrying out various socio-economic activities for the upliftment of the Lodha people with limited resources. Almost working for about six decades, Bidisa is now home to about 100 tribal families, including Lodha, Santhal, Munda, Mahali, Kora, Bhumij tribes. Within the *ashramic* folds of Bidisha, a social laboratory exists where research regarding tribal welfare and tribal development used to take place frequently every year. The laboratory mainly concentrates on working with tribal communities towards their integration into the society, imbibing in them the values of the mainstream society and teaching various skills for their sustainable development. Bidisha is being engaged continuously working and bringing social transformation for undeveloped and nomadic tribes by providing them space and where needed by rehabilitating also an opportunity to learn and sustain themselves. This was initiated by late Prof. Probodh Kumar Bhowmick, who was time and again discouraged by his friends, contemporary anthropologists, local leadership, government officials, and all his well-wishers. However, Prof. Bhowmick was firm in his life mission of working with and for the welfare and development of Lodha's and did not change his stand at all. He decided to work from Bidisha to start with, though later, it became the headquarters of social scientists to gather to exchange their ideas about the development of tribal people in India in general and the Lodha's in particular. It became their annual pilgrimage which they must visit, pay their tributes to the messiah of Lodha's, and attend the annual conference organized by the institute.

Since Prof. Bhowmick's time various training programmes, seminars, and workshops are being conducted from time to time to teach the tribes about various training skills and methods such as beekeeping, vermin-composting, mulberry, and *tussar* cultivation. A biogas unit and a vermicompost plan were installed to impart training facilities to the local tribal youth to provide a means of sustainable livelihood to the local people. Recently, the District Sericulture Board established a *tussar*-cum-mulberry cultivation, training-cum-production unit at Bidisha for employment and income generation in Paschim Medinipur. Through various training activities, the people here are forming self-help groups to ensure their self-dependency. From 2006 to 2008, a project called 'Empowerment of Tribal women through Batik Print: Training Cum Production' sponsored by the Department of Science and Technology, Government of India has been implemented at Bidisha. As a part of the project altogether 90 tribal women belonging to various tribal communities in and around Bidisha have been formed into 9 self-help groups given their interests. Bidisha strives to preserve the tribal art and culture, at the same time to teach them skills to survive in today's needs of the day. At present Bidisha is currently running 3 Ashram Hostels – 2 for boys and 1 for girls – exclusively for Lodha children. Ashram hostels provide free food and lodging facilities to the children. The tribal children study at the Daharpur Junior High School. Bidisha also houses an eco-museum and a library, Probodh Kumar Bhowmick Memorial Library. It publishes a biannual journal on social sciences namely, 'Man and Life' which has been running for the past 47 years.

To preserve, revive, and promote tribal art and culture, Bidisha used to organize the *Nabanna Utsav* every year. At this annual event, different tribal communities perform various cultural songs and dance programmes along with the Lodha inmates of Bidisha. Bidisha is putting its endeavour to provide a platform where the missing tribal cultural traits are being staged and this happens to be the eye-opener before the younger generation of various communities as a source of motivation and challenges. Finally, Bidisha is also a place for applied and action research by students of anthropology, rural development, and sociology, who come from all parts of the country. While tourists come to this place for visits, a lot of students used to come here for research, to study the model of Bidisha, and its role in the welfare of the tribal communities.

We may now conclude and summarise on observations that though noteworthy changes have taken place in the lives of Lodha's who were looked down on as the deadly terror by the mainstream society, the journey to come out of the tribal identity still lies far away. The changes that have taken place are mostly confined to the development of physical infrastructure which is though essential for a comfortable life. Besides, food security is significantly improved because of several welfare schemes run by the states and the central government. They need not worry anymore about the two square meals which was the biggest challenge at the beginning of the planned development of the country in the 50s. Similarly, the strange look which they were used to face in the interaction with the mainstream society has considerably disappeared. They are much more acceptable today without much inhibition and fear than what was present at the time of independence of the country. They do participate like any normal economic activities and social festivities like any normal member of the society. However, from society's point of view, soft integration which is the ultimate is still very elusive. The foremost reason for this appears to be a lack of education which has not yet become popular and firmly grounded, and without which, real change may not be realized. The very process of socialization of children is to be approached by counseling their parents about the importance of education and by making the school environment children-friendly.

On 13th December 2002, Professor Bhowmick met a severe road accident, which cause bone fracture and for that had a major operation. He improved and was taken home however, after a few days, he had met a stroke and left for his heavenly abode on 5th February 2003 at 10:10 p.m.

Chapter – 8

Life and Works of Dr. Tulika Sen

Rumjhum Ray Chaudhuri

Dr (Mrs) Tulika Sen, a distinguished physical anthropologist and retired senior faculty of the Department of Anthropology under the University of Calcutta, hailed from a very notable family. She was born on the 8th of May 1926 in Dhaka District of pre-independent India and was the youngest of seven siblings. Dr. Sen's mother, Late Charubala Sen, was a judicious homemaker; and her father Late Surnendra Nath Sen was a judge during the British period. Being the youngest in the family, she was loved by all the members and other relatives. Dr. Sen had her education in Kolkata up to post-graduation. Dr. Sen was fondly called Tulika Di or Didi (elder sister) by her students and younger colleagues. She was special to the students not only for her excellent systematic teaching but also for her nurturing the students with motherly affection. Besides being a proficient anthropologist and a great teacher, she was a good human being with a great soul, pleasant behaviour, and affectionate as well as supporting attitude towards all she knew. She was a kind-hearted, straightforward and courageous personality. Her love for animals, especially cats and dogs, was well known; even she cared for the plants deeply. Many senior professionals remember her smiling face, loving gesture, affection, and probing nature.

Tulika Di finished her schooling at Sir Ramesh Mitter Girls' High School in Kolkata and graduated with Anthropology Honours from the University of Calcutta in 1946. After finishing her post-graduation from the same university in 1948, the next year she joined as a junior technical assistant in the Anthropological Survey of India (AnSI). She served there until 1951, then got admission to Harvard University with a scholarship, and finished her master's in 1955. An ex-administrator of AnSI acknowledge that she was jolly and full of energy. She was the gold medallist in both BSc and MSc examinations at the University of Calcutta. She earned the distinction of being the first Indian woman graduate from Radcliffe College, Harvard. There she had the opportunity to receive the mentorship of Professor William W Howells, an anthropologist of great repute. She returned to India and during 1956-58 she worked in one ICMR project on the growth and development of children at Lucknow Centre. From 1958-63 she was a lecturer in anthropology in Loreto College, Lucknow. She was a passionate learner of Anthropology- she did not even hesitate to learn from her students, even at the last part of her life. She was keen to know about the nature of their work.

She was married to Late Dr. Dilip K Sen, a renowned Anthropologist and former director of AnSI on 14 June 1951. Her husband breathed his last at an early age in harness. She sometimes mentioned that she married him against the wish of her family, as none, at that time, liked any anthropologist as a son-in-law. However, she had enjoyed her married life for 21 years. Her husband always encouraged her studies and professional life.

During July 1965 and July 1968 she had a fellowship from the University Grants Commission and researched growth and development. She received her Ph.D. degree in Anthropology from the University of Calcutta in 1971 for her work on the *Growth and Development of Bengalee Girls* under the guidance and supervision of Prof Dr. M N Basu. This piece of work was published as a book by the AnSI.

Dr. Sen was appointed as a lecturer in anthropology at the University of Calcutta in 1972 and retired as Reader in 1991. She was closely associated with the Indian Anthropological Society, The Asiatic Society, the Indian Institute of Bio-Social Research and Development (IBRAD), and the Association of Gerontology (India). She was elected as Council Member and Anthropological Secretary of Asiatic Society, Kolkata (April 2000-March 2006). In this connection, one of her former students recollects that during 1972 there was some unpleasant incidence in the Department when the relationship of a few students with Dr. Sen turned painful and there was no interaction for long. Nevertheless, Tulika di herself took the initiative to normalise that, and hence after they had a very decent and respectable relationship till the end.

She was among the pioneers in the study of the Growth, Development, and Nutrition of Children in India. Her fields of interest and research are relevant in understanding population and health dynamics in India. She was equally prominent in the field of research on primatology, demography; biosocial anthropology, fertility, mortality, migration, and associated factors in respect of global *vis-à-vis* Indian populations, *Physiological and Physical Changes in Male and Female Populations in Different Environmental Setting* (ICSSR Project), etc. Her students still remember how methodical and systematic she was. Her students carried out studies on those areas of research, for example - *The Effect of Birth Control Programme on Rural and Urban Communities in West Bengal; Some Biological and Demographical Studies on Oraons and Mundas in two Different Settings; A Demographic Study on two Culturally Diverse Communities in Calcutta*, in the form of Ph.D. dissertations.

Tulika Di had contributed to the development of the logo of the Anthropological Society of India. For that purpose, she suggested the wordings **अमृतस्य पुत्रा**, which is still on the logo. Dr. S.B. Roy mentions that her association with IBRAD was a turning point for the institute. She promoted a participatory approach, besides the traditional one. She even wanted to offer financial support for IBRAD. In every meeting, she used to follow up on the decision taken during the previous meeting.

Dr. Tulika Sen has several papers presented in national and international seminars and published by the organisers, besides other papers in reputed journals. She had authored two books and edited three books. Her book on Anthropometry has been quite beneficial to the students of anthropology.

She attended various seminars and conferences; she also visited several countries for her profession. She had a very close working relationship with biological anthropologist Prof DF Robert and

Eleanor Kathleen Gough Aberle (British Anthropologist). Despite all these associations, she had kept a very low profile throughout her life.

My association with her began in the year 1974 when our undergraduate classes started in January at the University Colleges of Science at Ballygunge Campus. We became closer during our MSc classes, especially at the time of dissertation, and our intimacy continued till the last days of her life. I was out of West Bengal almost throughout my service life- she used to miss me a lot. I ensured seeing her whenever I came home. She felt very happy to meet her students. Ultimately, I resigned from my job in 2001 and started working as an independent consultant. Therefore, my opportunity of meeting her reduced as I started traveling more and my homecoming also reduced. At that time, we used to communicate over the telephone. She used to wait for me and complained a lot that I don't see her often. But she was able to understand my inability. For the last few years, she has broken into tears often that none comes to see her that frequently so that she is unable to converse meaningfully with somebody. She valued even a very small gift from her students. We used to celebrate her birthday sometimes, especially for the last two years or so. However, since March this year my visiting her has become infrequent due to the recent pandemic. These days a few of her students and I used to talk to her maid, Sachibala, who was with her for about 50 years (with a few years break), as Dr. Sen was not in a position to talk over the telephone. I could manage a visit to meet her a few weeks before her ultimate departure.

Dr. Mrs. Sen passed away at 20:00 hours on the 18th of October 2020 at her Kolkata residence, *Saptaparni*. She was 94+ years old and was suffering from complications mainly due to aging for her last few months. Though she did not have any child of her own, she left behind her countless children who really enjoyed her motherly affection and now miss her badly. Arnab Das, an ex-student and now an Associate Professor in the University of Calcutta expressed 'on getting the news tears filled my eyes and I had very heavy mental state'. It is worth mentioning the feelings of a few individuals after her demise recently-

One of her former students Dr. SS Saha says - 'Lots of memories. connecting her students like with umbilical cord. Nourished me in every necessity, academically or otherwise…'

Renowned anthropologist Prof KC Malhotra says '…I lost someone whom I respected so much. Will always cherish the love and affection I received. Anthropology lost an outstanding teacher, human and academician…'

Prof. K. Bhattacharya, says 'in the MSc Part 1 examination hall in 1977 Dr. Sen was the invigilator. I was hurrying and a bit restless for submitting on time. Suddenly found Dr. Sen coming close to my seat and kept her wristwatch on my bench'- she noticed that this student did not have a watch on his wrist!

I remember we - few students went for fieldwork for preparing dissertation with her to Medinipur District and put up in a bungalow under the fishery department. One day it was the birthday of our batchmate Sangeeta - we wished her and left for fieldwork. On our return, to our great astonishment, we found Dr. Sen in the morning ordered for prawns and then started preparing a great recipe for celebrating her birthday. I still remember the size of those prawns, our happiness, and above all Dr. Sen's motherly affection.

Her students had taken an initiative to compile all her publications and unpublished works, but to date; it has not been materialized due to certain constraints. I hope that we could complete this mission in near future.

'…When great souls die,
the air around us becomes
light, rare, sterile.
We breathe, briefly
Our eyes, briefly,
see with
a hurtful clarity.
Our memory, suddenly sharpened,
examines,
gnaws on kind words
unsaid,
promised walks…'

Maya Angelou

Some important Research Publications

Baker, PT., Hunt (Jr) EE, and Sen Tulika,1958. The growth and interrelations of skinfolds and brachial tissues in man. *American Journal of Physical Anthropology,* 16, 1: 39-58.

Banerjee, B. and Sen Tulika, 1984. Aging in the marine fisherman community of Balasore, Orissa. *Indian Anthropologis*t 14, 2: 105-120.

Basu, M; Sen Tulika, Sarkar A; and Mukhopadhyay, S. 2004. Fertility behaviour of two communities in a small village in West Bengal. *Journal of Indian Anthropological Society*, 39: 301-305.

Nandy, S and Sen Tulika, 1993. Menarcheal age among some rural Muslim women of 24 Parganas. *Journal of Human Ecology*, 4: 81-82.

Sen, Tulika and Dutta N.C. 2006 *Aspects of History of Science*, Kolkata, The Asiatic Society.

Sen, Tulika, 1969. Subcutaneous fat of the Bengali school and college girls. *Journal of Indian Anthropological Society,* 4, 1-2.

Sen, Tulika, 1975. A study on the age at menarche of the urban Bengali girls: a search for its secular trend. *Journal of Indian Anthropological Society*, 10, 2.

Sen, Tulika, 2010. New challenges in Anthropology, *The Eastern Anthropologist* 63, 2: 141-156.

Sen, Tulika, 2003. *Nirmal Kumar Bose: Life, Works and Vision,* Asiatic Society, Kolkata.

Sen, T. 1953. Reproductive life of some Indian women. *Man in India* 33: 31-35.

Sen, T. and Das, B.1983. Acceptance and non-acceptance of birth control methods and associated facts in rural areas of Midnapur District of West Bengal. *Man in India* 63, 4: 379-385.

Sen, Tulika, 1988. Growth, and Development of Bengalee Girls. *Anthropological Survey of India*, Kolkata.

Sen, Tulika, 1994. *Guide to Anthropometry*. The World Press. Kolkata.

Chapter – 9

Life and Works of Hirendra Kishore Rakshit

Sikha Chatterjee

H. K. Rakshit, former Director of Anthropological Survey of India (AnSI), was one of the most eminent Anthropologists and a versatile scholar, whose researches, writings, deliberations, guidance, and supervision have enriched Indian classical anthropology.

Birth, family, and education

H.K. Rakshit was born on December 1st, 1927 in the district of Dacca of the erstwhile Bengal province of India (now in Bangladesh). His father, Debendra Kishore Rakshit was a famous industrialist. H.K. Rakshit completed his primary and secondary education in Dacca. His family moved to India during the pre-independence time, where he was admitted for his Intermediate Science Course (ISc) in Presidency College, Calcutta. He passed his graduation from Calcutta University with honours in anthropology, and physiology, and psychology as pass subjects in the year 1949, followed by a masters' degree in physical anthropology in 1951. Some of his renowned classmates during post-graduation were Prof. K.D. Banerjee, Prof. Ajit Kishor Roy, Prof. D. P. Mukherjee, Prof. Pranab Kumar Ganguli, and Prof. Probodh Kumar Bhowmik. They all became great stalwarts in Anthropology later in their respective fields.

Research, service, and contribution

After his post-graduation, he started his career as an investigator in Prof K. P. Chattopadhyay's project on *'Somatometry of University Students'*. He was a research scholar and was registered for Ph.D. under Prof A. N. Chatterjee, a well-known Medical Professor and Anatomist of Nil Ratan Sarkar Medical College (NRS), Calcutta. His research topic was *'Factors Governing The Shape of the Human Skull'*. Then he was sent to work under Dr. S.K. Bose of Nil Ratan Sarkar Medical College for training on human anatomy and radiological study of human orbits, which unfortunately remained incomplete. He joined ICMR Growth Study at Coonoor for a brief period.

In 1957, he joined the Anthropological Survey of India as an Anthropologist (Physical Anthropology) in Central Regional Centre, Nagpur. During this period (1957-1969) he conducted an extensive field investigation in demography and anthropometry among some tribes of Bastar district, Madhya Pradesh. This time he also designed and supervised the *'All India Anthropometric Study, Southern Zone'*. This assignment was given to him by Prof N.K. Bose, the then Director of Anthropological Survey of India, also spent a short spell at Ootacamund and Southern Regional Centre, Mysore of AnSI in succession. It was the most important and largest anthropometric survey in the entire country covering a large number of populations. The purpose of this study was not only to achieve a large number of data but also to overcome the limitation of the earlier study. The basic data generated from the All India Anthropometric Survey, Southern Zone has been compiled and jointly published in 1988 and numerous students utilized these data for their doctoral research.

In 1964, he was invited to deliver a lecture at the All India Summer School of Anthropology, Dalhousie, organized by Prof. P.C. Biswas. In this gathering, all eminent Anthropologists of the country discussed the latest methodologies of anthropological studies, standardization of anthropometric measurements, professional ethics of anthropology, border area research problem, and other issues of national importance. Here he presented a paper on *'A perspective for Anthropometric work in India'*. He has made four major historical reviews with reanalysis of published anthropometric data for population across the country of undivided India. Of those, the first one has been presented in the Summer School of Anthropology. In this paper, he pointed out that there are three phases of anthropometric work in India, of these first by British administrators (1890-1910), second by professional anthropologists like Guha and Eickstedt (during the 1930s), and third by Majumdar, Karve and their colleagues (1940-1959). His critical comments are mainly based on four aspects:

1. Methodology of sampling
2. Analytical procedures
3. Horizontal and vertical variation
4. Clinal formation.

Rakshit accepted that the sampling procedure taken by Guha and Majumdar was meaningful in the circumstance in which anthropologists' worked. He also mentioned that their use of the term 'random' was utterly wrong and it could not be equivalent to actual random sampling. Rakshit's discussion in this connection was instructive for students of anthropological methods.

In analytical procedures number of comments with statistical insights like the multivariate Coefficient of Racial Likeness (CRL), method of testing normality, χ^2 test, D^2 analysis used by normality different authors in anthropometric character made in this review deserves the attention of the students of biometrical anthropology.

Regarding horizontal and vertical variation, he concluded that the two-dimensional variations (i.e. spatial and horizontal variation was observed in the first two phases of anthropometric survey, whereas the third phase of the anthropometric survey showed vertical variation) combined with the modern outlook of ongoing human evolution, will provide a useful framework for better understanding of anthropometric variation among the people of India.

Regarding the concept of clines or characters gradient, Rakshit thought that mapping of spatial clines in respect of various anthropometric characters together with blood groups and other genetic markers (at present DNA sequence analysis) could provide the basis for the reconstruction of migrational history and affinities of Indian populations that should be a treasure for anthropologists. He also differentiates geno-cline due to migration or hybridization for eco-cline due to environmental variation, although the two may sometimes interact. This comprehensive review was reflected with the planning and designing of *'All Indian Anthropometric Survey of the South Zone'*, which he described as the fourth phase of the anthropometric survey in India.

Besides, the basic data he also published in two reports of this Survey. In the first, he pointed out personal errors of measurements. Here he mentioned that large-scale surveys should be conducted by a few investigators to reduce the number of personal errors. On the other, he made a comparative study of the people of southern states and classified groups into different categories based on anthropometric traits and socio-cultural backgrounds like occupation, marital status, and language. This adds a new dimension to the ethnological analysis. Rakshit also worked at geographical variation among the Brahman populations of India in respect of available anthropometric data. He stated for justification of this study by saying that the Brahman caste represents a Varna, which occupied the uppermost position in the social hierarchy and represents a single Sanskritic tradition all over India. He also stated that this Sanskritic tradition all over India was built up in this area by several waves of people.

Similarly, Rakshit analyzed available anthropometric data on the Muslim populations of India. Based on regional variation, he divided the Muslim population into three main clusters:

1. The North-Western Clusters (the Muslim of Kashmir, Punjab, and Uttar Pradesh),
2. The Eastern Cluster (Muslims of undivided Bengal),
3. The Southern Cluster (Muslims of Andhra Pradesh, Karnataka, Kerala, Tamil Nadu, and Gujarat).

This was followed by his service as a Superintending Anthropologist (physical) and posted at Head Office, AnSI, Calcutta. During this period (1969 - 1979), he directed the 'All India Bio-Anthropological Survey' (The AIBAS project) Rakshit's most important contribution to anthropology was, for organizing, planning, and supervising the 'All India Bio-Anthropological Survey' through the Anthropological Survey of India (1972 - 1980). In 1972, Dr. S.C. Sinha, the then Director of the Anthropological Survey of India, called for a meeting among the staff members of the Survey. He took initiation a free exchange of ideas on the plans and programmes of the Survey. During this deliberation, Dr. Sinha referred to the project on All India Bio-Anthropological Survey, which was later executed by H. K. Rakshit, the then Superintending Anthropologist (physical), AnSI. It was followed by a discussion with the medical scientist, scholars from the Indian Statistical Institutes and Department of Anthropology, Calcutta University, and members of the Physical Anthropology division of Head Office, Calcutta.

It was a unique and well-designed project based on the cartographic method according to the demand situation in the survey. The uniqueness of this project lay in its objective and methodology. The main objective of this project was to make qualitative information on the physique in general, major bodily disabilities, diseases and abnormalities, food habits, and aspects of breeding structure for future studies in secular trends. Solo consideration of this study was spatial distribution of the population. Information was taken from 100 households of each 351 locations on the quarter-inch map of the Survey of India. Adjacent rural locations were about 100 km apart from each other and the few urban locations represented population densities between 0.5 to 1 million people. Thus, the rural as well as urban centres are distributed all over the state and union territories of India, except Sikkim. The entire field investigation was conducted by 54 teams through 108 field trips. Each team was composed of two investigators and altogether 43 scientific personnel were engaged.

A three-day first workshop seminar of 1975 discussed the preliminary findings in respect of specific information collected from 96 locations during the first round field investigation from 14 states, excluding the entire areas of Andhra Pradesh, West Bengal, and Kashmir states. Altogether seventeen papers were presented.

The result of this deliberation was published by Rakshit in 1976. Data and some further details were published later in 1988 by AnSI, although a lot of unknown useful population information in a holistic integrative manner remains unpublished. This valuable treasure that he marshaled together with a team of colleagues, were preserved by the data archive of the Anthropological Survey of India, Calcutta. It is hoped that further scholars will become intellectually indebted to him for this valuable information.

Subsequently, he became Deputy Director 1974-1978 and letter became Director of Anthropological Survey of India (1978-1982). He was more an academician than an administrator and did not like the bureaucracy of government policy. Ultimately he resigned from his position in 1982 at the age of fifty-four.

Being a Deputy Director, Anthropological Survey of India, he had also taken initiative to organise another project on *'Small population of genetical demography*' and it was completed successfully. Papers of this seminar, presented by the members of the survey were published in a book by AnSI, for detecting a small sub-population of a larger population. During this time he had also introduced a method i.e. 'snow-ball sampling technique' for detecting a small sub-population of a larger population. But he has not been able to give its mathematical shape due to his ailment.

As a director, he designed and supervised the know-how of Portrait Building System (PBS), a collaborative project with the Central Forensic Institute, Calcutta. Later this was conceived and executed by Dr. M.P. Basu (one of his Ph.D. students).

He served Anthropological Survey of India for 25 years in various capacities and contributed his valuable time and energy in just not building up his professional carrier but for enriching the discipline in various ways.

Initially, his area of research was focused on skeletal biology, race, classical anthropometry, micro-demography, cross-cultural analysis, etc. Gradually he shifted to population genetics. Ethno-historical studies of Indian populations, statistical reformations, medical anthropology, forensic anthropology, and so on. In between, there are a few exploratory or verification studies like Armitage, non-rejection of an obscure theory of foetalization, and analytical models for future researchers.

As a classical anthropologist, he has shown an enormous interest in ethnohistorical studies of Indian populations, which dealt with the interaction between biology and culture, i.e. holistic view of Anthropology. Four of his articles are directly focused on this topic itself. The first one was a historical review of Mongolian traits that has some indirect value for students of the history of anthropology. Another contribution under this topic concerns the ethnohistory of the tribal population of middle and southern India. This paper mainly dealt with population problems, especially identity problems, affiliation, and sub-group formation. He reconstructs different waves of migration among these tribal populations through a comparison of cultural traits including language. Rakshit's basic ideas of ethnohistorical analysis of tribal populations of middle India were deliberated elaborately in the first K. S. Mathur memorial lecture in 1961.

Rakshit, like Guha (1935), firmly believed the different waves of immigration are the main factor for the physical variation of the entire population of India. The facts and information he gathers together in the ethnohistorical analysis will be valuable for searching of micro-evolutionary process.

Rakshit did not write profusely and his contribution to anthropological research is not confined to his published works rather it covered a wide range of interaction and wide depth of analysis. He had contributed to 23 scientific papers, a summary of talks in two Summer Schools, a volume of anthropometric tables from southern Indian states, and two edited books. He also published a few Bengali articles and he has left some unpublished manuscripts.

Besides playing a leading role in the Anthropological Survey of India, he successfully supervised six doctoral students, and his major area of interest is also depicted in the dissertation works for his Ph.D. students.

Honours and memberships

He achieved his academic distinctions and honours like President, Research Director, and a long-time member of the editorial board of the Indian Anthropological Society. He was also Assistant Editor of *Man in India* and a member of the Editorial board of several reputed National and International Journal of Anthropology. He taught a variety of courses at the graduate and post-graduate level of physical anthropology and gave extensive lectures in physical anthropology at the School of Archaeology, New Delhi, Banaras Hindu University, Andhra University, and Calcutta University, and others on the invitation. He also deliberated the first K. S. Mathur Memorial Lecture in 1961.

Other interests

H.K. Rakshit was a man of diverse interests from painting to astronomy and classical music to Rabindra sangeet. He was influenced by Marxist Philosophy. He had high regard for Leo Trotsky, Bertrand Russel, and Winston Churchill. He loved poetry and was fond of playing chess and caroms. The Russian grandmaster Michal Tal was his favourite chess player. He also participated in Indoor- game competitions organized by the Anthropological Survey of India.

Personal life

Rakshit was very kind and gentle with a deep sense of humour, but had a strong personality and determination. He married Sipra Guha, an anthropologist in 1956. His only son Ananda Rakshit (Mining Engineer) is settled in the USA. He was an affectionate father and a great cook. He used to cook special dishes of chicken and tortoise for his son.

He could handle any critical situation with tranquility and his usual saying was 'take it easy'. He was passionate about reading books and donated books to the Indian Anthropological Society, Calcutta.

Some personal reminiscences about H. K. Rakshit that reflected from his son, friends, associates, and students are mentioned here. According to Prof. Ajit Kr. Roy, 'he was a private and sensitive person, a scientist with artistic inclinations'. Dr. Biman Dasgupta said, 'I was deeply impressed because I found him immaculately dressed, intensely absorbed in his researches around the clock'. Dr. Bharati Devi mentioned him as 'a store-house of knowledge'. Ananda Rakshit remembers his father, saying, 'he was a firm believer of technology but he always cautioned about the potential pitfalls of technology'. According to Dr. M. P. Basu, 'I was one surprized to see his mental strength when he easily ate fried beetle and half-cooked meat without spices offered by tribal families in Bastar'. Prof. D. P. Mukherjee said, 'being individualistic' and 'doing without doing' in his own words, has made his life bigger than 'anthropology' as he once said. But I feel the large amount of data, information, and ideas that Rakshit has left behind should provide enough work for future scholars in search of life through anthropology.'

I go down memory lane when sir Rakshit visited my field for supervising the Ph.D. work at Bhatpara in 1978. This allowed me an opportunity to interact with Rakshit Sir more closely and I rediscovered him as a true Anthropologist. His devotion, passion, and guidance were unparalleled to extract the best from his students. In the field, he taught me how to go deep into a problem and collect data methodically, systematically, meticulously, and honestly. I began to realise that he was always accessible to his students for the exchange of ideas and the dissemination of knowledge. I was deeply impressed by his utopian character. To me as a teacher, he was an understandable and affectionate person. I feel proud to have worked under the guidance of a stalwart person like H. K. Rakshit. Rakshit sir passed away on 4th July 1992 after a brief illness at a nursing home in Calcutta.

Though he is no more with us, his legacy will guide us in the present-day understanding of Anthropology in India.

His publications

1960. The Mahars of Maharashtra: an anthropometric appraisal. *Bulletin Anthropological Survey of India,* 9: 61-67.

1960. A short note on the anthropometry of the Dorlas and Dhurwas of Bastar. *Man in India*, 40: 56-64.

1960. Birth order, sibship size, and sex ratio. *Eastern Anthropologist*, 13: 93-104.

1961. The study of mid-phalangeal hair. *Man in India*, 41: 100-110.

1961. Mongolian element - real and alleged in Indian population Abstract and Discussion. *Proceedings Summer School in Anthropology*.

1961. Kodai Kanal *Bulletin Anthropological Survey of India,* 10: 37-39.

1963. A note on the anthropology of the Bhatra and the Muria (Kondagaon) of Bastar. *Man in India*, 43: 55-56.

1964. A perspective for anthropometric work in India. *Proceeding volume of the Summer School in Anthropology*, 1964, Dalhousie, pp. 25-56. Anthropological Survey of India, Calcutta.

1965. Incidence of phalangeal hair among two tribes of Bastar, *Eastern Anthropologist,* 18: 125-137.

1965. Anthropometry and personal error. *Journal of Social Research*, 2: 54-62.

1965. The Mongolian element in Indian population: real and alleged. *Anthropos.*, 60: 49-64.

1966. The Brahmans of India: an anthropometric study. *Man in India*, 46: 33-58.

1968. On the logic cross-cultural analysis: Discussion and criticism. *Current Anthropology*, 9: 64-65.

1969. Application of rank statistics in anthropometry. *Journal of Indian Anthropological Society*, 4: 51-78.

1970. Language, culture and race in South India. *Journal of Indian Anthropological Society,* 5: 205-232.

1971. The Muslims of India: an anthropometric study. *Man in India*, 51: 304-316.

1971. Aspects of marriage pattern in nine population groups of Maharashtra. *Man in India*, 51: 83-91 (with J. Dasgupta)

1972. The Dorlas and the Dhurwa of Bastar: A demographics profile. *Journal of Indian Anthropological Society,* 7: 115-128.

1974. Anthropometry of Bastar tribes. *Man in India* 54: 101-128.

1975. *Bio-Anthropological Research in India*. Anthropological Survey of India. Calcutta. (Edited volume).

1975. Understanding caste for demographic studies. In H. K. Rakshit (Ed.): *Bio-Anthropological Research in India.* Anthropological Survey of India, Calcutta - 16 pp. 230-243 (with F. Huq).

1975. Marriage distance and consanguinity in three Muslim villages in Murshidabad. In H. K. Rakshit (Ed.): *Bio-Anthropological Research in India,* Anthropological Survey of India, Calcutta 16, pp. 230-243 (with F. Huq).

1975. How big are the demes (Abstract). *Proceedings of Annual Meeting of the Indian Anthropological Society*, Calcutta, July 12-13, No. 47, p. 182.

1976. *Anthropology in India*: *Physical Anthropology*. Vol. 2, Anthropological Survey of India, Calcutta (Edited volume).

1976. Need for research in anthropological demography in India. In H. K. Rakshit (Ed.): *Anthropology in India: Physical Anthropology*, Vol. 2 Anthropological Survey of India, Calcutta, pp. 45-60.

1976. Seminar on All India Bio-Anthropological Survey. *Man in India* 56: 165-178.

1977. The contents of anthropology. *Abstracts of Papers Anthropology and Archaeology 64th Session, Indian Science Congress,* p. 1.

1980. Ethnohistory of the tribal population of middle India. *Journal of Indian Anthropological Society,* 15: 97-112.

1982. On some socio-cultural practices among the tribes of middle and south India. *Eastern Anthropologist,* 35: 95-114.

1988. *All India Anthropometric Survey, South Zone, Basic Anthropometric Data,* Vol. 2: Anthropological Survey of India, Calcutta - 16 (with R.D. Singh, S.H. Ahmed, D. B. Sastry, S. G. M. Ali and R. B. Bhale).

Acknowledgement

I thank Subhra Bhattacharyya of the Anthropological Survey of India for her help in bringing the manuscript to the present form. I am also grateful to Sri Sandip Mukhopadhyay for his useful comments and constant encouragement during the writing of the biography.

References

Armitage, P. 1995. Tests for linear trends in proportions and frequencies. *Biometrics,* 11: 375- 386.

Eichstedt, V. 1939. The history of anthropological research in India, In LAK. Iyer (Ed): *The Travancore Tribes and Castes*, 2: 12-54.

Guha, BS. 1935. Racial affinities of the people of India. *Census of India* 1931. Part 3: AI- LXXI.

Karve, I and Dandekar VM. 1951. Anthropometric measurement of Maharashtra, *Deccan College Monograph Series* - 8, Poona.

Mahalanobis, PC, Mazumdar DN. and Rao CR.. 1949. Anthropometric survey of the United Provinces 1941: A statistical study, *Sankhya,* 9: 90-374.

Mukherjee, DP, and Chatterjee Sikha. 1996. Anthropological writings of H. K. Rakshit. *Journal of Indian Anthropological Society*, 31: 1-19.

Risley, HH. 1907. *Anthropometric Data from Bombay*: Calcutta.

Risley, HH. 1939. Cited by V. Eichstedt, 1939.

Chapter – 10

Dr. K. S. Mathur

Nadeem Hasnain

At a time when we are celebrating 100 years of anthropology in India, it is in the fitness of things to remember all such anthropologists who contributed significantly to the development of the discipline and mentoring many budding anthropologists who rose to become important anthropologists.

Kripa Shankar Mathur (1929-1977) may rightly be described as one of the doyens of Indian anthropology. I cherish his memory as an outstanding teacher and mentor of several anthropologists including me. I count him as one of the few anthropologists of the world who would have contributed immensely and very significantly had they not passed away so early (Mathur died suddenly when he was just 47). At the time of his passing away, new ideas were churning in his mind which he used to share with some of his friends and close students and colleagues.

Born on 9th April 1929 in Shahjahanpur, Uttar Pradesh, he had his schooling in this district where his father was in serving in the department of agriculture, Government of Uttar Pradesh. Later, he had his education in Bareilly, Uttar Pradesh. Born and brought up in a traditional Kayastha family he imbibed traditional values but marched with modernity. During this time Allahabad and Lucknow were the best centers of higher education and their universities were also known as Oxford and Cambridge of the east. He joined Lucknow University for his undergraduate and post-graduate studies. Popularly known as KSM, he married Mrs. Vimla Mathur in 1953 and had a pleasant and popular family of two sons and a daughter.

Dr. Mathur came to anthropology via commerce and economics at Lucknow University. Several people may not be knowing that up to 1951, there was no independent department of anthropology in this University. Sociology and anthropology courses were being taught under the umbrella of economics. DN Majumdar was the only teacher of anthropology in this department appointed in 1928 to teach the paper on the primitive economic system. While taking his classes, he was able to attract a number of his students who have been his illustrious disciples and made a name in the disciplines of sociology and anthropology. KSM was one of his favourite students drawn to him and stayed with him all along till his sudden death in 1960.

After obtaining his Master's degree in 1950 with a specialization in anthropology, Dr. Mathur decided to do his Ph.D. in Social-Cultural anthropology. He was keenly interested in the Dudhi region of Uttar Pradesh for his anthropological research in the future. This was an eventful decade for anthropology in Lucknow as well as for Dr. Mathur; sociology had already established itself as an independent department but the University administration took years despite the persistent efforts of Dr. Majumdar for getting a separate department of anthropology. It was only in the year 1951 that the department of anthropology emerged with Dr. Majumdar as its founder- head of the department. In the very year, KS Mathur was appointed as a lecturer in the department. He worked closely and tirelessly with Majumdar to develop it as a prominent centre for anthropological research in South Asia.

In the year 1953, Mathur was awarded a research fellowship by the Australian National University, Canberra. The Department was still in a nascent stage and he was reluctant to leave it but his teacher-mentor DN Majumdar encouraged him to join this research assignment for his personal as well as departmental well-being. He left for Canberra along with his wife. He was fortunate to get the guidance of one of the most prominent anthropologists of his time, SF Nadel who took him under his wings for his Ph.D. work. This was the time when Nadel was keenly interested in expanding his department's research programme to South Asia. Adryn C. Meyer was already in Central India working on the secular aspects of caste; Mathur was persuaded to do his research work on the religious aspects of caste in the Malwa region of Central India. Dr. Mathur had to reluctantly drop his proposal on Dudhi. While still engaged in the field for data collection Nadel passed away. He later completed his dissertation and was awarded the degree of Ph.D. in anthropology under another prominent anthropologist JD Freeman in 1960. His Ph.D. dissertation was published in 1964 under the title *Caste and Ritual in a Malwa Village.*

His work on Malwa was acclaimed internationally as a seminal contribution to this field of knowledge. The objective of this field research was to analyze the function of Hinduism in the integration of caste society. Implicit in this method is a comparison of caste and ritual concepts as they occur in Patlod village. Here Mathur tried to relate Hinduism of the sacred text and All India Hinduism. The emphasis was on the underlying unity and similarity of Hinduism despite some local variations. This attempt to understand the village Potlad as an aspect of All India Hinduism (popular Hinduism) and Hinduism of the texts is the strength of this work while some reviewers looked at it as both strengths as well as weaknesses. A systematic attempt to interpret local beliefs and practices in terms of universal Hindu values was long needed. That is why Mathur's contribution in this field of knowledge has been accepted as an important contribution. The main thesis of the researcher is based on his conclusion that Hindu philosophy is the principal determinant of caste-based behaviour. Thus, Mathur asserted that ideology was a determinant of behaviour.

Besides his academic pursuit the couple, Mr. and Mrs. Mathur, was extremely popular on the campus as well as the city because of their involvement and promotion of cultural activities. They were like the 'cultural ambassador' of India.

After the completion of his Ph.D. work in Australia National University, Canberra, Mathur returned to Lucknow in 1957 and resumed his duties in the department.

The discipline of anthropology in India, the department of anthropology of Lucknow University, and Dr. Mathur and other close associates of Majumdar received a major setback when DN Majumdar passed away suddenly in 1960. He was like a banyan tree for the nascent department. Recovering from this shock Mathur involved himself in conducting a comprehensive survey of primitive tribes of Madhya Pradesh on their socio-economic condition. This was sponsored by the National Council of Applied Economic Research, New Delhi. The survey was spread throughout 1960-62. Later, he become the Head of the Department of Anthropology in 1962 and continued to occupy this chair till his sudden and untimely death in 1977.

DN Majumdar founded the *Ethnographic and Folk Culture Society* in 1945 and the research journal *The Eastern Anthropologist* in 1947. Mathur was one of the closest associates of Majumdar in both these ventures. He inherited both these responsibilities and worked tirelessly from the death of his mentor in 1960, till his death in 1977. In a short span of 17 years, the Society became a recognized organization, especially for ethnographic research. Most of the eminent anthropologists and sociologists became the life members of EFCS. Some distinguished life members/fellows from abroad have been Louis Dumont, Cora Debois, Mickim Marriott, Harold Gould, etc. Among the Honorary Fellows of the EFCS, the names of C Von Furer. Haimendorf, David Mandelbaum, Sol Tax, Fred Eggan, Levi-Strauss and others may be mentioned. The organ of EFCS, *The Eastern Anthropologist* made rapid strides during his tenure and counted as one of the best-known journals of Anthropology in the world. During his tenure, two more research journals – *Indian Journal of Physical Anthropology and Human Genetics* and *Manav*, the first and the only research journal of Anthropology and allied sciences in Hindi were started adding another feather to his cap.

In 1972, Mathur got the EFCS to initiate a biennial lecture series in memory of Majumdar. It had already become a prestigious academic event and several world-renowned anthropologists have delivered the memorial lectures. Just before he passed away the institution builder had one more institution to build. It was *DN Majumdar Museum of Folklife and Culture*, another wing of EFCS, established in 1975. It has galleries exhibiting ethnography and material culture mainly of the folk and tribal communicates of Uttar Pradesh.

Like a true mentor, he always encouraged his students to take up new ventures. Three of his research scholars, including me launched a bi-annual research journal *Research Bulletin*. He made it a point to introduce us to several eminent anthropologists visiting the department and requesting them to subscribe to this journal.

Since the Department of Anthropology was located in the heart of Hindi land and many students were coming to the University through Hindi medium background. There should have been some textbooks and translations of English books for the requirements of such students. Because of his persistent persuasion, the Uttar Pradesh Hindi Academy published some books of Anthropology in Hindi as well as the translations of some books. He wrote books in Hindi to motivate and inspire others.

Mathur's contribution was not confirmed to only anthropology or academia. When Lucknow Festival was started by the Uttar Pradesh government in 1975, he was actively involved in its organization. He took a keen interest to propagate the culture of Lucknow and its arts and crafts. He was deeply interested in the lives of the artisans and their crafts and skills and always supported their cause.

Mathur also enjoyed international repute. He was a member of the permanent council of the *International Union of Anthropological and Ethnological Sciences* and Vice-President of the Indian Anthropologist Association and was associated with several academic bodies.

A super organiser, an outstanding anthropologist, a visionary, a mentor, and an inspiring teacher he has left behind hundreds of his students, some of whom are now prominent anthropologists based in different parts of the world.

Chapter – 11

Prof. Tarun Chandra Sharma

Sukanya Sharma

Introduction

Prof. T. C. Sharma ended up in archaeology maybe as a result of a long-held romantic notion of making great discoveries and solving mysteries. As a kid, he might have always had his head buried in books, lost in the realms of the great ancient civilizations of the world because he would always talk of the past when it was about 'casual talk'. He had fantastical expectations of archaeology but not to travel the world and be a globe-trotting treasure hunter but to instill in all human beings a pride that 'we are all achievers'.

Born in April 1929 in Dakshingaon village under Nalbari district, Assam, Tarun Chandra Sharma received his early education from Nalbari Gurdon High School, Assam. He then pursued his B.Sc. Honours in Anthropology from Cotton College; Gauhati (1951) standing first in the order of merit and further obtained his M.Sc. in Anthropology from Gauhati University in 1958 with distinction and gold medal. Finally, in 1966, he was awarded his Ph.D. in Archaeology by the Institute of Archaeology, University of London. It was his association with fellow archaeologists in this Institute that changed his perspectives towards the archaeology of North-east India. Adding to his early achievement, he was the recipient of the Commonwealth Scholarship by the British Government for conducting a Ph.D. research project on Prehistoric Archaeology of Assam between 1963-1966. For the merit of his Ph.D. thesis and also his contribution to the Archaeology of the region, he was awarded the prestigious *Gordon Childe Memorial Prize* by the University of London in 1966.

Having retired as Professor of Anthropology, Gauhati University in 1989, he was subsequently appointed as Visiting Professor of Archaeology in the Department of History and Archaeology, North Eastern Hill University, Shillong, in Kohima Campus, Nagaland from 1990 to 1994. After the establishment of Nagaland University in 1994, he was again appointed Visiting Professor of Archaeology in the Department of History and Archaeology, Nagaland University, Kohima, from 1995 until his retirement in December 1997. His areas of specialization were chiefly Old World Prehistory, the Stone Age Cultures of North-east India and Southeast Asia, and the Megaliths of North-east India.

Several archaeological explorations and excavations in parts of North-east India were conducted by Tarun Chandra Sharma, among which to his credit are his excavations at Daojali Hading (North Cachar Hills), Selbalgiri in the Northwest Garo Hills, and Ambari in the heart of Guwahati city. Systematic explorations were also undertaken in an attempt to discover Stone Age sites in North-east India in parts of Garo Hills, Khasi Hills, Nagaland, and Manipur.

He successfully supervised five Ph.D. dissertations on different archaeological topics with emphasis on the investigations and studies of prehistoric Stone Age Cultures of North-east India and the Ethno-archaeology of Megaliths:

Sharma, H. C. 1974. *Stone Age Cultures of the Garo Hills, Meghalaya*, Gauhati University.

Sonowal, Minerva. 1986. *Flake and Blade Industries of the Garo Hills, Meghalaya*, Gauhati University.

Ramesh, N.R. 1991. *Geomorphology and Associated Cultural Remains of West Tripura district, Tripura*, Gauhati University.

Binodini Devi, P. 1994. *Studies on Megalithic Remains of Manipur*, Gauhati University.

Jamir, Watijungshi. 1997. *Megalithic Tradition in Nagaland: An Ethno-archaeological Study*, Gauhati University.

He also had to his credit three books and more than 135 research papers and popular articles on different aspects of Anthropology and Archaeology in several national and international journals. He was an Indian delegate to various conferences, including the 2nd *International Conference on Asian Archaeology*, Colombo (1969); the 9th *International Congress of Anthropological and Ethnological Sciences*, Chicago, U.S.A. (1973); the 9th *Congress of the Indo-Pacific Prehistory Association*, Pune (1978); and the 1st International *Congress of South Asian Archaeology* of the SAARC Countries, New Delhi (1985). He was elected President of the *Anthropological Society of Northeast India* (1976-77 and 1977-78); elected President of *Indian Society for Prehistory and Quaternary Studies*, Pune (1984). He delivered the *Panchanan Mitra Memorial Lectures* (2 Lecturers) on invitation by the Asiatic Society, Calcutta (1987) and delivered the Platinum Jubilee Lecture, at the 82nd Session of the *Indian Science Congress*, Jadavpur University, Calcutta (1995).

His association with a few of the academic bodies includes – *Kamrupa Anusandhana Samiti*, *North-East India History Association*, *North-East India Council for Social Science Research*, *Assam Science Society*, and *Anthropological Society of Northeast India*; as Associate, *Current Anthropology*, Chicago, USA. (1973); elected Fellow, *Royal Asiatic Society of Great Britain* (1965). He was a Life Member of the *Indian Archaeological Society*, New Delhi; the *Indian Society for Prehistoric and Quaternary Studies*, Pune; *Assam Science Society*, Guwahati and was a Member of the *Indo-Pacific Prehistory Association*, Canberra, Australia.

Prof. Sharma also participated in excavations at Nevasa, Maharashtra (1960-61); co-field Director in excavations at the Neolithic site of Daojali Hading, Assam (1961-63); as a student excavator in the British Museum Excavations at High Lodge, Suffolk, UK (1965); the Cambridge University Excavations at Norman Castle Site, Northampton, UK (1965). He was co-field Director, Archaeological Explorations and Excavations in the Garo Hills, Meghalaya (1967 onwards) and at the Ambari excavations, Guwahati, Assam (1969-71, 1996-97). He also studied museum collections at the Archaeology Museum, Deccan College Post-Graduate and Research Institute, Pune (1960-61); British Museum, London (1963-64); Museum of Archaeology and Ethnology, University of Cambridge, UK, (1964); Pitt Rivers Museum; Oxford University,

(1964); Mus de L'Homme, Paris, (1965); Muse Von Volke Kunde, Leiden University, Netherlands, (1966).

Major contributions

I am quoting below excerpts from the summary and conclusion of the thesis of Prof. T C Sharma to highlight the Neolithic story he told to us 40 years back. The title of his thesis is '*Prehistoric Archaeology of Assam (A study of Neolithic Cultures)*'. He completed it in June 1966 from the University of London.

The state of Assam possesses a marked physical and cultural individuality. It is a marginal area between eastern Asia and India, and in a sense transitional towards Southeast Asia and China. It is a flat alluvial plain, high mountains, big rivers, excessive rainfall, floods, earthquakes, and thick forests present, so to say, an extreme environment in which man wrests for his existence.

Stone tools that have been found in large numbers in almost every part of the state on the surface of the ground, as well as in stratified deposits, form the most important item of the relics of Neolithic man in Assam. Pottery has also been found recently in one stratified deposit. Almost all the stone implements and pottery preserved in museums in India and Great Britain, including my collection from the stratified site, have been studied by me independently and included in this work. A typological classification of the stone implements based primarily on the technique of manufacture has been developed. It is revealed that the implements are divisible into four large groups, i.e. Group A – Chipped stone implements; Group B – Edge-ground stone implements; Group C –Pecked-and-ground stone implements; and Group D – Fully ground stone implements. Each of these groups is again divisible into types and varieties based on the form and cross-section of the tool. The system of classification shows that altogether 30 swell-defined types of tools are present in Assam, besides a few unique and aberrant types. There are 7 types of Group A, 4 types of Group B, 8 types of Group C, and 17 types of Group D. In addition to these, a large number of non-edged tools have been discovered. These are grooved hammers, belted or notched pebble hammers, grinding slabs, polishing and sharpening stones for making wooden spears, flat and concave mealing stones, spheroid, ovoid and elongated rubbers, mullers, and pistles. The majority of these tools were found in stratified deposits.

All the pottery included in this study comes from the stratified site. There are four classes of Neolithic pottery. Among them, the cord-impressed group is the most numerous. Pottery showing incised decoration forms a minor element. The dull red tamped ware is also rare. The fine brick-red were, which is also rare, seems to be foreign to the ceramic industry of Daojali Hading. In the colour and texture of the fabric, this pottery is comparable to the Yang Shao red pottery of North China. The specimens found in Assam were most probably imported from Szechwan. The cord-impressed group of ware is characterized by its peculiar method of construction which is the dominant and basic Neolithic ceramic technique in eastern Asia. Its presence in Assam provides clear evidence of a culture spread from that direction. On this evidence alone, it can be firmly established that the Neolithic culture of Assam belongs to the eastern Asiatic Neolithic complex.

Other evidence supplied by the stone tools further supports the theory of a long-standing cultural relationship between Assam and eastern Asia. The stone industries of different parts of Assam exhibit a general homogeneity so far as the tool types are concerned, although local specialization arising mainly out of the utilization of locally available raw material gave rise to regional specialization. This is reflected in the technique of manufacture which differs from place to place depending upon the types of rocks used and also in certain tool-types showing restricted distribution. The influence of raw material upon the technique of stone-working is a potent factor in bringing about variations among the tools of the same type, as could be seen among different varieties of the shouldered axes.

The technological and typological aspects of the Neolithic stone industries of Assam have been thoroughly analyzed. The analysis reveals that the main material used in the Garo Hills is dolerite, in the Naga Hills greenstone, while in the North Cachar Hills and Kamrup district a variety of indurated shale was extensively used for making edged tools, and sandstone for other implements. The technique of manufacture also varies from region to region. In the Naga Hills, pecking and edge grinding is the dominant technique. In the North Cachar Hills, the Garo Hills, and other parts of Assam it is chipping and partial or overall grinding. The method of flaking and grinding could be inferred from the instruments used for these purposes. Pebbles and prepared hammers were used for flaking and portable sandstone blocks for grinding. Some of the pebble hammers are grooved or notched for hafting. Tools showing partially sawn marks and partially boring holes have also been found. It can be inferred from them that the sawing of jadeite was probably done with a sliver of sandstone and boring was done with a hollow borer which might be a piece of reed or bamboo using sand as abrasive. A sliver of bamboo with sand was probably used for cutting out the tang of the rectilinear shouldered axes. There is no evidence of using a wire-saw for this purpose.

Among all the groups of tools, the fully ground implements are by far the most numerous. They are widely distributed throughout the state, the largest concentration being found in the Garo Hills. This tradition is very thin in the Naga Hills where tools are generally made by pecking-and-edge grinding techniques. Stone axes made by flaking alone in the palaeolithic fashion are also found to be concentrated in one area i.e., in the Garo Hills. The distribution of the different groups of tools seems to be largely governed by the availability of the particular rocks used for their manufacture.

Among the tool-types, the shouldered axes are by far the most numerous. They have been put into a stratigraphical context at Daojali Hading where they are associated with small axes, some of which are characterized by flat grinding on the sides, quadrangular adzes, and cord-impressed pottery. This complex has an exact parallel in Southwest China and Indo-China. It also clearly brings out the difference with those of Malaya and Siam where shouldered axes are very rare and none has so far been found in a stratified context. Moreover, the absence of the beaked adze clearly distinguishes the Malayan Neolithic from that of Assam. In the absence of stratified data, a close comparison with Burma is not possible. It is therefore plain that the Assamese Neolithic is oriented more towards the Southwest Chinese and Indo-Chinese complexes. The Daojali Hading assemblage as a whole is comparable to the Late Bacsonian of

Southeast Asia with a few exceptions that might have developed under the influence received directly from China. The suggestion, on the present showing, is that the Upper Yangtze Valley of Szechwan and Yunnan played a major role in the development of the Neolithic cultures of Assam.

The implements of Group A *i.e.* the chipped axes include several examples comparable to those of the Hoabinhian type of Indo-China. The industry as a whole may also be compared with the early Bacsonian of Indo-China. However, it must be admitted that more systematic work is necessary for this area to be able to produce a clear picture of this industry.

The pecked-and-edge-ground axes of the Naga Hills have no parallel in Southeast Asia except for a few examples from the Kachin Hills of Upper Burma. They are however comparable with the pecked-and-edge-ground axes excavated at Yang Shao Tsun in Honan, North China. The pecking technique seems to have been introduced into Assam from China. The influence of the Chinese Neolithic culture seems to be stronger in the Naga Hills than in other parts of Assam. The presence of jadeite axes of Chinese type further strengthens this view.

There is at present no evidence to prove any influence of South Indian or Western Asiatic Neolithic cultures over Assam. Among all the areas of India, only Chota Nagpur and the Darjeeling area of the Himalayan district have yielded a few comparable types of stone implements, but in the absence of pottery and excavated materials in those areas, it is not possible to determine the exact relationship between the two cultures. Nevertheless, on the present showing, we may reach certain conclusions regarding the genesis of the Assamese Neolithic culture. It is clear from our comparative study that the entire Assam falls within the boundary of the eastern Asiatic Neolithic complex. Most probably from the Hoabinhian period up to the Neolithic the area remained as a cultural province of eastern Asia. The Indianization of Assam is only a recent phenomenon, the beginning of which can be traced to the time of the Indo-Aryan immigration from the Ganges Valley. Although the exact date and the cultural period in which the early Indo-Aryans entered Assam is not known, we are almost certain from the history of the Aryanization of India that it was post-neolithic. Thus, one is justified in concluding that Assam forms the western outpost of the eastern Asiatic Neolithic complex, and the meeting ground of the eastern and Indian traditions, as pointed out by Dr. Allchin (1962, p. 326), could be traced in the Chota Nagpur Plateau. It is amply borne out by the evidence of the materials discovered in Darjeeling and Assam that Chota Nagpur received much of its eastern Asiatic traits overland through Assam and the Himalayan districts. Such a situation would indeed have been brought about if Assam was the corridor through which eastern Asiatic traditions entered India.

The affinities of the pointed butt axes of the Naga Hills are thoroughly discussed. It is evident that these axes, being associated with shouldered axes, seem to assert their east Asiatic affinity, and their typological similarity with the South Indian type is superficial. We have also rejected the method adopted by some earlier writers (Worman, 1949, p. 186; Wheeler, 1959, p. 89) for showing cross-continental culture affinities based on typological similarity of some stone tools. Some basic types of tools, such as the axes with a pointed or conical butt might have evolved independently in different centers regardless of cultural affiliation. The important point here is to regard the tool-type as an integral part of the culture of which it is a product and not as a wandering isolated trait irrespective of cultural relationship. The culture to which the pointed butt axes of Assam belong has no relationship with that of South India; it, therefore, follows that these axes are not related to those of South India.

The problem regarding the origin of the shouldered axes has also been thoroughly discussed. It has been shown that there is no justification in assuming, as did Dani and others (Dani, 1960, p. 226; Wheeler 1959, p. 88), that these axes were copied from the highly characteristic bronze shouldered axes of the Shang dynasty of North China. On the contrary, we have sufficient archaeological data to prove that the stone form originated in the pebble chipping Hoabinhian industry and its prototype consists of axes made on a naturally tanged pebble. Some examples of the prototype, as already referred to, have been found in the cave of SAO-DONG in Hoa-Binh (Colani, 1927, Pl. III:8).

The Neolithic settlement of Assam appears to have been very extensive. The major part of the state seems to have been inhabited during this period. The hills were more thickly populated than the malarious flood plain of the Brahmaputra Valley. Those who were settled along the edge of the plain or on the high gerunds in the valley were probably equipped with advanced techniques of agriculture.

We have no precise information regarding the racial affinities of the Neolithic people of this area, but there is no reason to doubt that they were not Mongoloid. If this is so they may well be regarded as the ancestors of the present-day tribal population of the state.

In the absence of adequate data, nothing can be said about the house type, food habits, and burial customs of the people. However, at Daojali Hading some appliances used for the preparation of food have been found in stratified deposits, but because of the absence of food remains it is not possible to say what kind of food was prepared in them. We have already mentioned that rice and millet are grown wild on and around the site. These two kinds of grain were probably cultivated by the Neolithic people living in this area.

Assam being the home of many primitive aboriginal tribes offers great scope for linking the buried cultures of the Neolithic period with the living ones. Among so many Neolithic survivals that could easily be detected among the tribal societies, we have noted only a few important items viz., the shifting cultivation, the method of making barkcloth, and cord-impressed pottery. It systematically investigated this would indeed be an interesting subject of research.

There is clear identification of stone implements and pottery with those of Southeast Asia and China. Unfortunately, the absolute dates of these objects are not yet known in any of these countries. There are, however, several postulated dates as well as a few radiocarbon dates of the Late Neolithic Cultures from the outlying islands. These show that the whole of Southeast Asia including Assam entered into the Late Neolithic phase around 2000 BC.

The data in hand show that only the Late Neolithic Cultures were well developed in Assam, but this does not mean that during the Hoabinhian and the Early Neolithic periods this area was unpopulated. From our present survey, we can at least say that some parts of Assam probably came under the Hoabinhian influence. If this is true, in the absence of Palaeolithic Cultures, the Hoabinhian seems to be the earliest prehistoric culture in Assam.

We are therefore justified in proposing the following culture sequence for Assam:

4. Aeneolithic
3. Late Neolithic
2. Early Neolithic
1. Hoabinhian.

The tentative nature of the scheme is quite apparent. Its confirmation, however, depends upon the archaeology of the future rather than the past. It is only hoped that this chronological framework might form a basis for future reference in the archeology of Assam. It is therefore urgent to put into effect an intelligently planned programme of archaeological investigation in this area to solve the many interesting problems of the prehistory of Assam.

The Assamese Neolithic Culture which he talked about in the present context is the North-east Indian Neolithic Culture. The confirmation of the occurrence of shouldered celts and chord-marked pottery in a single stratigraphical layer was his major contribution. That gave the North-east Indian Neolithic an identifiable characteristic feature of its own.

His second noteworthy contribution in prehistoric studies of the region was the discovery of sites in Garo Hills, Meghalaya. His surveys 'on foot' in central and west Garo Hills resulted in the discovery of more than 20 sites in the Ganol and Rongram river valley. These were mainly late Pleistocene-early Holocene formations capped by a mid-Holocene alluvial formation. Of particular interest were the pebble tools, bifaces, and tools made on dolerite flakes. Sizes of these flake tools varied from site to site. Some were large, 15 cm to 20 cm in length and some were micro-sized 0.5 cm to 2 cm in length. He called them microliths. Missimagiri in west Garo was one site he discovered which had just the microliths. With his doctoral student, Minerva Sonowal undertook an in-depth study of the microliths of Garo Hills. These he concluded were composite tools that were hafted into wooden or bamboo handles and used as saws and sickles.

He closely observed the Garo society to find the meaning of the archaeological record of the area. In the process, he reconstructed their age-old system of making barkcloth, fishing techniques, etc. To understand the cultivation pattern he actively participated in different activities of *jhum* cultivation starting from firing. He spoke fluent Garo and could easily make himself feel at home in any Garo household. This gave him an added advantage to understand their way of life as an insider. These villagers would often visit his quarter no. 2, in the Gauhati University Campus. Every year when he went back to the field he would carry medicines, slippers, shoes, toys, etc. for his friends there. In the process, he would get to spend quality time in a Garo household to observe them. He would observe how they would hold a big iron knife (*dao*) in their hands to slit a bamboo, chop a tree trunk, or cut vegetables in the kitchen. Amidst the activity, he would offer them a similar stone tool and ask them to perform the same activity with the stone tool. These villagers keeping his request would tell him if it worked. Sometimes they would tell it partially worked and sometimes they would completely reject it also. He kept repeating these experiments to come closer to the truth. Now when I teach my students methodologies like contextual validity, hermeneutics, etc. I see the relevance of his actions. He never came to his conclusions without logical reasoning.

The whole controversy regarding the Neolithic and pre-Neolithic in North-east India disturbed him. His whole argument was that the Neolithic in Northeast India can be dated to 3000 BC to 4000 BC and there exists evidence of human activities on the landscape before this period. He came to this conclusion based on the stratigraphical position of the tools and the radiocarbon dates of the geological layers. These layers have been dated by the Geological Survey of India (GSI). Some Neolithic sites in North-east India have been recently dated and all the dates fall within this bracket proving his argument right. The GSI has mapped the quaternary deposits in Garo Hills and they have identified 2 layers of alluvium. One of Pleistocene origin and one of the Holocene period. Recent geomorphological studies of these 2 deposits have confirmed that in the Ganol and Rongram river valley of Garo hills the bottom layer is a late Pleistocene formation while the top layer is Holocene. In the bottom layer which consists of strong brown alluvium, we find large, medium, and small-sized flake tools, bifaces, and pebble tools like short axes and choppers. This is not Neolithic for which he opposed the fact that this can be called pre-neolithic.

In his typo-technological analysis of Neolithic tools, he explained the local variations of the Neolithic Celts found in the region. This he said was because of the difference in raw material and also because of the difference inactivity. In Garo Hills, almost all the Neolithic Celts were ground and polished while in Naga Hills pecking and edge grinding were the dominant types. The reasons behind this were: (1) In Garo hills the late-Pleistocene-early Holocene people who used the bifaces, pebble tools, and the flake tools had already cleared patches of the jungles for making it convenient for the dwelling (defence purpose) or for laying traps for hunting or for allowing wild varieties of cereals, fruits, etc. to proliferate receiving ample air, water, and light. As a result, the cultivators of the Neolithic period of Garo hills had a friendly landscape, to begin with. While for the cultivators of Naga Hills it was a virgin land that they occupied. To clear the land they required effective tools that they repeatedly sharpened by the edge-grinding.

His next milestone was the studies on the living megalithic culture of Nagaland and Manipur. The types and varieties and also the rituals connected with the megaliths are enormous in the Naga society. These memorials in stone found all over the world in the prehistoric context have always been a puzzle. Why were they erected by people of a particular period? How were they erected? This has been studied by various people but the enigma attached to these stones remains. With two of his very dedicated students, Dr. Wati Jungsi Jamir of Nagaland and Dr. Binodini Devi from Manipur he completed exhaustive surveys covering all the districts within the political boundaries of both the states. Both these works now stand as milestones for understanding the living Megalithic culture of North-east India. These works provide us primary data for understanding the past or rather they can be called windows through which we can peep into the past.

He had a vision of finding evidence of domestication of rice in North-east India. In 1977, to transform this vision into reality he, in collaboration with Dr. R.M. Rowlett from the Department of

Anthropology, University of Missouri-Columbia, and Prof. S.N. Rao of Department of History, North-Eastern Hill University prepared a research project 'Early Plant Domestication in North-east India'. Extensive exploration was planned all over Northeast India after which excavations were to be conducted in the potential areas. The whole project was funded by U.S.P.L. 480 Rupee Funds. The University of Missouri-Columbia promised full technical help. They had planned for collecting samples for dating, both by using radiocarbon and thermoluminescence methods. The Department of Anthropology at the University of Missouri-Columbia had developed a flotation machine suitable for working in North-east India and they had plans to bring it here. The University Grants Commission (UGC) had approved the project and the Govt. of India provided the clearance for the required staff from the University of Missouri-Columbia. It was decided that the whole project staff will be under the direct supervision of T.C. Sharma and S.N. Rao. But it was destiny that the concerned university here did not give clearance to the project. If he could have undertaken the project several prehistoric sites would have been excavated and dated. Chronology, stratigraphy which are plaguing prehistoric archaeology of North-east India today would have been solved in 1977. It was his dream project. It weighed heavily on his heart that he was not allowed by the university to undertake it. It was an opportunity lost by the region. If we are backward in archeological studies today it is because we chose to be. The project was a 38-page document that included minute details like who will maintain the daily logbook to how many plastic and paper bags they will need for packing the samples. The funding agency even provided insurance coverage to those who worked on the project. They had planned and also had the approval for 30 carbon dates at the rate of $175 each and 30 Thermoluminescence dates at the rate of $60 each. These were the rates in the US laboratories then.

But even after these setbacks he tirelessly continued his work. After he retired from Gauhati University in 1988 he went off to Kohima to join the North Eastern Hill University campus there as visiting professor. He carried his enthusiasm there. He undertook explorations in different parts of Nagaland for locating prehistoric sites. In association with the Art and Culture department of the Govt.

of Nagaland, he undertook explorations in the Ukhrul and Phek districts. He had enthusiastic students there to whom he could transfer his zeal and enthusiasm. The result was a joint venture by a team of archaeologists and other social scientists from the Department of History and Archaeology, North Eastern Hill University, Kohima Campus, together with the Directorate of Art and Culture, Government of Nagaland, at Chungliyimti in 1992. The team undertook a trial excavation in the site and reported evidence of Neolithic tradition such as polished stone axes, grinding stone, spindle whorls, pottery vessels, beads of rare stones, and earrings made of stone. The Neolithic Celts found at the site are of the quasi-shouldered type prepared by grinding technique, spindle whorls of sandstone, mullers, and pestles made from a fine variety of sandstone. Pottery is handmade, coarse with gritty tempering material, made by the beater and pad technique, and ill-fired, with grooved beater impressions visible on the exterior surface of the potsherds (IAR, 1993). During his stay in Kohima whenever it was possible he would visit archaeological sites. The Government of Nagaland in 1992 had organized a Megalithic festival in which rituals like stone dragging, erection of the megalith were performed in great detail. For him, it was a lifetime experience to see the performance of a prehistoric tradition.

In 1980, he had written a piece titled '*Prehistoric Archaeology in Northeast India- A Review of Progress*' in the book 'Eastern Himalayas' which he jointly edited with D.N. Majumdar, his esteemed colleague from the Department of Anthropology, Gauhati University, and a dear friend. There he had outlined the problems of prehistoric Archaeology in North-eastern India awaiting our urgent attention. I am quoting this here for the benefit of young researchers in the field and also because they are true even today.

The Problem:

> In this context, it is apt to outline the problems of prehistoric Archaeology in North-eastern India awaiting our urgent attention.
>
> 1. Firstly, on the problem of the origin of man and his culture in North-east India, inhabited by some species of primitive primates and anthropoid apes may yield evidence related to the origin of man. The works of Gauhati University (Lal, 1967-1968), and the scientific expedition in Arunachal

Pradesh (Bopardikar, 1972) have proved that Palaeolithic man lived in this part of India. In all these cases only some tools have been collected, leaving aside a hols to problems to be tackled by future anthropologists and archaeologists. These are the problems of Pleistocene Geology, Palaeo-Climatology, and Palaeontology which are still untouched in this part of India. If we are to know the life and culture of Palaeolithic man in North-east India, these problems cannot wait for a long. It is not too much to expect that we have here ample opportunities for the young anthropologists.

2. The next problem of the prehistory of North-east India is about Mesolithic cultures which evolved after the Palaeolithic. We have, so far, no authentic evidence of Mesolithic culture from the whole of North-east India. Although some Mesoliths have been found in Garo hills (Sharma, 1973), we still don't know whether they are the relics of the Mesolithic period unless well-attested materials are available. There is therefore urgent need to engage some scholars to investigate this problem.

Conclusion

Archeologists need a combination of technical and interpersonal skills. Prof. T. C. Sharma continuously persevered to learn the technical skills for which he attended excavations under stalwarts like Prof. H.D. Sankalia and others. In India and abroad he had friends from the field who would continuously update him about recent works. He would receive long letters from his friends from across the world to whom also he would write back about his work. That is how he was well informed and uptodate with the latest information from across the globe. An archaeologist needs physical agility to perform actions such as exploring and digging. Maybe because of that he maintained a strict daily routine. His waking up hours were fixed and also the time when he went to bed in the night. He loved food but never overate. An archeologist needs to be vigilant and a torch was always by his below and he never forgot it when he traveled. He took extreme care, replaced the batteries on time, and kept checking the little tiny bulb continuously. He always carried extra batteries and bulbs with him when he traveled and always stressed the ability to communicate clearly with others. Would always encourage students to publish their research work and attend conferences to present their research work. He advised archaeologists to develop a deep understanding of the history of human civilization when carrying out professional duties. To identify artifacts, to accurately determine the chronology and what they are and how they were used he focussed on a clear understanding of the historical context. That is why he read profusely about societies, about culture, about civilizations, and the present world too. He was inquisitive and naturally inclined to investigate and seek out information about things. Thus, his world was every day new. He lived to bring joy to it and the day he realized that unhappiness dominated it broke his heart. He decided to go. It was a fall that fractured his hip bone. A successful surgery could not lift his body and neither his spirits. It was in the autumn of 2011 that he left the world.

Maybe
'*The old order changes, yielding place to new.*' — 'Idylls of the King: the Passing of Arthur,' Lord Alfred Tennyson or
Maybe *the old remains as the most loved, most revered.*

Some selected Research works / Publications of T.C. Sharma

1966. *Prehistoric Archaeology of Assam: A Study of Neolithic Cultures.* Unpublished Ph.D. Thesis, University of London, London.

1967. A note on the neolithic pottery of Assam, *Man* (N.S) 2,1: 126-128.

1979. *Eastern Himalaya: A Study on Anthropology and Tribalism.* (with D.N. Majumdar), Cosmo Publications, New Delhi.

1974. Prehistoric archaeology in North-east India-Its problems and prospects, in B.M. Das (Ed.): *Contemporary Anthropological Research in North East India*, pp. 147-155. Dibrugarh University.

1978. A note on the microlithic industry of the Garo Hills, In Prematileka and Van Lohufzon (Eds.): *Sanarat Paranavanita Communication,* pp. 215-217. Leiden: E.J. Brill.

1981. Neolithic pattern of Northeast India, in M. S. Nagaraja Rao (Ed.): *Madhu: Recent Researches in Indian Archaeology and Art History,* pp. 41-52. Delhi: Agam Kala Prakashan.

1983. North-east India in prehistoric times, in S. Karotemprel (Ed.): *The Tribes in North East India*, pp. 1-21. Calcutta: Firma KLM.

1985. Problems of upper palaeolithic in Northeast India, in V.N. Misra and P. Bellwood (Eds.): *Recent Advances in Indo-Pacific Prehistory* pp.171-173. New Delhi: Oxford and IBH Publishing Co.

1990. *The prehistoric age*, (with H.D.Sankalia), in H. K. Barpujari (Ed.): *Comprehensive History of Assam*. pp. 25-43. Assam: Publication Board.

1991. Prehistoric situation in Northeast India, in J.P. Singh and G. Sengupta (Eds.): *Archaeology of Northeastern India,* pp. 41–58. New Delhi: Vikas Publishing House.

References

Allchin, FR.1962. The Neolithic stone industry of the Santhal Parganas. *Bulletin of the School of Oriental and African Studies.* 25: 306-330.

Bopardikar, BP. 1972. Prehistoric investigation of Daphabhum scientific survey expedition (NEFA). In *Archaeological Congress and Seminar Paper.* 1-8, Nagpur, Nagpur University.

Colani, M.1927. L'age de pierreactans la province de Hoa Binh (Tonkin). *Mem. Serv. Geol. Indochine.*14: 1-60.

Dani, AH. 1960. *Prehistory and Protohistory of Eastern India*, Calcutta, Firma KLM.

Lal, BB.1967-1968.*Indian Archaeology: A Review.*Archaeological Survey of India, Government of India. New Delhi.

Sharma, TC. 1980. Prehistoric archaeology in North-Eastern India: A review of progress. In T.C. Sharma and D.N. Majumdar (Eds): *Eastern Himalayas: A Study on Anthropology and Tribalism.* pp. 102-125, New Delhi: Cosmo.

Wheeler, M 1959. *Early India and Pakisthan,* Thames and Hodson, London.

Woorman, EC., 1949. The Neolithic problem in the prehistory of India. *Journal of the Washington Academy of Sciences.* 39, 6: 181-201.

Chapter – 12

Dr. Abhimanyu Sharma

Anup K. Kapoor

Dr. Abhimanyu Sharma was born on 20th January 1930. He received his B.Sc (Hons) degree in Physics and M.Sc degree in Anthropology from the University of Delhi. Soon after he joined the Faculty of Rangoon University in Burma as a lecturer and remained there for three years. During his stay in Burma, he collected a large series of data on the palmar dermatoglyphics of the Kachins. On his return to India, he joined his alma mater as a lecturer on 26th July 1955.

He worked for his doctoral thesis on the palmar dermatoglyphics of the Burmans under the supervision of Dr. P.C. Biswas. His Ph.D. thesis entitled, 'A study of palmar dermatoglyphics of Burmans: Certain fresh methodological approaches as based on the Burman data', was a landmark in dermatoglyphic studies. Besides, dermatoglyphics, he also worked in other fields of physical anthropology, viz. Indian ethnology, palaeoanthropology, human growth and development, and biometrics. On 20th July 1968, he was appointed a Reader in Physical Anthropology. He supervised five Ph.D. theses and was the author of more than 110 articles and papers published in various scientific journals. Apart from the fact that he was passionately devoted to the growth of Anthropology, he was one of the best teachers of the Department. He tried to improvise new methods of teaching. With his death, we have lost an excellent teacher of Anthropology, who will always be remembered among Anthropologists as a distinguished scholar, teacher, and friend.

He served the Anthropological Survey of India, knew German, and had translated the sources where Anthropometric techniques were discussed. Dr. Sharma did not confine himself to the biological aspects as one would have imagined, since he was a physical anthropologist. In his teaching, he incorporated the element of time, in the form of evolution in biology, and history in the study of culture. He was scholarly in everything he did, whether it was a paper on Kachin kin terms or handprints. Dr. Sharma was innovative in the research topics he sometimes advised his students to pursue. For instance, he advised one of his female doctoral students to study the growth of mammary glands among women.

It is interesting to mention here that Anthropology was introduced at the University of Delhi at the B.Sc level in 1965 and still it is continuing in the department. Dr. Sharma used to teach material culture and technology in the second-year class. I joined as a faculty in 1983, it was noticed that classes were taken as per the rotation among teachers. He used to teach us the Ethnology of India concerning Australoid, Negroid problems, blondism, and about race and caste aspects. He also taught pair-bond relationships, which was extremely popular among students, and each student used to attend his class regularly. He was the first teacher to start with an overhead projector, slide show and newspaper cutting, research articles, with various photographs. He was always punctual to the class and specific to the topic of the lecture. I still remember the time when he presented a photograph of a naked Andamanese or Onge woman in the class. All the students turn down their heads so nobody looked at the women. It was a very conservative time in the 1970s. Dr. Sharma told the whole class 'if you can't look at the women, how will you become an anthropologist in the future'. After that whatever he showed to the students, they used to see and discuss in the class.

He also taught Palaeoanthropology at M.Sc (1st Semester) with all types of photographs and notes. That time impact was very good on the students. He also used to take somatometry, somatotopy, osteometry, and Osteology practicals in M.Sc. (1st and 4th Semester). He was very particular about landmarks while telling the students and he used to go to each student to locate the landmarks. I followed the same practice while taking the practicals in M.Sc 1st semester.

He also taught us about diaptograph which was very useful in forensic anthropology, osteometery, palaeoanthropology, forensic science, etc. Now in the present scenario, this technique has been omitted by the faculty. I want to emphasize here that whatever he taught us in M.Sc., we followed his style, way of presentation with cuttings of research papers and slide shows in our classes for the next generations of Anthropology. He also attended the first-ever Summer School in Anthropology in Dalhousie (HP, India) and presented his research work.

He used to present papers on dermatoglyphics, growth, and development, and ethnological dynamics of Indian populations, etc. He also developed an instrument which was known as Pelvimeter to measure the human pelvis, somehow it lost its applicability after his death. Department of Anthropology, University of Delhi, Delhi initiated an award in the name of Dr. A Sharma Memorial best paper award 2014 and continued till 2018. He was a recognized authority on the Ethnology of India, palaeoanthropology, dermatoglyphics, and human growth and development. He was known for his seriousness as well as a good sense of humour and his students and colleagues. He is survived by his wife, son, and grandchildren. Dr. Sharma was a true inspiration not only to his students and research scholars but also to the laboratory staff and technical staff. On 24th September 1987, Dr. Sharma breathed his last in All India Institute of Medical Sciences, New Delhi, after illness following cardiac surgery.

Important research publications of Dr. Sharma

1957. Notes on palmar main-line index and transversality. *The Anthropologist* 4: 20-27.

1959. A methodological note on the geometric basis of MLI determination. *Anthropologist* 6, 1-2:

1960. Symmetry of four palmar main lines collectively and modal types in the Burman series. *Anthropologist* 7: 21-32.

1962 (1978). A study of the association between finger ball and fingertip configurational complexes. *Anthropologie* (1962-) 16, 3: 205-209.

1962. *A study of palmar dermatoglyphics of Burmans: certain fresh methodologic approaches as based on Burman data.* Unpublished Ph.D. Thesis 1-503.

1963. Geometric basis of MLI determination. *Proceedings of the Second International Conference of Human Genetics,* Gregor Mendel Institute, Rome, 15: 32-33.

1963. Relative positioning of digital triradii d and a and the axial triradius with respect to each other determines the angle atd values. *Homo* 14: 218-222.

1963. Suggested two-fold groupings of mainlines D, C, B, A terminations and locations of axial triradius. *Acta Geneticae Medicae Et Gemellologiae: Twin Research* 12, 4: 369-373.

1963. Negrito problems in India: New perspective. In L K Bara Ratnam (Ed): *Anthropology on the March*, pp. 89-103, The Book Centre.

1963. Usefulness of listing different mainline formulae. *The Anthropologist* 10, 13.

1963. Zur variation der lagebeziehungen zwischen den palmaren triradien a, d und t. *Anthropologischer Anzeiger*, H-4: 274-278.

1964. Comparative methodology in dermatoglyphics International Committee for Standardization in Human Biology.

1964. A methodological study on angle atd (t, t', t') distribution on the palmar prints. *Zeitschrift Für Morphologie Und Anthropologie*, 24-31.

1964. Anthropology and the third World. *Eastern Anthropologist* 37, 2: 171-174.

1964. Cummins' summational MLI (1936) as an expression of the significance of D and A lines: an alternative approach *Anthropologica,* 175-182.

1964. Direct angle measure: A new instrument. *Man* 64, 18-19.

1964. Morphologically evidenced extent of fluctuation of BHI values at t, t' and t' for the corresponding different single angular values of angle atd. *Eastern Anthropologist* 17: 23-30.

1964.Some clarifications about a metric method of locating the proximo-distal anatomical positions of the axial triradius and the proposed t-index. *South African Journal of Science* 60, 6: 167-171.

1965. Correlation between proximo-distal positioning of axial triradii (t, t2, t 3) and the nine-grade scale of angle atd values in palmar dermatoglyphics: A methodological study. *Anthropologie* (1962-) 3, 2: 43-46.

1965. Rules governing the choice of proximal digital triradiant and successor ridge in relationship with facultative and obligative behaviour of palmar mainlines. *Zeitschrift Für Morphologie Und Anthropologie*, 232-248.

1966. Axial triradii formulation and certain fresh indexes giving metric expression of variable positioning of axial triradii and digital triradii c and b. *Proc. of the Summer School in Anthropology, Dalhousie* 1964, 81-82.

1966. The linear coordinate-cum-angle measure: A multi-purpose tool. *Current Anthropology* 7, 2: 235-239.

1968. Effects of variable digital spreading on radio-ulnar trends of deviation. *The Anthropologist;* Special Volume, 121.

1968. Methodological study of flexional angle in quantitative palmar dermatoglyphics. *Eastern Anthropologist* 21, 3: 257-266.

1968. Standardized position of digital spreading for quantitative palmar dermatoglyphics. *The Anthropologist* 15: 11-16.

1969. Effects of variable digital spreading on radio-ulnar trends of deviation quotient. *The Anthropologist* (Special Volume): 121-131.

1970. Definite meaning of Cummins' summational mainline index *The Eastern Anthropologist* 23: 37-44.

1972. A study of positional index as compared to deviation quotient. *The Eastern Anthropologist* 25: 51-56.

1975. Effects of age-changes in some segmental measurements in Mundas/Oraons of Chota Nagpur. *Ind J Phys Anthrop and Hum Genet* 1: 9-16.

1975. Inclination of longitudinal axis of palmar print with inter-triradial distance Ad, PMPC, and DWC. *Acta Geneticae Medicae Et Gemellologiae: Twin Research* 24, 3-4: 319-320.

1976. Application of pelvic area as a new morphometric variable in man. *Zeitschrift Für Morphologie Und Anthropologie,* 320-332.

1976. Multiple regression equations for estimating age in primitive communities. *Archaeology and Physical Anthropology in Oceania* 11, 2: 156-161.

1977. A cross-sectional growth study of some modified fresh pelvic measurements and the correlation matrices. *Anthropologie* (1962-), 141-147.

1977. A fresh perspective on parent-child stature correlations. *Zeitschrift Für Morphologie Und Anthropologie,* 286-292.

1977. A method for adjusting sample means in growth and development studies. *Current Anthropology* 18, 1: 95-96.

Chapter – 13

Contributions of Dr. Dhirendra Narayan Majumdar towards Anthropological Studies in North-east India

Rajendra Prasad Athparia

Dhirendra Narayan Majumdar was born in a highly regarded Assamese Mauzadar Hindu family of Guwahati in May 1930. He was known among the anthropological community as Dr. D.N. Majumdar who rose to the height of proving himself as one of the illustrious disciples of the legendary anthropologist of the same name, the late Professor D.N. Majumdar of Lucknow University. He did his M.A. in Anthropology from that university in the early fifties under the guidance of Professor D.N. Majumdar. From the beginning of his academic career, he had a pre-conceived mind to know about mankind. That is why he opted to study anthropology. He was destined to be born for anthropology. His premature demise within two months of his retirement on 25th July 1990 has created a great loss in the field of anthropology that it would be difficult to fill up for many generations to come. His research contribution was a source of envy to many of his compeers who created for him a life of challenge as well as achievements because there could be no success where there is no challenge. At the beginning of his academic career, he was found disqualified in an interview for the post of lecturer in a college. Since then he had to face this kind of challenge till the last phase of his service career. Each time, the Anthropological Survey of India acts as a savior by offering him at the formative stage, a Junior Research Fellowship, and in the very last phase by honouring him with Visiting Fellowship. He took up the ups and downs of his life with such great strides that within two decades of his career he proved himself that there was none equal to him in the field of anthropology in contemporary North-east India in terms of completed research projects, standard published books, and research papers as well as supervising Ph.D. thesis of as many as fifteen scholars of various branches of social sciences. His contribution to Social Science Research did not confine his reputation in the country only, it spread abroad also. In response to the invitation to an International Social Scientists Conference at Zagreb in Yogoslavia in May 1989, he presents a paper on the *jhum* cultivation of North-east India which was highly appreciated by the social scientists of the different countries of the world. He was also invited to deliver a series of lectures on the cultures of North-east Indian tribes to the Ethnological Museum at Osaka, Japan in April 1990. His deliberation and depth insight of the view and analytical approach was highly appreciated by Japanese scholars.

In collaboration with the Japanese Social Scientists counterparts, he completed the research project on '*Production and Consumption of Fermented Fish of South East Asia with special reference to North-East India.*' Moreover, with financial assistance from the Ethnological Museum of Osaka, Japan he conducted a research project on the panoramic display of the emblematic study of dress and ornaments of different communities of North-east India.

Tribal ethnography being his primary interest developed while he was in Garo Hills first as a social worker of a voluntary welfare organization known as 'Assam Seva Samiti' and then as Block Development Officer. Once again, destiny seems to have played its role, when he chose to marry a Garo girl, Claris Momin, from a very remote and underdeveloped village in the Eastern Garo Hills. It proved to be a great fortune for an anthropologist like Dr. D.N. Majumdar to marry a Garo girl, who under the rigid matriarchal system found to have assumed the role of a queen of the household and the family property, leaving her husband free to devote intensively in his pursuit in search of new facts and true knowledge in anthropology. This understanding not only allowed him to be completely assimilated into a tribal society, thus setting a unique example of cultural adaptation, but also enabled him to seize the unique opportunity of moulding himself into an anthropologist of a unique type. To achieve this he had to sacrifice his own aristocratic Assamese Hindu identity. He was not only the master of Garo dialect but also adapted to Garo's way of life in all respects.

With the unique background, he assumed the role of a great strider extending his area of operation first to every nook and corner of the Garo Hills then gradually extending to all parts of North-east India which are called 'a paradise for anthropologists'. Dr. D.N. Majumdar dominated over the so-called paradise not like the Indra Devta but like a Pasupati Mahadev Shiva, who is unconquerable. In doing this, he discarded all the earthly pleasures that always accompany the urbanite anthropologists. *Balapha* as the Garos calls him thus perfected the participant observation method in anthropology in recording the minutest details of the lifeways of the relatively unknown tribal community which hardly opened up the inner core of their social intricacies to the stranger anthropologist. He can in this respect be compared with Verrier Elwin, the famous anthropologist who married a Gond girl to know the Gond culture authentically.

The Garos was his focal point of research and he spent all his later life studying the Garos and their culture. He was equally familiar with other tribal groups of Garo Hills like Song Koch, Rangdani Rabha, Hajong, and Mech and he published research articles on these tribes also.

He was a field anthropologist rather than a theoretician. He studied language, food habits, dress and ornaments, agriculture practice, kinship system, marriage, family, clan organization, political organization, and customary laws of these tribes and he described minutely everything he saw and learned. He never propagated a theory. His way of treating the tribal people was as they were and in this respect, he had a resemblance with a portrait painter. Portrait painting or descriptive analysis was the core of his study. He did his Ph.D. under the guidance of Professor M.C. Goswami in the Department of Anthropology of Gauhati University and the topic of his thesis was *'Study of Culture Change of two Garo Villages of Garo Hill'* and joined the Department of Anthropology as a lecturer.

In addition to his successful teaching career in the Department of Anthropology at Gauhati University, he undertook several research projects either individually or in collaboration with other reputed social scientists of the country and abroad. He also served in the Department of Sociology, Dibrugarh University for about a year in 1978-79 as Reader. As a leading anthropologist of India, he was attached to different Social Science Institutions as a member of the Executive or Advisory Committee. Mention may be made of the North-east India Council for Social Science Research, Shillong; North-eastern Institute of Anthropological Research; Anthropological Society of North-east India. He was also a Guest Lecturer in the Assam Administrative Staff College, Guwahati for a brief spell and also associated with the Tribal Research Departments of the different states of North-east India including Assam.

Dr. D.N. Majumdar was a prolific writer. His published works include more than 15 books and about 70 research papers. Some of his volumes were written in Garo and Assamese languages, but most of his works are in English.

Dr. Majumdar's contribution to cultural anthropology

The major part of Dr. D.N. Majumdar's contribution to cultural anthropology was in the area of ethnography. As a student of the behavioural aspect of man, his approach was that of a cultural anthropologist. He regarded the works of man or the products of human activity, i.e., language, marriage, family, kinship, economy, magic, religion, art, political, etc., as the subject matter of anthropology. His approach to the study of human culture was that of functionalist. He regarded functionalism as the best method for the collection and interpretation of data concerning human behaviour. Dr. Majumdar studied the cultural aspects of tribal groups rather than their problems. In nearly all his works whether monographs or articles, he included a discussion of cultural dynamics. He maintained and followed Malinowski's teaching that although changes are occurring in culture yet it retains its character of being an integrated whole. His study has grown out of the fieldwork in the Garo Hills of Meghalaya since 1953. In the initial stage, he did not start investigations with any particular aspect of tribal life. Their religion, law, the social structure was as fascinating topics for investigation as the problems which they were facing due to their contact with the outside world. He just wanted to know the people, by living with them, by learning their language, by sharing their joys and sorrows, and by trying to understand their day-to-day problems. At that stage of the investigation, his mind was not oriented towards any particular school of anthropological thought. He collected data on all aspects of their life. He intended to know them in their totality. Thus, a general idea about the tribe was formed. Later, he concentrated upon the problem-oriented study of cultural change among the Garos.

He found that the descriptive accounts of the Garos were available right from their early contacts to the present times. Playfair gave a comprehensive account of the Garos in 1909. Again in 1954-56, Robbins Burling, an anthropologist from Harvard made an extensive study of the Garos in a village named Rengsengiri in present Bangladesh which in those days conserved the traditional culture to a great extent. Many fragmental studies of the tribe focusing upon particular aspects, such as kinship, law, inheritance, etc were made in the intervening period by several workers. So, another descriptive study of the Garos as a whole or any particular aspect of it would have meant the only duplication of work. At the time of his first acquaintance with the Garos from 1953 to 1962, he noticed rapid changes in society. These changes took place when he visited some interior villages in 1953 which he revisited a decade later. He witnesses several perceptible changes in the material culture; Christian Garos no longer built traditional houses; the perineal band of the male and the shortened skirt of the females were gradually disappearing; handmade pottery was replaced by the wheel made pottery brought by the traders from the Assam plains.

What was the significance of these changes? How far did the basic institutions of their social change? What were the degrees of change? These were some of the questions which Dr. Majumdar attempted to analyze and discuss in his monumental Ph.D work on

'Study of Culture Change in two Garo villages in Meghalaya'. His focal objective was to examine the effects of permanent agriculture in a culture that has changed over from shifting cultivation to permanent cultivation. For this study, he had selected two villages, Wajadagiri and Matchakolgiri, and investigate their permanent agriculture. The general aspects of these two villages upon which he focused the study of culture change were within the same Ambeng sub-tribe of the Garos. The inhabitants of Wajadagiri village were the followers of both Christian as well as non-Christian (*Songserek*). Matchakolgiri village was inhabited by Christian Garos only. Among the Garos, there was a predominance of the particular clan in the sub-tribe while some particular clans were limited to certain sub-tribe. In the Ambeng sub-tribe, Chambugong and Agitok clans were predominant.

All the households of Wajadagiri village had migrated from the nearby hill areas depended on shifting cultivation but now reclaimed land for permanent cultivation. Though the village was a homogenous population, the area as a whole had greater diversity. From early times, Koch and Hajong people came to this area in search of land and settled in the vast arable land of Galwang valley. Within a radius of four miles of Wajadagiri village, some small villages belonging to communities of Wansang Koch, Pani Koch, Satbari Koch, Hajong, *Songsarek* Garo (follower of traditional faith), Baptist Christian Garo, and Roman Catholic Christians were found at the time of his field investigation. Though the villagers of Wajadagiri were settled cultivators yet the hilly areas of this village depended on shifting cultivation.

The other village Matchakolgiri is located at a distance of a furlong west of the Tura-Mankachar road. This is the main connecting road of the village with the plains of Assam. The village was named Matchakolgiri because there was a tiger's den near the village. The original village was in a corner of its *adok* means shifting cultivation. The village was shifted to the present site in 1947 due to the man-animal conflict and the epidemic *Kala Azar* which had wiped out many of the populace. After coming to the new village site the villagers have converted to Christianity and all the converted families along with some migrant Christian families formed the new village and came to be known as *Christian Gitim.* The inhabitants of this village were shifting cultivators and all were at the same level as the economy.

Dr. Majumdar has highlighted that the culture change in both the Garo villages is ecological determined. In both the villages' impoverishment of shifting land was the basic reason for a change in the economic patterns. Though it was ecologically determined other factors were also responsible for the changes. In Wajadagiri, the villagers have adopted wet rice paddy cultivation because: (1) they could observe as well as pick up the technique from their neighbouring people like Koch and Hajong, and (2) they had land suitable for permanent cultivation at their disposal. On the other hand, Matchakolgiri people took up non-agriculture occupations because of their proximity to an urban population. Even if they would have liked to adopt plough cultivation they had no land suitable for this type of cultivation. So, the problems posed by ecological factors are solved by different peoples in different ways according to varying circumstances. However, Dr. Majumdar was silent about how the problem of the impoverishment of shifting cultivation be solved by people who have neither the possibility of opening up new cultivable land nor any opportunity of changing over to other occupations. He was hopeful that future investigators might be able to solve this problem. He further said that other problems of these two Garo villages were: the rapid rise of population, lack of proper incentive to educate the children, and lack of medical care. Despite all these problems, in Wajadagiri there was a vital change in the system of agriculture which Elwin recognizes as 'A way of life and an aspect of culture, for culture has been defined as the force of adhesion between people and environment'. The Garo society is described as in the state of 'Eunomia' (borrowed the term from Radcliffe Brown). On the other hand, though there was no such major change in any of its vital aspects of culture in Matchakolgiri, it was in a state which Radcliffe Brown would have described as 'dysnomia'. But they were struggling hard towards a state of 'Eunomia'. Dr. Majumdar's study on these two Garo villages has opened up a new vista for further anthropological research in culture change.

Study on the tribe-caste continuum

The term continuum was used for the first time by Robert Redfield in his book '*The Folk Culture of Yucatan*' (1941) to understand the interaction between tribal, folk, semi-urban, and urban communities. The study of caste dynamics in terms of the tribe-caste continuum also attracted Dr. Majumdar to understand the process of caste formulation among the tribes of North-east India. The concepts of the Tribe-Caste continuum, Tribe-Rajput continuum, Hinduization, and Sanskritization refer to the same or similar process of 'caste formation' from the tribal matrix under the impact of caste-dominated major regional societies.

Since the bulk of the tribal communities has lived for centuries in close interaction with the Hindu social order, so Hinduization is a very long process in North-east India. Dr. Majumdar's valuable research work on the study of Sanskritization among the Bodo-speaking tribes of Garo Hills was published in K.S. Singh's book on '*Tribal Situation in India*' in 1972 is in the same way as mentioned by G.S. Ghurye in his work. '*The Scheduled Tribe*' (1957) characterized the tribals as a backward class and Prof. B.K. Roy Burman in his article entitled 'Tribal Demography: A Preliminary Appraisal' in K.S. Singh's edited book on '*Tribal Situation in India*' in 1972 has attempted a classification of Indian tribes in terms of their orientation towards Hindu social order. In this case, Dr. Majumdar has opined that the Bodo-speaking tribals of Garo Hills like Koch, Rabha, and Hajong have been fully incorporated into the Hindu social order. They have almost turned into castes and can hardly be differentiated from the neighbouring Hindu peasantry.

Dr. Majumdar believes that Sanskritization is part of a similar process and starts with the simple claim of the group as being members of the greater Hindu society. This varies in direct proportion with their giving up of unclean non-Hindu habits such as beef-eating, rearing of pigs and fowls, and eating of pork and fowls. Abstaining from beef-eating is an indication that the group in question wants acceptance in Hindu society. Those, who give up beef-eating or pig-rearing, look down upon those who do not do so. The second step in Sanskritization is the suspension in belief in tribal deities and gradual adoption of the Hindu deities along with their traditional rituals. They also celebrate Hindu festivals. In the third or final stage, the tribals seek to give up their clan organization and also in some cases give up matrilineal inheritance and adoption of the patrilineal complex. In many cases, tribal language is also given up.

Dr. Majumdar's work on '*A Comparative Study of Boro and Koch Kinship Terminologies*' in 1972 aimed to examine how far differences in the anthropological factors manifest in kinship terminologies. The Koch have a matrilineal descent group while the Boro have no such groups and their society is patrilineal. The study shows that the existence of matrilineal descent groups among the Koch has not been able to exert its full impact on its kinship terminology. Dr. Majumdar said that due to the adoption of some terms from Indo-Aryan kinship terminology the traditional shape of the terminology has been obliterated. On the other hand, some aspects of terminology which can be expected in the matrilineal framework are found in the Boro kinship terminology though at present there is no trace of it in the society.

To sum up it can be said that Dr. Majumdar was the authority of the Garos. As an anthropologist, he used to visit the interior areas of Garo hills and observe the Garo society from close quarters as a participant observer. Fieldwork was the soul of his study of the tribal groups. He used to stay with the people for months together whom he wanted to study. He used to say that fieldwork is an important means for the anthropologist to explore and analyze the data to develop a theory on that basis. Dr. Majumdar could overcome all the problems faced by researchers through his uncanny research-oriented mind and what is known as 'Participant Observation' in the parlance of Anthropology. He is specialized in the study of the Garos with whom he had intimate and direct contact and knowledge for several decades. He could visit even the remotest and interior areas and collect data from the primary sources with unending and indefatigable zeal and accuracy. He had an eye and ear for details. The works he had left behind are eloquent testimony to this. Some of his published works are as follows:

1. 1960. Garo Pahar (in Assamese), In *Pabitra Assam*. Assam Sahitya Sabha, Jorhat.

2. 1962. Garo (in Assamese) In : *Asomar Janajati*, Assam Sahitya Sabha, Jorhat.
3. 1965a. Mahari among the Garo, *Journal of the University of Gauhati*, Vol. 2: Science.
4. 1965b. A study of women's position among the Garos of Assam, *Man in India*, 45, 1.
5. 1966a. A study of legal concepts of the Garos, *Journal of the Assam Science Society*, Vol. IX.
6. 1966b. *The Garos: An Account of the Garos of the Present Day.* 2nd edition Lawyers Book Stall, Guwahati, Assam.
7. 1967a. Clan organization among the Garos of Assam, *Man in India,* 47, 4.
8. 1967b. Social organization of the Song Koch of Garo Hills, Assam, In *Common Perspective for North East India*, edited by Pannalal Dasgupta, Calcutta.
9. 1968a. A study of social attitudes among the Garo, *Man in India*, 48,1.
10. 1968b. A note on Hajong marriage. *Bulletin of the Anthropological Survey of India*, XVII, 1-2.
11. 1968c. A study of religious practices of Song Koch of Garo Hills, *Bulletin of the Anthropological Survey of India,* XVII, 3-4.
12. 1968d. An account of magico-religious rites and beliefs of the Rangdani Rabha. *Bulletin of the Anthropological Survey of India*, XVII, 3-4.
13. 1969a. An appraisal of administrative policies economic development of the people of the Hill Areas of North-east India. *Tribe*, V, 1 Udaipur.
14. 1969b. A comparative study of three kinship systems of Assam (*presented at the All India Sociological Conference*, Delhi).
15. 1970a. Clan degeneration of the Song Koch of Meghalaya. *Journal of the Assam Science Society,* XIII.
16. 1970b. Changing family patterns of the Garos (*presented at the Summer School on the Sociology of North-eastern Hill Areas of India*, Kohima).

17. 1972a. *Social Institutions of the Garo of Meghalaya: An Analytical Study*. Calcutta.
18. 1972b. A study of tribe – caste continuum and the process of sanskrititization among the Bodo-speaking tribes of Garo Hill, In KS Singh (Ed): *Tribal Situation in India,* Institute of Advanced Studies, Simla.
19. 1972c. Acculturation among the Hajong of Meghalaya, *Man in India,* 52, 1.
20. 1972d. A comparative analysis of Bodo and Koch Kinship terminological. *Bulletin of the Department of Anthropology*, Gauhati University, 1.
21. 1972e. A study of the kingship terminology of the Koch of Garo Hills (Proceeding of 58 Indian Science Congress).
22. 1972f. Concept of law and justice among three socio-cultural groups of North-East India, *Gauhati University Law Journal*.
23. 1972g. Matriliny in North-east India. *Vivekananda Kendra Patrika,* Madras.
24. 1973a. A glimpse of Garo policies, *North-eastern Affairs*, Shillong.
25. 1973b. Size-shape categories of the languages of North-east India. An exploration of the Sapir-Whorf hypothesis, *Bulletin of the Department of Anthropology.* Gauhati University, Vol. 2.
26. 1974a. *Garo Sanskritir Ruprekha*, Assam Sahitya Sabha, Jorhat.
27. 1974b. Effect of bilingualism in the phonemic structure of the Song Koch language, *Bulletin of the Department of Anthropology*, Gauhati University, Vol. 3.
28. 1975a. A review of Fr. Costas Garo Code of Law, *Bulletin Department of Anthropology,* Gauhati University, Vol. 4.
29. 1976. Economic changes among the Garos of Meghalaya, *North-eastern Research Bulletin*, Dibrugarh, Vol. VII.
30. 1977a. Education among the Garos: Its prospect, *The Thinker*, Kohima, Vol. V, No. 1.
31. 1977b. Shifting cultivation: Is it a way of life? *Shifting cultivation in North-east India*, Shillong.

32. 1978. The practicability of Terrace cultivation in Garo Hills, *North-east India*, Delhi.
33. 1979a. Garo in pre-British period, sources of the history of India, Vol. II, *Institute of Historical Studies*, Calcutta.
34. 1979b. Problem of identity in a multi-ethnic setting. *Bulletin of the Department of Anthropology*, Dibrugarh University.
35. 1980a. *A Study of Culture Change in two Garo Villages of Meghalaya*. Gauhati University Publication, Guwahati.
36. 1980b. North-east India: A profile, *Eastern Himalayas*, Delhi.
37. 1980c. Growth of ethnological studies in North-eastern India, *Eastern Himalaya,* Delhi.
38. 1980d. *Eastern Himalayas* (ed. with TC Sharma), Delhi.
39. 1980e. *Some Aspects of Urbanization in the Garo Hill: Family, Marriage and Social Change on the Indian Fringes*, Cosco Publication, Delhi.
40. 1984. *Tribal Occupational Mobility* (jointly with B Datta Ray), Research India Publications, Calcutta.
41. 1986. *Crime Perspective in North-east India* (jointly with B. Datta Ray and D. Doley), Omsons Publications, Gauhati, and Delhi.

Chapter – 14

Life and Works of Prof. S.R.K. Chopra towards Anthropological Research in India

Indu Talwar

The most important people who shape our lives and careers are our parents and teachers. The only and most beautiful way to pay them respect and gratitude is by celebrating and glorifying their life achievements. In India, we celebrated 100 years of teaching Anthropology in the year 2020, by organising webinars through which the contributions of founding fathers and distinguished scholars in the development of the subject of Anthropology were highlighted. It has been very thoughtful to celebrate this occasion by deliberating upon the life, works, and significant contributions of doyens of Anthropology, who established academic excellence in the various fields of Anthropology. Their contributions will inspire budding anthropologists and enrich their knowledge. It was the happiest moment for me when I was invited to contribute an article on the life and works of Prof. S.R.K. Chopra towards anthropological research in India. I deem it as a rare honour and privilege to have this opportunity to pay my gratitude and have attempted sincerely to throw light on the life and works of internationally renowned scholar, distinguished anthropologist Prof. Shiv Raj Kumar Chopra, F.N.A., founder Head of the Department of Anthropology at Panjab University, Chandigarh, my esteemed teacher, mentor, guide, philosopher and a true visionary.

Academic and research contributions

Prof. S.R.K.Chopra was born at Ludhiana in Panjab on 8th October 1931 in an educated family. His father, a learned scholar, was a Professor of English literature at the University of Delhi. His mother was a homemaker, a very affectionate noble soul. I had the opportunity to meet his parents on many occasions and had their blessings. He did his B.Sc. Honours in Zoology in 1951 and Masters in Anthropology in 1953 from University of Delhi. He was awarded his Ph.D. in 1955 from Zurich, Switzerland. His doctorate research work on the cranial suture closure in the old world and new world monkeys was a significant contribution and was published in 1957. Chopra (1957) studied 10 genera of old and new world monkeys, observed high intra-specific and intra-generic variability in suture closure of monkeys, and specified that each genus had a regular sequence. His findings described phylogenetic relationships between higher and lower primates. From 1955-56, he received a grant under Wenner–Gren Foundation, at the University of Birmingham for anthropological research and designed Pelvimeter, for the measurement of angles of torsion on the pelvis and other bones of primates including man. This design was published in 1958 in the journal *MAN* by the Royal Anthropological Institute, London. After having served as an invited lecturer at the Duckworth Laboratory, University of Cambridge, UK from 1957 to 1958, he returned to India in 1959, to join as a Reader in Anthropology in the Department of Zoology at Panjab University, Chandigarh. Being a true visionary, in 1960, he established an independent Department of Anthropology at Panjab University and became its founder head at a very young age of 30. He served as Chair of the Department till 1981. He got married in the year 1960 to the most graceful woman named Krishna Taneja who was a very warm person and an excellent host. They have three children, two daughters, and a son. The eldest daughter Ms. Shalini Vahi did her Masters in Anthropology from the Department of Anthropology, Panjab University, Chandigarh, and is a practicing socio-cultural anthropologist settled in Australia. She has recently contributed an in-depth article on her fathers' life for the United Indian Anthropology Forum. I acknowledge her help which I got from her article in writing about the life and works of Prof. Chopra.

Prof. Chopra had great academic and administrative skills. The Department grew in strength in terms of faculty, infrastructure as well as in the number of students under his leadership. From 1967 onwards, painstaking investigations was undertaken by him and his team in the Sivaliks yielded large primate fossil material, which played an important role in understanding the evolution of man. He has to his credit the discovery of a new fossil Gibonoid tooth from the Sivalik hills. A nearly complete mandible of Gigantopithecus representing a new species *Gigantopithecus bilaspurensis* was found in the Dhok Pathan beds of Northwest of Haritalayangar, Himachal Pradesh, India. This find was the first reported discovery by Chopra (1968a, b) and Simons and Chopra (1969) of the joint Chandigarh –Yale research programme in the search of early hominids and related apes in North India and published by the Peabody Museum of Natural History, Yale University. His contributions also include the discovery of fossils like *Pliopithecus Krishnaii* (in the Miocene beds) described by Chopra (1978) and Chopra and Kaul (1979). Chopra (1983) described a new genus and species *Sivasimia chinjiensis* (in the Chinjis). Descriptions of lower primates consisting of Tree Shrews (Chopra et al, 1979; Chopra and Vashisht, 1979), Adapids (Chopra and Vashisht, 1980a), and Indraloris (Chopra and Vashisht, 1980b) were also published. His work has been well documented and cited in research papers, textbooks as well as recently in Wikipedia. He was known as a leading paleoanthropologist of the world. Besides palaeoanthropology, he has made seminal contributions in the field of primatology, human growth, and human adaptability.

Being a very ambitious and passionate researcher, besides Chandigarh -Yale research project he had many collaborative research projects and procured funding at the international as well as a national level like funds from Kiel University in collaboration with the German Research Council to undertake studies on the biological surveys of select Himalayan Populations; funding by Panjab Government and CSIR (1964 -1968) to conduct biological surveys in Lahul Spiti; funding by INSA from 1972-74 to continue these studies in the same area. He attended the 5th International Congress of Primatology held in 1974 at Nagoya Japan and presented his paper on Dryopithecine material from the Shivaliks, which got published in *Contemporary*

Primatology in 1975. In 1979, he undertook studies on human adaptability in varying climatic zones in association with the Cambridge Himalayan High Altitude Research Expedition, and the research was funded by the Medical Research Council and the Royal Society, UK, Cambridge. The report of this work got published in the *International Compendium*, Cambridge University Press. Due to these collaborations, the Department of Anthropology benefitted a lot and had the opportunity to meet visiting faculties from various parts of the world. This kind of exposure widened the horizons of anthropological knowledge at the departmental level and helped the faculty to achieve excellence.

The Department of Anthropology was recognized worldwide as a center of excellence for paleoanthropological studies. Under his leadership, the Department of Anthropology offered not only undergraduate and post-graduate programmes in anthropology but also became one of the first departments in the country to introduce a diploma course in Forensic Science and Criminology. Initially, the department had more faculty with specialization in Physical Anthropology, he recruited faculty in Social Anthropology to maintain the holistic and integrated nature of Anthropology. Facilities for research work at the doctorate level were made available not only in physical and social anthropology but also in Archaeology. Fieldwork for three to four weeks was mandatory to collect data for the M.Sc. dissertation. Every year students were taken to Haritalayngarh, Himachal Pradesh for fossil collection to impart training in paleoanthropology. This practice is still going on and students are taken to nearby Sivalik hills for fossil collection. He was proficient in English, Hindi, Punjabi, and German languages. He has published more than 100 research papers in national and international journals of repute like *Nature, Journal of Human Evolution, Human Biology*, etc. He supervised 19 Ph.D. students in diverse fields of anthropology. He was an excellent teacher and always motivated and inspired his students to give their best in studies and research. His charismatic personality, humility and leadership qualities, love, and commitment to the subject made him a unique person. He emphasizes intensive fieldwork, discipline, dedication, empathetic and innovative approach for becoming a good researcher. His focus was to disseminate anthropological knowledge, popularise and promote the subject of anthropology, and his concern was to create job opportunities for his students. He and his colleagues at the department trained his students so well that they got jobs in prestigious institutes in India as well as abroad. He was a member of various professional bodies at Punjab University and various other Universities. He acted as a paper setter /examiner for postgraduate and doctorate examinations at the national and international levels. He was elected Fellow of the Indian National Academy in 1984. The unique and nationally acclaimed Museum of Man in the department was conceived by Professor Chopra in 1974. Life-size models based on the fossil material collected from Sivaliks were reconstructed by the artisans from Kolkata and it was inaugurated by the then Chief Minister of Punjab, Giani Zail Singh. Besides having a living primate gallery it has human evolution gallery, ethnographic gallery, and pre-proto historic gallery. The museum has been posthumously named the *SRK Chopra Museum of Man* in his honour.

His vision and legacy have been carried forward by the faculty and the department is well known for its researches in the fields of palaeoanthropology, palaeoecology, human growth and development, forensic anthropology, genetic epidemiology, twin studies, medical anthropology, and socio-cultural anthropology. It is a UGC-funded Centre for Advanced Studies in Anthropology since 2011.

Anthropological Survey of India, Government of India, 27 Jawaharlal Nehru Road, Kolkata, West Bengal, 700016

Prof. Chopra received Wenner-Gren Foundation Award for Excellence twice from 1955 to1956 and then from 1966-1967. Excellence Award by the Shiromani Nehru Centenary Committee was bestowed on him in 1989 for his contributions towards National Development. He was the President of the Indian Association of Physical Anthropology from 1976 to 1978. He was the recipient of the Dr. Panchanan Mitra Memorial Lectureship award in 1985 of the Asiatic Society, Kolkata for his significant contributions to the subject. He was a fellow of the Royal Anthropological Institute of Great Britain and Ireland, a fellow of the Zoological Society of London, a member of, Permanent Council of the International Congress of Anthropological and Ethnological Sciences, and a member of the

International Association of Human Biologists. He also served as the editor of *Everyday Science* and as a member of the Advisory Committee of Anthropological Survey of India, and the Indira Gandhi National Museum of Man, Ministry of Culture. He delivered the Presidential Address (Anthropology Section) of the Indian Science Congress in 1974 at Nagpur on a topic *Palaeo-primatological studies in India with special reference to recent findings in Sivaliks* (LXVI Session) which was published in the proceedings. He delivered the *D.N. Majumdar Memorial Lecture* in 1976 and received a silver plaque from the Ethnographic and Folk Culture Society, Lucknow. He served as the UGC National Lecturer from 1980-81. *M.R. Sahni Memorial lecture* was delivered by him in 1984 under the auspices of the Palaeontological Society of India. He chaired many sessions in conferences in India as well as abroad. The session on Palaeo-Biology, and Evolution for the 7th Congress of International Primatological Society in 1979 was chaired by him. His research contributions helped in promoting scientific explorations in the field of fossil primate discoveries and due to this recognition, he was nominated as a member of the Explorers Club of the USA.

Prof. Chopra was the most widely traveled person. He visited various Universities in connection with international assignments. To name a few, he was a visiting Professor at the Institute of Anthropology at the University of Kiel in West Germany from 1965-1967. In 1979, he was invited as a Visiting Professor to Primate Research Institute at Kyoto University in Inuyana, Japan. Being a famous palaeontologist, he was invited in 1980, as an expert by the President of the 8th Congress of International Primatological Society, Professor A.B. Chiarelli of Florence University to deliberate upon Shivalik *Fossils Remains* with other experts and delegates of the congress. His hard work brought him laurels but he compromised on his health. In 1988, Prof. Chopra developed health problems and had to undergo a kidney transplant which remained successful and he was back to his ongoing academic commitments. Soon after fully recovering in the same year, he served as a Visiting Professor for one year, at the United Medical and Dental School, University of London. S.R.K Chopras Festschrift volume was published in his honour for his immense contributions in anthropology in 1989 by the distinguished geologist Professor Ashok Sahni and Prof. Rajan Gaur who did his Ph.D. in palaeoanthropology under Prof. Chopra.

Prof. Chopra remained head of the Anthropology Department for nearly 21 years. He was appointed Pro-Vice-Chancellor of Punjabi University, Patiala from 1983 -1986 and thereafter he became Vice-Chancellor of Kurukshetra University, Haryana from 1986-1989. He is remembered for his outstanding administrative skills not only at Panjab University but also at both these Universities where he worked selflessly to raise the standards of teaching and research. After completion of his term at Kurukshetra University, he joined his parent department and was assigned the prestigious position of Dean of University Instructions, Panjab University till his retirement on 31st October 1991.

Prof. Chopra was a very sophisticated, grounded, humble, warm, kind, and fine human being with a very pleasing personality. He was a strict teacher and professional to the core but had a heart of gold. He treated his faculty and research scholars like his family members. Both Prof. Chopra and Mrs. Chopra were very hospitable and we all enjoyed their hospitality and style several times. We learned not only Anthropology from him but imbibed many qualities which have helped us in our career and our day-to-day life. He believed in the overall development of the students and encouraged them to participate in extracurricular activities and formed an Anthropological association where students were given awards based on their academic performance, participation in sports, declamation, debates, and cultural activities. To promote the discipline he not only contributed academically but motivated undergraduate and postgraduate students for excellence in the discipline. In 1962, his family came forward and donated money for instituting the Rai Bahadur Wali Ram Taneja Medal in memory of his father-in-law which was given to the topper of the B.Sc (Hons. School), final year. Since 2005, SRK Chopra Memorial Scholarship has been instituted in his memory with the financial contributions made by his family, and this scholarship is given to the topper in B.Sc (Hons. School) in Anthropology. Postgraduate students were awarded the University medal for standing first class first in the order of merit.

Prof. Chopra left for his heavenly abode on 3rd July 1994, leaving behind a void which can never be filled but he will be remembered for generations to come for his immense contributions in the field of anthropology and as a founder head of the department of anthropology at Panjab University, Chandigarh. He was an institution in himself, a scholar par excellence, and a noble soul revered by the Anthropological fraternity at the national and international level. Such teachers and visionaries are rare. I feel it as a personal loss and offer my sincere gratitude and tributes to him for shaping my life. Unfortunately this year in May 2021 his wife became a victim of Covid-19 and left for heavenly abode to join him. She was a gem of a person. My respect, regards, and tributes to the noble soul.

Some selected publications

Chopra, SRK 1957. The cranial suture closure in monkeys. *Proc Zool Soc* Lond 128, 67-112.

Chopra, SRK 1968a. The early man in Sivalik. Part I. *Akashvani* 33, 45: 5.

Chopra, SRK 1968b. The early man in Sivalik Part II. *Akashvani* 33, 47: 9.

Chopra, SRK 1978. New fossil evidence on the evolution of Hominoidea in the Sivaliks and its bearing on the problem of the evolution of early man in India. *Journal of Human Evolution*, 7, 3-9.

Chopra, SRK and Kaul, S. 1979. A new species of Pliopithecus from the Indian Sivaliks. *Journal of Human Evolution*, 8: 475-477.

Chopra, SRK and Vasishat, RN. 1979. Sivalik fossil tree shrew from Haritalyangar, India. *Nature*, 281: 214-215.

Chopra, SRK and Vasishat, RN. 1980. A new mio-pliocene Indraloris (primate) material with comments on the taxonomic status of Sivanasua (carnivore) from the Sivaliks of the Indian subcontinent. *Journal of Human Evolution*, 9: 129-132.

Chopra, SRK, Kaul, S., and Vasishat, RN. 1979. Miocene tree shrews from the Indian Sivaliks. *Nature,* 281: 213-214.

Chopra, SRK 1974. *Palaeo-primatological studies in India with special reference to recent findings in Shivalik.* Presidential address, Proc. LXVI Session, Indian Science Congress Association, Part II, pp. 1-16.

Chopra, SRK 1983. Significance of recent Hominoid discoveries from the Sivalik Hills of India: In A.L. Ciochon and R.S.Corruccini (Eds): *New Interpretations of Ape and Human Ancestry:* pp. 539-567. New York, Plenum.

Chopra, SRK 1984. Evolution of early man in India –Perspectives and Issues. *Journal of the Palaeontological Society of India*. 29: 1-5.

Gaur, R., and Chopra, SRK 1983. Palaeoecology of the middle Miocene Siwalik sediments of a part of Jammu and Kashmir state (India). *Palaeogeography, Palaeoclimatology, Palaeoecology*, 43: 313-327.

Simons, EL., and Chopra, SRK 1969. Gigantopithecus (Pongidae, Hominoidea): a new species from North India. *Postilla,* 138: 1-18.

Vasishat, RN., Gaur, R., and Chopra, SRK 1978. Community structure of middle Sivalik vertebrates from Haritalyangar (H.P.), India. *Palaeogeography, Palaeoclimatology, Palaeoecology*, 23: 131-140.

Vasishat, RN., Gaur, R., and Chopra, SRK. 1978. Geology, fauna, and palaeoenvironments of lower Sivalik deposits around Ramnagar, India. *Nature,* 275: 736 -737.

Chapter - 15

Prof. Deba Prasad Mukherjee: A Doyen in Indian Anthropology

Tilak Bagchi and Palash Chandra Coomar

Introduction

Prof. Deba Prasad Mukherjee, popularly known as Prof. D.P. Mukherjee represents a unique tradition in Indian anthropology which is the juxtaposition of Indian heritage and philosophy in one hand and contemporary advancement in anthropological thoughts and tradition in the field of biological anthropology in general and holistic anthropology in particular. He firmly believed that the development of anthropology depends on the creation of an approach, which combines biological and cultural attributes of mankind both in time and space. A renowned scholar in anthropology Prof. Pranab Ganguly (1997) in this regard remarked, Professor Deba Prasad Mukherjee is an outstanding scholar who has made a significant contribution. By his keen interest and great zeal in scientific research, he has already made a remarkable impact on the people around him over the last several decades, the science of anthropology has made phenomenal progress. This has been made possible primarily by the painstaking efforts of the scholars like Deba Prasad in the gathering of empirical data, their analysis and interpretation, the test of hypothesis, and the building of theory.

Another celebrated scholar and his colleague in the Department of Anthropology, University of Calcutta Prof. A.R. Banerjee (1997) observed that one of the most characteristic features of Prof. D.P. Mukherjee is that what he believes, he practices it with conviction. Another eminent scholar Prof. Amitabha Basu (1997) wrote that Prof. Mukherjee belonged to a near-extinct variety of teachers/scientists – with all their frailties and eccentricities – which the society hasn't carried to preserve. He represents the old social order which is now dead. Dr. Satya Bbrata Chakrabarti, a well known cultural anthropologist and General Secretary of the Asiatic Society (1997) evaluated Professor Mukherjee in the words - Biology according to him, can be explained to a certain extent through culture, and evolution and adaptation are to be considered as complementary in understanding biology and culture.

Prof. Ashok K. Ghosh, an outstanding paleo-anthropologist, made a tribute by saying that 'Mukherjee tries to consider the discipline in a holistic manner' (Ghosh, 1997). Prof. V. R. Rao, former Director-in-Charge of the Anthropological Survey of India and former Professor of Anthropology, University of Delhi commented about him that his most significant contribution to the subject (anthropology) is the creation of highly motivated students in research (Rao, 1997). Under the above backdrop in the present chapter, an attempt has been made to highlight the academic profile of Professor D.P. Mukherjee modestly.

Family background and life sketch

D.P. Mukherjee was born in a village Azimnagar of Dacca, presently in Bangladesh, on 2nd February 1931 at the house of his maternal grandparents. His maternal grandfather Shri Purna Chandra Chakraborty was a local landlord (*Jamindar*). Mukherjee is the first child of Shri Prabhakar Mukherjee and Smt. Niharkana Devi. He is the eldest among eleven sibships. His father Prabhakar was the son of Upendra Nath Mukherjee, who was a typical Bengali Hindu Brahman and had remarkable command over both English and Sanskrit literature. The unique quality of his grandfather was inherited by Mukherjee in letter and spirit.

His father was a patriot, who was a disciple of Rastraguru Surendra Nath Banerjee. His father also met with Rabindranath Tagore and Netaji Subhas Chandra Bose in Mahajati Sadan as revealed from an old photograph. Although Prabhakar Mukherjee joined the police service he always cooperated with India's freedom movement in his way. Niharkana Devi, the mother of D.P. Mukherjee, was a kind-hearted true homemaker.

Prof. Mukherjee's second brother Shiva Prasad Mukherjee is the direct student of Professor Nirmal Kumar Bose in the Department of Geography, University of Calcutta. Immediately after passing post-graduation in Geography, he joined Maharaja Manindra Chandra College as a part-time lecturer. He then joined the Anthropological Survey of India as the cartographer and was instrumental in preparing the Tribal Map of India under the able guidance of Prof. N.K. Bose. Shiva Prasad motivated his elder brother to join the Anthropological Survey of India, Shillong as a Research Associate in 1957. Later Shiva Prasad joined the Indian Police Service and retired as Director General (Prosecution) in West Bengal.

Mukherjee's third brother Shri Rama Prasad Mukherjee was an expert mountaineer, who successfully climbed Mt. Abru in Sikkim, with world-famous mountaineer Tenzing Norge. Like Shiba Prasad, he was a post-graduate in Geography and an alumni of the Presidency College, Calcutta. He joined NCC and retired as a Major in NCC. During the Indo-Pak war in 1971, he was a Station Commandant, NCC in Tripura.

Mukherjee's fourth brother Shakti Nath received B.Sc. with Honours in Physiology from Presidency College, Calcutta; M.Sc. in Biochemistry from the University of Calcutta; M.D. in Medicine, and D.Sc. from the USA. He was also a PRS from the University of Calcutta. He served as a lecturer in Physiology at Krishna Nath College, Bahrampur, Murshidabad before he moved to the USA. He also served as one of the Director of Research and Development in Science and Advisor to the U.S. President in the concerned subject.

The youngest brother of Prof Mukherjee, Sandeep Mukherjee was a political worker. Thus, not only D.P. Mukherjee but most of his brothers were inherited academic aptitude with a spirit of nationalism and love for the country and its heritage from the forefathers of D.P. Mukherjee.

Till the age of about three and a half years, Debi Prasad lived in a joint family in Baldiapara Road near Maniktala. He also lived in Sambhunath Pandit Road near Bhowanipur, and Rahmetpur in Barisal now in Bangladesh, and Kotalpur of Bankura district for a brief period. His initial name was Debdas, later his parents changed his name to Deba Prasad. During the late 1930s, his family shifted to Nilambar Mukherjee Street, Kolkata, in a rented house, where he and his family lived almost till his death barring the period when he was settled elsewhere for education and job.

In 1938, Deba Prasad was admitted to the Park Institution in the third standard. Prof. Pranab Ganguly was his class-fellow till his school days. Dr. Subhendu Mukherjee, a teacher of Bengali in a reputed college in Calcutta was also contemporary to him in school. His illustrated teachers in the Park Institution were S/Shri P.C. Kanjilal, Amulya Nath Lahiri, Nitya Gopal Chattopadhyay, Gopal Chandra Bhattacharya, and many more. During his school days, he witnessed the Great Bengal Famine of 1943, the Azad Hind Movement of Netaji Subhas Chandra Bose, before and immediately after passing Matriculation securing the First Division. He had the opportunity to see Veer Savarkar, Mahatma Gandhi, Pandit Jawaharlal Nehru, and many national leaders in Desbandhu Park which is very close to his residence. All these have made an ever-lasting imprint of patriotism with a spirit of Indianness in the mind of young Deba Prasad. Throughout his life, he was a member Alumni Association of the school and presented many prizes and medals to the bright students of the school.

After passing Matriculation he was admitted in I.Sc. Course in Bangabasi College with scholarship. He also passed Bachelor of Science with Honours in Anthropology from the Bangabasi College. In his college days, he had the opportunity to study under able teachers like Prof. Girish Bose, Prof. Satkari Mitra whose maternal uncle was Swami Vivekananda. Their impacts further strengthen the spirit of nationalism in the mind of young Deba Prasad. He passed M.Sc. in Anthropology in 1951 from the University of Calcutta. His illustrious university teachers were Dr. S.S. Sarkar, Dr. T.C. Das, Dr. T.C. Raychaudhury, Dr. M.N. Basu, Prof. Dharani Sen, Prof. K.P. Chattopadhyay, and many more. He got Prof. P.K. Bhowmick,

Mr. Hirendra K. Rakshit, Prof. Pranab Ganguly, Prof. Manish Ranjan Chakrabortti as his classmate in Bangabasi College and/or Ballygunge Science College of the University of Calcutta. After passing M.Sc. in Anthropology he joined Brahma Boys School as Assistant Head Master and also as a part-time lecturer in Bangabasi College. He earned a B.T. degree, in 1957 and DMS from Calcutta Homeopathy College in 1963, and completed a Statisticians Certificate Course from Indian Statistical Institute, Calcutta in 1956. During this period young Deba Prasad came in contact with Smt. Sima Maitra, Sima Maitra came from a traditionally affluent family of Baranagar near Calcutta. She was associated with the Bratachary Movement launched by Gurusaday Dutta and a very good Rabindra Sangeet singer and used to recite excellent Bengali poems. She was also associated with the Mahila Mahal Programme of All India Radio, Kolkata. Deba Prasad married Sima Maitra in 1959. They were blessed with a son and three daughters.

Their elder daughter Dr. Subidita Chatterjee is a gynaecologist, obstetrician, and infertility specialist. The second issue of Prof. Mukherjee is Dr. Arindam Mukherjee, who is a renowned anthropologist, an Ishan scholar from the University of Calcutta, recipient of the University Gold Medal for securing the first position in first class in Anthropology from the University of Calcutta. He also received Ph.D. in Anthropology and did quality research and teaching in Anthropology in the USA. He also received a Master's degree in Statistics and a postgraduate diploma in Genetics from the USA. Presently he occupied a very senior post in an LG company in the USA. Their second daughter Dr. Samadrita Mukherjee is a Ph.D. in Zoology and presently runs the School of Human Genetics and Population Health founded by her father. Dr. Paramita Mukherjee a Ph.D. in Botany now settled in Mumbai is their youngest daughter. She was a Principal in a Private College, Gujarat and wrote a good number of books and articles. It would not be exaggerated to state that D.P. Mukherjee and his wife Sima Mukherjee were successful to infuse academic bent and other extra curriculum activities in the life and activity of their children.

After working in Bramha Boys School for a very brief period D.P. Mukherjee joined Kandi Raj College in 1952 as a founder

Lecturer and Head, Biology Department. He worked in the said college till 1955. During 1955 – 1956, Mukherjee worked as a Senior Investigator of a UNESCO Project of the Planning Commission titled *Effect of Industrialization*. Again he came in the main orbit of Anthropology and joined the Anthropological Survey of India as a Research Associate and was posted in its North-East India Station, Shillong from 1957 to 1964. During 1958 he worked as a Research Officer in the Planning Commission project in New Delhi on lien. Prof. Ruggles Gates appointed him as an Investigator for his survey on Anglo Indians as a part of the massive project *Race Crossing* sponsored and supported by the Indian Statistical Institute. In 1964, Mukherjee got a Commonwealth Scholarship and went to the United Kingdom and joined the Galton Laboratory under London University where he worked as a Commonwealth Scholar and Honorary Faculty Member. He got his Ph.D. while working in Galton Laboratory from University College of London in 1967 for his Ph.D. thesis titled *Quantitative Genetics of Dermal Ridges* with special reference to an Indian population. He got Ph.D. under the joint supervision of S.B. Halt, C.A.B. Smith, and L.S. Penrose. After being awarded of Ph.D. degree he got an MRC Fellowship at Kennedy – Galton Centre and returned to India in 1969.

After returning to India Dr. Mukherjee joined the National Institute of Family Planning in the capacity of Assistant Director. During his tenure in the said Institute, he created Population Genetics and Human Development, Division. During his tenure, he was also a visiting faculty in the Department of Anthropology, University of Delhi, Department of Social and Preventive Medicine, Lady Irwin Medical College, New Delhi, and was selected as an expert in Human Genetics in WHO, Geneva.

He left the National Institute of Family Planning, New Delhi in 1971 and joined the Department of Anthropology and Sociology in Sri Venkateswara University, Tirupati as a Reader cum Founder Head. He also was the Advisor of the Population Centre of the said university and worked there from 1971 to 1975 and produced a good number of anthropologists of repute.

In 1975, Dr. Mukherjee again joined the Anthropological Survey of India as a Deputy Director (Physical Anthropology) and Founder

Principal of the School of Anthropology of the Survey. He was also the Acting Director of the Anthropological Survey of India in 1976. He worked in the Anthropological Survey of India till 1981.

From 1981 to 1996 Mukherjee was a Professor in the Department of Anthropology, University of Calcutta. For a brief period, he also served as the Head of the said Department and worked as a Guest Professor in the Department of Anthropology, Vidyasagar University, Medinipur.

Prof. D.P. Mukherjee founded the School Human Genetics and Population Health in 1983 and was a President in Anthropology Section of Shiv Yogasram Institute (SYRI) in 1993, which is devoted to studying History of Science in India. He was elected as the President of the Anthropology and Archaeology Section of the Indian Science Congress held in Delhi in 1993. He was a Council Member and Executive Committee Member of Indian Science Congress Association in 1999 – 2000 and attended 90th Session in the Indian Science Congress at Pune in the said capacity. He delivered several memorial lectures including *Priyabala Das Memorial Lecture* in Gauhati University, *S.S. Sarkar Memorial Lecture* at Calcutta, and *R.P. Chandra Memorial Lecture* in Anthropology, and was awarded a *Centenary Medal of Sarat Chandra Roy* for his lifetime achievement in Anthropology in 2007 by the Asiatic Society, Kolkata. Mukherjee passaway on 1st July 2015 at the age of 84 years after a brief illness at a nursing home in Kolkata (Vasalu, 2016). He supervised several Ph.D. students from Universities all over India.

Prof. D.P. Mukherjee as an anthropologist

D.P. Mukherjee made significant anthropological contributions in the varied field of research disciplines ranging from Haemoglobinopathies, Epidemiologies, Dermatologyphics, Tribal Studies, Reproductive Health, and Menarchial Age, Gerontology, Medical Anthropology and so on. He is the author/co-author of three books namely:

1. 2007. *Outline of Population Genetics*, Allied Publisher, New Delhi under the aegis of the Anthropological Survey of India, Kolkata.

2. 2009. *A Laboratory Manual of Biological Anthropology* (with Dr. Dipak Mukherjee and Prof. Premananda Bharati) Scholar Publisher, Kolkata, (2nd Edition, 2018).
3. 2014. *Theories of Evolution at a Glance*, School of Human Genetics and Population Health, Kolkata.

He wrote the above three books mainly for the budding researchers and students of anthropology. One of the book reviews was published in the *Journal of the Indian Anthropological Society*.

He had published more than 300 research papers in international and national journals of high repute including high-impact international journals like *American Journal of Human Biology, American Journal of Physical Anthropology, American Journal of Human Genetics, Anthropos, Annals of Human Genetics, Acta Genet. Med. Gemellol., Current Science, Current Anthropology, Human Biology, Human Heredity, Man, Z. Morph. Anthrop,* amongst others. He had also published peer-reviewed chapters published by various reputed international publishers like Cambridge University Press (Bose, 2015).

Dr. Deba Prasad Mukherjee while working in the Anthropological Survey of India in its North-east India Station, Shillong as Research Associate from 1957 to 1964 has made extensive fieldwork among the tribal population of North-eastern India namely the Khasi, Naga, Manipuri, Mizo of Nagaland, Meghalaya, and Assam along with Prof. M.R. Chakravartti and also by himself alone. He had collected several anthropometric, dermatoglyphics, cultural, and bio-anthropological information. This has given him a lifelong interest in dermatoglyphic research on palm and toe to understand human variation and disease associated with the dermatoglyphic traits. Later his work with Prof. Ruggles Gates, a renowned persona in human genetics advised him to investigate the inheritance of recessive characters like hypertrichosis or tuff of hair on the outer rim of the external ear. He collected detailed pedigrees from among the families where the trait is noticed to know the pattern of inheritance of the traits. Mukherjee was also deeply interested in dermatoglyphic research of finger, toe, palm, and sole for pattern configuration, ridge count, triradius particularly t-triradius of palms, and other characters with their possible association with certain genetic disorders and studied in detail the palmer and finger patterns among the Mahar and few other communities. This study led him to come in contact with Prof. L.S. Penrose, who is well known for his classical research on the association of elevated t-triradius and some other distinguished dermal patterns among some chromosomal disorders including Down Syndrome patients. Being highly influenced by his quality of research Prof. Penrose invited him to join Galton Laboratory, England. It has already been said that Mukherjee in Galton Laboratory not only has conducted quality research on dermatoglyphics but has been awarded a Ph.D. degree from the UK. His work on Anglo Indians has generated disagreement about the inheritance of hypertrichosis of ear rim whether autosomal or Y linked trait. Dr. Mukherjee was in favour of its Y-linkage while many others considered the trait to be autosomal.

As an expert in the WHO committee on Human Genetics, he has presented a paper on *Patterns of Marriage and Family Formation in Rural India and Genetic Implication of Family Planning*, which is noteworthy to understand the long-term impact of national family planning programmes affecting the course of human evolution. In the same year, he communicated a paper *Biologic Age and Population Trend* which was highly praised in the symposium of Biological Relativity held in Philadelphia, USA although he was not personally present in the said symposium.

In S.V. University, Tirupati, Dr. Mukherjee has not only carried out research work in biological anthropology but has opened areas of teaching in the field of Sociology, Social Anthropology, and Pre-historic Archaeology. Dr. Mukherjee and his students collected and documented several stone tools from Tirupati town itself.

During his tenure as Deputy Director of the Anthropological Survey of India, he was one of the Organizing Secretaries of the International Congress of Anthropology and Ethnological Sciences held in India in 1978 under the Chairmanship of Prof. L.P. Vidyarthi. Dr. Mukherjee also contributed his mite to make the event a grand success.

During his tenure in the S.V. University, Tirupati he has published several papers mainly with his students. It includes association between digital formulae of hands and feet (with V.R. Rao); earlobe attachment, hand crisping and arm folding among the Tamil Brahmins in relation to cultural and ethnic affiliation (with S. Srinivasan); pregnancy spacing in breathing (with M. Lakshmanudu); seasonality of birth weight in Tirupati Hospital during November, 1973 and October, 1974 (with K. Ramamma); pattern of inheritance on genetics and PTC test (with BM Reddy); inheritance in menarchial age (with T. Siddamma); population structure of the Pattusali, a genetic isolates from Andhra Pradesh (with P.G. Reddy); consanguinity and breeding effects of fertility, mortality and morbidity among the Pattusali, a small population of Tirupati (with A. Papa Rao and P.G. Reddy); inbreeding effects of finger print patterns (with S. Sarbani); cross-sectional growth at adolescence in Renigunta (with K.N. Reddy); quantitative genetics of relative toe length (with V.R. Rao); inbreeding among some Brahmin population of Tamil Nadu (with S. Srinivasan); effects of inbreeding in some endogamous population in Chittoor district of Andhra Pradesh (with S. Bhaskar and M. Lakshmanudu); marriage distance in Mala and Madiga, two scheduled caste population of Chittoor district of Andhra Pradesh (with P.C. Reddy); offspring survival and patents stature among the Boya population in a village of Kurnool district of Andhra Pradesh (with M. Santadevi); seasonal variation of pregnancy and birth weight in and around Tirupati as observed from Hospital records (with K. Ramamma); taste sensitivity among the Mala of Chittoor district of Andhra Pradesh (with P.C. Reddy); ABO blood groups and ABH saliva secretion in Reddys and Kamas of Andhra Pradesh (with J. N. Naidu and P. Veeraraju); ethnic variability of pattern intensity on palms in Khasi and Kuki-Chin population of Manipur, Nagaland and plains of Assam (with M. Lakshmanudu); A_1A_2BO Blood groups among the Mala of Andhra Pradesh (with P.C. Reddy); quantitative genetics of palmer dermatoglyphics of Mala and Madiga of Tirupati, Andhra Pradesh (with M. Sirajuddin); inheritance pattern of dermal ridges (with S. Yaseen Saheb); and so on. The above account is merely a cross-sectional report of the study that has been carried by Dr. D.P. Mukherjee mainly with his students of S.V. University, Tirupati. The above observation also suggests that Dr. Mukherjee not only encouraged and supervised his students to research along with him in different branches of biological anthropology but different aspects of social-cultural anthropology and prehistoric archaeology in the form of collection and documentation of lithic tools of the stone age era.

Apart from his biological anthropological contribution to Indian anthropology Dr. Mukherjee also contributed significantly to social-cultural anthropology. Some of his major contributions in the above domain are rain cults and rituals in the Rayalaseema region of Andhra Pradesh (with K.V. Reddy); the prevalence of the Basavis system, which is the dedication of the female child to some popular deities by her parents in Chittoor district of Andhra Pradesh (with P. Rajyalaskshmi and M. Suryanayana) and so on.

During his tenure in the Anthropological Survey of India (1975-1981), he also carried out research work in India either independently or jointly with his colleagues in the Survey, students, and his family members. It includes trends of dermatoglyphics research in India (with H.K. Rakshit, former Director of Anthropological Survey of India); quantitative variability of ABH antigen in a Bengali sample (with Mani Kanchan Das); studies on middle pharyngeal hair among the Meiteis of Manipur (with K.S. Singh of Manipur University); congenital digital anomalies in Kandi of Murshidabad; variation of the type of palmer C line in some population of Maharashtra, Odisha and Madhya Pradesh (with Guru Charan Ghosh); hemoglobin level with age, sex and OAH blood groups in Bengali samples of Sodepur, North 24 Parganas, West Bengal (with Mani Kanchan Das); palmer patterns among Jatavas of U.P. and some other Indian population (with I. Sircar and G.C. Ghosh); hemoglobin and diurnal variation in vegetarians and non-vegetarians (with Arindam Mukherjee and Mani Kanchan Das); Inbreeding effect on dermatoglyphics (with P.C. Reddy and M. Lakshamanudu); congenital malformation of neonates with special reference to anencephaly (with Anima Guha); influence of A_1A_2BO blood groups on hemoglobin level (with Mani Kanchan Das); dermatoglyphic data, mid phalangeal hair and occipital hair whorl of the Toto, a small Particularly Vulnerable Tribal Group (with M.R. Chakravartti); and so on.

Besides, Prof. Mukherjee also wrote several popular articles and review articles in the field of anthropology. Some of the articles which may be put under this canopy are micro demography of social change among the Mizo of Shillong (with R.D. Pathak and Sima Mukherjee);

population education in Anthropology and Sociology; extending horizons of Physical Anthropology; bathing customs and practices in India (with Sima Mukherjee). Later Sima Mukherjee published a book on hygienic practices in bathing customs, etc. in India mainly with the data of All India Material Trait Survey of Prof. N.K. Bose and the first-hand data collected both by Prof. Mukherjee and Sima Mukherjee; action physical anthropology for MCH Services among the tribal population; distribution of blood groups among the tribal population of West Bengal (with Chumki Piplai); review of the distribution of blood groups in the Bengali population (with Sikha Chatterjee) and so on.

In 1981, Dr. Mukherjee joined the Department of Anthropology, the University of Calcutta as a Professor of Anthropology. He served at the University of Calcutta till 1996. Even after his superannuation, he was equally active in his research almost till his death. During this phase, he continued to work with his erstwhile junior colleague of Anthropological Survey of India as well as his students of the University of Calcutta, S.V. University as well as Vidyasagar University. Some of the interesting works carried by him during this phase includes ontogenic interrelationship of hemoglobin level with breathing rate, pulse rate, skin fold thickness and body dimension (with Mani Kanchan Das); A_1A_2BO blood groups among the Mala of Andhra Pradesh (with P.C. Reddy); quantitative genetics of palmer dermatoglyphics of Tirupati population (with S.M. Sirajuddin); low hemoglobin level in A_1 and O blood groups (with Mani Kanchan Das); growth surveillance among Kanwar and Oraon tribal children of Surguja district of Madhya Pradesh (with S.K. Biswas and N.K. Das); anthropology of tribal health among Asur of Netarhat Pleteau (with Shyamal Kumar Nandy); biological affinities between the migrant groups of fisher folk of Puri coast of Odisha (with B. M. Reddy and V.P. Chopra); variation and interrelationship of menarche, menopause and fertility among Bengali speaking rural Christian population of Southern Bengal (with Sikha Chatterjee and Chumki Piplai); effect of inbreeding in stature (with M. Lakshmanudu); influence of industrialization on healthcare and cure among the Kharia, Santal, and Kumhar population of Ghatshila town of Jharkhand; inheritance of finger triradii; new data on family and twin correlates and inbreeding effect (with Lili Kundu and Arindam Mukherjee); effect of dominant gene for Otosclerosis on the pattern intensity of finger (with N.K. Majumder and Samiran Roy); genetics and anthropology of consanguineous marriage; pattern intensity on finger and palms in four Nicobarese population (with G.C. Ghosh and Pranab Ganguly); consanguineous marriages and their genetical consequence in some Indian population; secular regression in stature among the Mahisya of West Bengal (with Dipak Mukhopadhyay); perspective on culture change and development (with Shyamal Kumar Nandy); variability of maternal age and selection potentiality among five Indian population (with Arindam Mukherjee); patterns of marriage among the Muslims of a Calcutta slum (with P. Guha, Bidhan Kanti Das and Abhijit Guha); nonlineal inbreeding effect on secondary sex ratio in relation to birth order and parental age (with Bidhan Kanti Das and Abhijit Guha); multidimensional genetical study of families with oculocutaneous albinism in Calcutta and Howrah (with Sudip Dutta Banik, D. Mukherjee, S. Chatterjee, C. Ganguly and K.N. Mukherjee); Indian contribution to dermatoglyphics from ancient period to 1900 A.D.

Articles contributed by Prof. Mukherjee during this phase in the domain of popular or general anthropological articles, review articles, contribution of eminent anthropologists in India besides application of statistics in studies on dermatoglyphics; inbreeding in genetics and quantitative traits in man; methodological issues in anthropological comparison; genetical implication of changing pattern of marriage; spastics and population aging - two emerging biological and bio-social issues; application of multi-variate distance analysis in anthropology; concept of biological and cultural adaptation of man; nature and scope of medical anthropology in India (with Shyamal Kumar Nandy); a profile of secretor status in India (with S. Das); some sources of biological anthropology in ancient India; some anthropological contribution of Hirendra Kishore Rakshit (with Sikha Chatterjee) and Biraja Sankar Guha; population genetics in human welfare; ethics in Anthropology (with Tilak Bagchi) and many more.

During his post-retirement life, he was particularly interested not only in different branches of anthropology but also in gerontology and ethical issues in anthropological research. He was Chairman of the ethical committee of the Anthropological Survey of India for some time. In his teaching, he always emphasised the holistic concept of anthropology and argued that the development of anthropology primarily depends on combining biological and cultural attributes of man rather than the study of biological and cultural anthropology in isolation. He also taught in detail various sampling methods because he firmly believed that the success of quantitative research in anthropology primarily depends on a proper and scientific way of sampling and proper use of statistics in research.

D.P. Mukherjee: an applied cum development anthropologist / social worker

Prof. D.P. Mukherjee strongly believed that apart from carrying basic research in anthropology, anthropologists should also use their anthropological knowledge for the welfare of human beings. He was highly influenced by great national leaders like Mahatma Gandhi, Netaji Subhas Chandra Bose, Iswar Chandra Vidyasagar, Rabindranath Tagore, and Swami Vivekananda in one hand and was also equally motivated with leftist Marxian philosophy. All these helped him to love the country and its heritage and to do something for the welfare of human beings. He once conducted night schools, work for the welfare of the *Bidi* workers and tea stall boys, and staged street drama for the down-trodden segment of the population. He was also involved in a UNESCO project on the effect of industrialization under the Planning Commission of India which is one of the pioneers working industrial anthropology in India and helped for planning for the welfare of the industrial workers. One of his work on research-cum-action project in Singur of Hooghly district, West Bengal helped him to learn from his teachers in anthropology regarding the use of anthropological knowledge in the construction of community latrines breaking the cultural/behavioural barriers for the use of orthodox females especially married women much before the work carried out by great action sociologist Prof. Bindeswar Pathak of Sulabh International. All these helped him to do something for the cause of his fellow mankind.

In his later life, Prof. Mukherjee founded the institution School of Human Genetics and Population Health (SOHGAPH) to build a platform between medical practitioners and biological anthropologists, especially human geneticists. The institution was established on 26th April 1993 as an anthropologist's attempt for service-oriented research in the field of human genetics and to address many problems affecting the population such as ethnicity, epidemics, and ethos of the common man.

He dreamed to build a hereditary register of all those genetic disorders and characteristics which were present in the community mostly unreported especially in the regions of eastern India. This he felt would be extremely useful to detect the variant of the genetic predisposition of diseases and their characteristics found in the region.

The institution under his active guidance has worked in the Pediatric Departments of Government Hospitals to do genetic counseling and dermatoglyphics studies therein. Prof. Mukherjee also encouraged and trained students in genetic counseling in a private infertility setup. The institution to date has been a major genetic counseling Centre following his mission. One of the main mottos of the Institute is to reach every doorstep with essential healthcare awareness and to prevent diseases, deformities and discrimination. This mission in term would bring direct sustainable community development as dreamed by Prof. Mukherjee.

School of Human Genetics and Population Health (SOHGAPH) took up rural and urban field projects viz.

1. Reproductive Child Health Project - RCH Phase I, 1999-2004.
2. HIV / AIDS prevention and control in the target population of clandestine sex workers in the north-east part of Kolkata, 2005-2008.

Both these projects were meant for awareness generation and modestly providing healthcare services. Mukherjee as the founder Director of SOHGAPH made the field workers trained in anthropological methods and brought out enormous data on the health-seeking behaviour of the community. The Institution had a facility for human genetics research where courses were conducted on population studies. In short, SOHGAPH not only generated data on different aspects of human genetics and population health-trained manpower in the said field but also helped the target population at large to create healthcare awareness.

Prof. D.P. Mukherjee and homeopathy

One of the prominent features in the character of Prof. Mukherjee is that what he beliefs he practices with conviction. He believed in homeopathic therapeutics and found pleasure in prescribing medicine to whoever approached him for that. Prof. Mukherjee administered homeopathic medicines even to those who are undergoing allopathic treatment by making them aware of the hazards and limitations of the allopathic systems and magic cure in homeopathy (Banerjee, *op.cit.*). He had a long association with the discipline of homeopathy. He was formally trained with a DMS degree and also a diploma in homeopathy from the UK during his period of stay as a Commonwealth Scholar for pursuing his Ph.D.

Prof. Mukherjee was extremely passionate about homeopathy. His family of four children was never exposed to any allopathic treatment during their growing up days. He was always ready with a remedy in a crisis of any ailment. He would not rest until the symptoms subsided. Mostly they did promptly as his intuition on the choice of medicine was effective. He claimed to have cured several malignant patients and chronic diseases. Being a biological anthropologist he had a natural sense of the biological body and felt homeopathy was triggering well-being and restoring health. There is hardly anybody who is not prescribed with a *homeodose* sometimes or the other. He also had a homeo clinic in a homeopathic medicine shop near his school the Park Institution. Much of his dislike he was put on an allopathic medical health check and had to take only routine blood pressure medicine in his 70s up to his end.

Concluding observation

Prof. Mukherjee was not only an excellent researcher, able administrator, and teacher in anthropology but he also loved social work for the welfare of his fellow people and patients. His academic activities attracted the attention of many universities where anthropology was taught (Lakshmanudu, 1997). His success lies in the fact that he always encouraged his students to conduct quality research and publications in reputed anthropological journals. The result was staggering and many of his students occupy important positions in Universities, Colleges, Research Organizations, and Hospitals all over India and even abroad carrying with them the mantle of biological (and social-cultural) anthropology that was so forcefully installed in them with so much vigour and commitment by none other than Prof. D.P. Mukherjee single-handedly (Lakshmanudu, *ibid*).

Last but not least it is to be stated that Indian Anthropology would be much more benefitted from Prof. Mukherjee if he would be a little less absent-minded and a little more organized in his academic endeavour. As a testimony for the same, we must refer that Prof. Mukherjee had completed a manuscript for the book titled *History of Biology in India*. The manuscript was the outcome of his painstaking and years-long research on the review of the genesis and development of biological anthropology in India from the ancient period to the present day. However, the book never sees the light of the day because of incomplete references. Prof. Mukherjee transferred all the references in the reference card but at the time of finalization, it has been found that numerous reference cards were misplaced.

References

Banerjee, AR,1997. Professor D.P. Mukherjee, as I have seen him. In D. Mukhopadhyay (Ed): *Profile of An Anthropologist,* pp. 67-68, D. Mukhopadhyay, Calcutta.

Basu, Amitabha 1997. The old social order is dead, long live the social order. In D. Mukhopadhyay (Ed): *Profile of An Anthropologist,* pp. 68-70, D. Mukhopadhyay, Calcutta.

Bose, Kaushik 2015. Deba Prasad Mukherjee, 1931-2015, *Journal of the Indian Anthropological Society.* 50, 2-3: 207-208.

Chakraborty, Satya Brata 1997. Professor D.P. Mukherjee, personal reminiscence. In D. Mukhopadhyay (Ed): *Profile of An Anthropologist,* pp. 70 - 71, D. Mukhopadhyay, Calcutta.

Ganguly, Pranab 1997. Foreword, In D.Mukhopadhyay (Ed): *Profile of an Anthropologist*, D. Mukhopadhyay, Calcutta.

Ghosh, Ashok. K. 1997. Professor Deba Prasad – as I know him in my way. In D. Mukhopadhyay (Ed): *Profile of An Anthropologist,* pp. 74-76, D. Mukhopadhyay, Calcutta.

Lakshmanudu, M. 1997. Saluting the great master: Dr. D.P. Mukherjee. In D. Mukhopadhyay (Ed): *Profile of An Anthropologist*, pp. 78-80, D. Mukhopadhyay, Calcutta.

Mukhopadhyay, Dipak. 1997. *Profile of An Anthropologist* (A tribute from D. Mukhopadhyay), D. Mukhopadhyay, Calcutta.

Rao, VR. 1997. D.P.The phenomenon. In D. Mukhopadhyay (Ed): *Profile of An Anthropologist*, pp. 81-83, D. Mukhopadhyay, Calcutta.

Vasalu, TS. 2015. Professor Deba Prasad Mukherjee (2nd February 1931 to 1st July 2015). *Journal of the Indian Anthropological Society.* 50, 2-3: 203-206.

Acknowledgments

We are thankful to Dr. Dipak Mukhopadhyay for providing the information to write this chapter. We are grateful to Dr. Samadrita Mukherjee for her constant encouragement and for providing valuable information that is incorporated in the present chapter; to Sri Sandip Mukherjee for providing information regarding the family background and grooming of Prof. D.P. Mukherjee. Finally, the authors are thankful to Sri Dibyajyoti Ganguly for his all-round help.

Chapter - 16

Prof. Raghunath Singh Negi

Richa Negi

To me, he was my father, a pillar of strength and protection. He was someone I could turn to in my difficult times and needs and; who enthused a feeling of security that every child feels around his/her parents. This is how I have known him during my formative years. Later, he became my role model as my mentor, guide, and confidante. My earliest memory of him is of someone whose presence was a great comfort and a learning experience in different stages of my life. After he was gone, whenever I feel myself in challenging situations, I sit quietly and reminiscence each moment savouring them and questioning myself what would he have advised me during these situations. He has left a big void in the lives of the people he had a close association with, his family, students, contemporaries, and colleagues.

Professor Raghunath Singh Negi (born 12.07.1932) was my parent, mentor, and guide, but for the world, he was an anthropologist with unique qualities and sensibilities towards his discipline and the studies/research he undertook in different phases of his life and career.

Trained as a Physical Anthropologist from the University of Lucknow; Uttar Pradesh, he excelled as a pioneer student and was awarded the Gold Medal as a University topper for his Post Graduation in Physical Anthropology. His name and photograph can still be seen in the Department of Anthropology, Lucknow University. Professor Raghunath Singh Negi was a physical anthropologist and was trained in traditional anthropology, under Professor D. N. Majumdar of Lucknow University.

Eldest siblings of three brothers and two sisters, he left his native place Pauri, Garhwal in the Central Himalayas, Uttarakhand to pursue his higher education in Allahabad and Lucknow respectively. It is said that he was the first among very few people who left his village and hometown to pursue higher studies and goals in life. He completed his formative education and Higher Secondary from Messmore Public School in Pauri Garhwal which was probably the first Missionary School of its time.

After completing his higher education from Lucknow University, he first joined the Anthropological Survey of India in 1953 as a trainee under a scheme for advanced scientific research in anthropology.

Among his phenomenal works, one must mention the most remarkable expedition and research on the discovery of human remains scattered all over the Rupkund Lake in the Central Himalayas which was undertaken during the initial stage of his career in the Anthropological Survey of India (AnSI). He was a member of the Human Biology section and was engaged in the Rupkund project from collection to finalization of the report for about two years. The expedition and the project/research was a very arduous and remarkable task in itself.

The Rupkund Lake in the Central Himalayas, Uttarakhand is a cup-shaped depression in a very higher altitude surrounded by glaciers, which at the time of the expedition was very difficult and inaccessible. It was a very arduous journey on foot for a human being to undertake at the time when communication was scarce or most of the time none and metal roads were non-existent. The journey was embarked mostly on foot. Prof. Raghunath Singh Negi was instrumental in leading an expedition initiated by the Government of India to Rupkund glacial area and bringing back a large number of human skeletal remains which included a full torso intact with flesh from the lake and was brought to the Anthropological Survey of India which was later added to its collection in the Headquarters (Kolkata) which can be viewed even to this day.

In his own words, while delivering a talk on the occasion of the NK Bose Memorial lecture at IGNCA he mentioned that, it was an extremely arduous task as there was very poor road connectivity at that time and the skeletal material was extremely fragile and decomposable with the bones having flesh and skin on them. I was not only successful in transporting this precious material but also did much scientific experimentation on these bones to ascertain their ethnicity and identity. He also explains further that, he joined the expedition team to Rupkund where human skeleton remains were found in the glacier. Three different expeditions were organized and were successful in reaching Rupkund between 4th and 18th September 1956 - one by the Department of Anthropology (now Anthropological Survey of India), Government of India, Calcutta, under the leadership of its Director, Dr. N. Dutta Majumdar; second by the Department of Anthropology, Lucknow University, under the leadership of Prof. D.N. Majumdar; and the third by Swami Pranavanand, Fellow of the Royal Geographical Society and a renowned explorer. All three expeditions were successful in bringing back sizeable collections of both skeletal remains as well as cultural artifacts for further scientific studies to determine the identity and origin of victims and the time of the tragedy (Negi, 1958, 1997, 2000, 2002, and 2009). The Anthropological Survey of India collection had a large segment of the human body which comprized a portion of a body from the waist to both the knees. The bones were fully covered with both dried-up and deteriorated flesh and skin. The sex of the individual could not be determined. In their collection, most of the bones were free from any attached soft tissues but few of them had muscular and cartilaginous tissues attached to them. The medullar cavity of such long bones was found to be full of soft and yellow pasty substance, presumably marrow. Several samples of flesh and bone marrow were collected on the spot in sealed sterilized tubes. The lines of investigation on the skeletal material were as follows: (1) Diagnosis of sex and maturity of the skeletal posts. (2) Anthropometric measurements of the skulls and long bones and estimation of stature from the long bones. (3) Determination of blood group substances A and B in the various tissues such as bone, marrow, and flesh. (4) Radio-Carbon dating from the wooden/skeletal material to establish the time of the tragedy.

Based on this expedition and research, his paper entitled, *Determination of A and B Blood Group-Specific Substance in the*

Rupkund Human Body Remains, was published by the Government of India.

During his association with the Anthropological Survey of India, he worked on different projects undertaking and conducting pivotal field studies and research. Among his pioneer studies and research area, one must mention his works on Sickle Cell Traits, among the tribals of Bastar, Nomads of Himalayas, Gujjars of Uttarakhand, Cis-transhumans, and many others.

His research works in the Bastar region mainly focused upon serological aspects including many landmark studies on Sickle-cell traits. Besides Bulletin of the Anthropological Survey of India, his paper which appeared in *Man*, published by the Royal Anthropological Institute of Great Britain and Ireland where he elaborated and explained in detail the incidence of sickle-cell trait in two Bastar tribes i.e. the Dorla and the Dhurwa (Negi, 1962). He was engaged in the genetic survey of tribal people of Bastar, which among other traits, also included the sickle-cell trait.

He served at various stations of the Anthropological Survey of India. Later he was instrumental in establishing the Indira Gandhi Rashtriya Manav Sangrahalaya, then known as Rashtriya Manav Sangrahalaya, Museum of Man as its Founder Director. It is through his initial efforts and vision that the Manav Sangrahalaya emerged as the most prestigious open-air museum of the country established in Bhopal, Madhya Pradesh.

His journey as a professional anthropologist began from the Headquarter of Anthropological Survey of India, Kolkata to other places in different capacities and in pursuance of his research/projects which encompassed different studies and breakthroughs in his research. At the same time, very few people are aware of the fact that he also served in the Indian Armed Forces (Army) and also served the country during the 1965-1971 war between India and Pakistan. The very Gold Medal which was awarded to him by Lucknow University as a University topper was donated by him in 1964 during the Sino-Indian war. Much later, my siblings and I were very curious about the Gold Medal which of course we did not see as it was donated much before we were born.

Prof. R. S. Negi was a leading Indian Anthropologist from the North-Western region of India and also the Founder Director of Indira Gandhi Rashtriya Manav Sangrahalaya, Bhopal. He was also the Professor and Head of the Department of Anthropology, Hemvati Nandan Bahuguna Central University in Srinagar, Garhwal, Uttarakhand; and also was instrumental in establishing a museum in the department of anthropology at the University. He undertook extensive fieldwork in different parts of the country and abroad.

Among his contributions in Physical Anthropology, he had contributed immensely to the study of blood groups, sickle cell traits, colour blindness, etc., among various Indian populations. He worked on population genetics and other studies on the Bhoksa of Dehradun, India.

His work of ethnic components in the distribution of sickle cell traits in India was commendable. He also investigated the presence of sickle-cell traits in the Dorla and the Dhurwa (1962). In his paper, he mentions that the incidence of sickle cell trait among tribals, there is a direct relationship with evolutionary stages of agricultural practices of different tribal groups. Also, he points out that, the frequency of sickle cell trait is significantly high among certain south Indian tribal groups who follow similar agricultural practices. Further investigations were carried out to ascertain the presence and distribution of the trait amongst the various other groups of Bastar (Bhatra, Muria, and Mahra) during the period from November 1959 to April 1960. Prof. R. S. Negi also explored the sporadic occurrence of sickle cell traits in Peninsular Gujarat, India. He also investigated the bio-cultural aspects of sickle cell traits among the South Indian tribal population.

Although Prof. Raghunath Singh Negi specialized in physical anthropology, other branches of anthropology were not kept untouched. He along with Dr. Jitendra Singh and Dr. J.C. Das have jointly dealt with the trade and trade routes in the Cis., and Trans-Himalayas. They have also thrown light on the pattern of traditional entrepreneurship among the Indian highlanders. An interesting picture of the Makar Sankranti festival as observed in the Garhwal Himalaya was explored. He also worked on, Symbiotic Relationships between Man, Animal, and Nature among the Gujjars of Garhwal, where he found that the major socio-economic, political, religious, and reproduction activities were centered around a *Dera* (household or homestead). They analyzed the pastoral community which has settled now focussing on their socio-economic aspirations. He also worked among the Bakerwal community, a nomadic tribe based in the Pir Panjal and Himalayan mountains of North India.

He had life membership in the Indian Anthropological Association, New Delhi; the Ethnographic and Folk Culture Society, Lucknow; the Indian Science Congress Association, Kolkata; and many others.

He also contributed to many renowned national and international journals and also edited books. Besides, he has also written numerous research articles which appeared in different reputed journals of India and abroad. In his final years, he had a lot of ideas and was planning to give them shape and direction. I hope one day I shall be able to take forward his work along with his students which will be a fitting tribute towards his life and journey in the field of anthropology.

References

Negi, RS. 1962. ABO blood groups, sickle cell trait, and colour blindness in the Maria of Bastar and Gond and Kanwar of Bilaspur. *Bulletin Anthropol. Surv. India*, 12: 149 -153.

Negi, RS. and Ahmad SH., 1963. A study of A_1A_2BO MN Rh blood groups, ABH secretion in saliva, and colour blindness in the Dorla and Dhurwa of Bastar. *Bulletin Anthropol. Surv. India*, 12: 21-29.

Negi, RS., Raha MK., Das JC. 1982. The Raji and their economy. In KS Singh (Ed): *Economies of the Tribes and their Transformation*, pp. 153–58. New Delhi: Concept.

Negi, RS. 1962. The incidence of sickle-cell trait in two Bastar tribes. *Man,* Vol. 62: pp. 84-86. https://jstor/stable/2796291

Negi, RS. 1964. New incidence of sickle-cell trait in Bastar, III. *Man*, Vol. 64 (Nov.- Dec.) pp. 171-174. DOI: 10.2307/2796574.

https://www.jstor.org/stable/2796574

Negi, RS. 1968. Incidence of sickle cell trait in South Gujarat. *Bulletin of Anthropological Survey of India*, Vol. XVII, No. 4. Calcutta.

Negi, RS. 1968. Sporadic occurrence of sickle cell trait in Peninsular Gujarat. *Bulletin of Anthropological Survey of India*, Vol. XVII, No. 4. Calcutta.

Negi, RS. 1987. Bio-cultural aspect of sickle-cell trait in tribal population of South India. In Viswanathan Nair (Ed): *Anthropology of Tribal Health and Medicine*, pp. 22-33. Kozhikode: KIRTADS Publication.

Negi, RS. 1995. The nomads: Man, animal, nature. In B. Saraswati, (ed).: *Primal Elements: The Oral Tradition.* IGNCA Central Vista Mess, Janpath, New Delhi.

Negi, RS. 1998. Symbiotic relationships between man, animal, and nature: A study of the Gujjars of Garhwal. In Vaidyanath Saraswati (Ed): *Lifestyle and Ecology*, New Delhi: Indira Gandhi National Centre for the Arts and D.K. Printworld Pvt. Ltd.

Websites:https://kirtads.kerala.gov.in/2017/10/25/anthropology-of-tribal-health-and-medicine-in-forest-environment/

Chapter – 17

Adhyapak Biswanath Banerjee: A Teacher *per* Excellence

Sekh Rahim Mondal

Introduction

Adhyapak Sri Biswanath Banerjee was popularly known as BNB. He was a legendry teacher of the Department of Anthropology, University of Calcutta, particularly from the late 1960s to mid-1990s. He was known for his unique teaching skills and original thoughts on anthropological studies and research. He was a social thinker, a good fieldworker, and an excellent mentor. His anthropological journey was started from the study of folk communities of North-east India and gradually expanded to the other communities and places of Eastern and Northern India. He possessed a versatile knowledge of tribes, peasants, and castes, other communities of hills rural areas, urban places, and cities. His ideas on Indian societies, cultures, and civilization were very inclusive and unique and which made him distinct from other anthropologists of his time.

In this chapter, a humble attempt has been made to highlight the life and works of Dr. Biswanath Banerjee as a tribute to remember him on the great occasion of 100 years of teaching and research on Anthropology in India. This write-up is based on facts obtained from published and unpublished sources as well as information gathered from his close students, friends, and colleagues. All these are finally supported by the author's own experience as one of his close associates and student for over four decades.

[2]

Early Life

Sri Biswanath Banerjee was born on 8th May 1932 in Gauhati, Assam, and died on 26th January 2009, in Kolkata. He was the third child and only son of Sri Kamaksha Prasad Banerjee and Smt. Champaklata Banerjee. His family pet name was Khokan. He was in between two elder sisters – Konika, Monika, and his youngest sister Mira. He was born and brought up joint family, which helped him to learn the art of sharing, caring, and sacrificing. At the age of 22 years, he lost his father, thus growing under the guidance of his father's elder brother (*Jathamasaya*) and mother (*Maa*). Thus, the situation made him shoulder family responsibilities at an early age.

Biswanath Banerjee's family members, trace their ancestry from the sisters' side of Maharaja Krishna Chandra Roy of Navadwip, Nadia of undivided Bengal. His family history suggests that Biswanath Banerjee's grandfather Sri Surendra Nath Banerjee along with his brother Sri Nonigopal Banerjee moved to Assam (Gauhati) from Bengal where they established business and settled near the famous Jubilee Park of this city. Biswanath Banerjee's family was very popular in the place of their residence and used to enjoy honour and respect from the members of local peoples.

Since his childhood days, Biswanath Banerjee was very simple and kind-hearted. He was not much fond of food, dress, and style. However, he was very naughty and witty. His simplicity and meritocracy attracted the attention of his relatives as well as neighbours. This made him very popular in his locality. It is to be noted here that famous Assamese Singer Sarboshree Dr. Bhupen Hazarika was Biswanath Banerjee's childhood friend. The relationship between the members of their families was also very deep and cordial.

[3]

Education and Carrier

Biswanath Banerjee was meritorious and studious since his childhood days. He was a meticulous learner and listener. His listening and learning habit was not only confined to classroom studies but also moved to other areas like singing, music, dancing, craft making, and so on. He had his basic education in Gauhati, where he passed Matriculation from Bengali High School of Gauhati in 1948 and secured first division with letter marks. He obtained I.Sc. degree from famous Cotton College (now Cotton University) in 1950 with anthropology as one of his core papers. He graduated (B.Sc.) from the same college with Honours in anthropology, in 1952. During his final year B.Sc. practical examination, he met Prof. K.P. Chattopadhyay, who happened to be his external examiner. Prof. Chattopadhyay was very much convinced by the performance of Biswanath Banerjee in the examination, thus motivated for higher education in anthropology from the University of Calcutta. He moved to Calcutta the capital city of Bengal and took admission in the Post-graduate course of Anthropology at the University of Calcutta. Biswanath Banerjee got an M.Sc. degree in Anthropology from the said University in 1954 with a specialization in Social-Cultural Anthropology. In the post-graduate class Biswanath Banerjee was theoretically and practically trained under several luminaries like Prof. K.P. Chattopadhyay, Prof.T.C. Das, Dr. S.S. Sarkar, Prof. M.N. Basu, Dr. D. Sen, Prof. G.S. Roy, Dr. J.K. Bose, Prof. T.C. Roychowdhury, and many others. His other mentor was Prof. N.K. Bose from whom he got the real interest in anthropology and its significance in understanding Indian societies, cultures, and civilization. During his student days, he was exposed to Prof. S.C. Sinha and was much motivated by his intelligence, personality, and academic excellence.

Biswanath Banerjee learned the art of fieldwork from Prof. T.C. Das, Prof. N.K. Bose, Prof. D. Sen, Prof. G.S. Roy, Prof. J.K. Bose, and Prof. S.C. Sinha and later proved themselves as excellent field workers. He is widely known for his anthropological fieldworks among the indigenous communities at various places of North-east India, Bihar, West Bengal, and some other states. His anthropological works on the city of Calcutta (Kolkata) and Varanasi deserve special mention.

Biswanath Banerjee started his professional carrier as a teacher after completing a post-graduate degree in Anthropology. He joined as a college teacher in Dinabandhu Mahavidyalaya, at Bongaon, North 24 Parganas in 1956, when he was only 24 years. He left Bongaon and joined as a teacher in the Department of Anthropology of Sri Chaitanya College of Habra, North 24 Parganas in 1958. During the days of teaching at the colleges, he used to teach courses of all the three major branches of anthropology and also accompanied the students for field training at various places of India.

Biswanath Banerjee joined the Department of Anthropology of the University of Calcutta on 20th February 1963, as Lecturer. He retired from the said esteemed Department as a Senior Reader on 5th April 1994. Altogether, he served more than three decades in the said Department as a most popular faculty.

It is necessary to mention that Biswanath Banerjee was acted as a centrifugal force to attract students not only students of the Department of Anthropology but also the students of many other disciplines of Ballygaunge Science College Campus of the University of Calcutta. This was primarily due to his versatile knowledge and expressions both in academic fields and performing arts (drama, dance, music), as well as his interests in games and sports. He possessed a versatile knowledge of Vedic literature, Vedanta, and Hindu views of life. He had a very deep knowledge of Hindu philosophy. Being influenced by Tagore's writings Biswanath Banerjee was very much motivated by his social and civilization thoughts of multi-cultural India.

In Calcutta University Post Graduate Department of Anthropology Biswanath Banerjee primarily engaged in teaching courses on social-cultural anthropology. The courses in which he had strong command were social structure, social organization, marriage, family, kinship, culture, and civilization. He was also used to taking classes on research methods and above all the thoughts and theories of anthropology. His classes on the history and growth of anthropology in general with India, in particular, were very attractive to the students.

In addition to classroom teaching of courses, Biswanath Banerjee was more interested to teach the students in his departmental chamber or his own home through informal ways for explaining the tough subjects in a very easy manner. His method of teaching was almost like the manner of *Guru-Shishya* relations. He was a methodical teacher i.e. a teacher per excellence.

For the reasons, unknown Biswanath Banerjee was never associated with any professional bodies and associations of anthropology as their formal member. But it is interesting to note that, he had very close and friendly relations with the members of the managing committees of several anthropological bodies and associations of Kolkata and other parts of India.

[4]

Academic Connections and Administration

Biswanath Banerjee was popularly known as an ultimate teacher and for which, many veteran anthropologists, sociologists, and experts of other disciplines knew him. Among Indian anthropologists, he had very close relations with Prof. N.K. bose, Prof. Madhab Chandra Goswami, Prof. S.C. Sinha, Prof. A. Betteillie, Prof. L.K. Mohapatra, Prof. S. N. Ratha, Prof. B.K. Roy Barman, Prof. R.K. Mukherjee, Prof. Manish Chakrabartti, Prof. B.N. Saraswati, Dr. A.K. Das, Dr. Sudhendu Mukherjee, Prof. B.M. Das, Prof. A.C. Bhagabati, Prof. Usha Deka, Prof. Gopala Sarana, Prof. Y. Singh, Mr. H.N. Rakshit, Prof. A.K. Danda, Prof. Suhas Biswas, Prof. Amitava Basu, Prof. Aloke K. Ghosh, and many others. He was also very close with his departmental colleagues inspired by his differences in opinions with many of them. Biswanath Banerjee had very close relations with some anthropologists of Great Britain, the USA, France, and Japan. Those scholars developed their relations with Biswanath Banerjee for some academic help and support to study folk and village societies of India as well as the study of Indian civilization.

It is to be noted here that one of his Japanese students, Dr. Swatoo, got an important position in anthropology in his country. This is also very true for other foreign scholars who had relations with Biswanath Banerjee. So far I know Biswanath Banerjee got some opportunities to visit many foreign Universities. But he had not shown any interest to accept those invitations for his unavoidable social bindings and values including the unique ways of life.

Biswanath Banerjee had shown his meticulousness in academic administrations by various means, among them, the most important were field works, examination works, the frequent calling of meetings for the academic boards constituted for under-graduate, Post Graduate, and Research studies. His colleagues and students opined that he was very active in performing his duties as a Chairman of the Board of Research Studies of Anthropology (C.U.), during his tenure. He had the habit to call the members personally through phone calls or through messengers to make the corum for conducting the meeting. In this way, he helped many students or scholars with their Ph.D. registration and submission of a thesis on due time.

For ill health, familial responsibilities (looking after the old mother), and for his routine religio-spiritual practices Biswanath Banerjee had never shown any interest in time-bound administrative works. Several times, he had declined the Departmental headship. Only once for a short period, he worked as a Head of the Department but was not able to continue and complete the tenure for illness. He used to believe that co-operation, dialogue, exchange of views, and consensuses are very necessary for getting success in administration. With this philosophy, he used to do the academic administration those were assigned to him during his days as a teacher in the Department of Anthropology, University of Calcutta.

Even though Biswanath Banerjee was not deeply associated with any professional associations. But he along with his other classmates like Prof. A.R. Banerjee, Prof. Gaurango Chattopadhyay, Prof. Suhas K. Biswas, Dr. Biman Dasgupta, Dr. Bikash Roychoudhury and some others played a very crucial role to form Indian Anthropological Society at its initial stage from the previous Anthropological Club (1921) of Calcutta University to Indian Anthropological Society (1954) under the active leadership of Dr. S S. Sarkar of the Department of Anthropology, University of Calcutta.

[5]

Identity and personality

Biswanath Banerjee was a man of a unique personality. He was a typical example of the modernization of tradition. A man of saintly appearance, dressed with a typical fashion. White *dhoti* and light saffron *kurta* (*Panjabi*) with gold button up to the neck, cotton side bag (*jhola*), and cane stick umbrella was his most favourite fashion.

The unique was his footwear, which was always an English boot of brown colour. A small leather wallet and a German-made pilot fountain pen in the pocket were very special of him. His casual shaving, smiling and charming face attracted the attention of his close ones. He was a man of very simple character and at the same time very tough in decision-making. The blending of these two made him a man of a unique personality. He was a very open-minded man as well as outspoken. He never compromised with any bad acts. He was known for tough fighter against wrongful acts. This he used to do to save the students from the hands of powerful persons.

Biswanath Banerjee was a highly religious and spiritual man and at the same time very secular by heart and mind. He always helped and did for others. By appearance, his look was very much traditional, but in mind, he was highly rational, logical, and liberal. He was a typical man who had many disagreements with his departmental colleagues, but always maintained friendly relations with them and even with their family members. One must learn this art of balancing between professional life on one hand and social life on the other, what the Biswanath Banerjee had. He never thought of himself, but always for the cause of his students and close ones by the kins or non-kin. I feel it is necessary to mention here that, he donated all of his last life savings to a non-kin member, who was a child and whose parents were very close to him during his last days.

Biswanath Banerjee was neither a rightist nor a leftist but a true humanist. He had constituted of his own identity and personality not just as a scholar but also as an ultimate teacher and mentor. This is the reason his students considered him as *Guru* or *Mastermohashai*.

[6]

Contributions to Anthropology - as scholar, teacher, and mentor

Biswanath Banerjee was a person who possessed a wide knowledge in various fields ranging from socio-cultural arena to music, dance, drama, drawing, and even in performing and fine arts. He was a man whose everyday life was compartmentalized into pragmatic and spiritual domains.

In his professional life, he established himself as a teacher of anthropology and specialized himself in the field of socio-cultural anthropology. In post-graduate classes, he used to teach anthropological thoughts, theories, methods and approaches, and other papers. He had a very clear-cut knowledge of the history and development of Anthropology in India. His ability and art of defining and describing anthropological concepts, theories, and facts simply were unique to him.

He had also a versatile knowledge of Indian rural and urban societies. The courses on Indian tribes, castes, and other village communities he used to teach simply and lucidly attracted the attention of the students and motivated them to research various aspects of those topics.

Theoretically, Biswanath Banerjee was much influenced by both historical and functional schools of thought. The theories of evolutionism, diffusionism, structure-functionalism, and structuralism he used to explain before his students in such a lucid manner that even those tough courses turned to be attractive to them. His most favourite topic of discussion was culture, which he used to narrate from various perspectives of anthropological thoughts and theories. The major concepts and theories of culture and its dynamic processes were his special focus of discussion and explanation in special classes. Those helped to grow interests among his students for studies and research in social-cultural anthropology. While discussing the issues of society his major concern was to explain its structure, institution, function, organization, and change. Unique of Biswanath Banerjee was instead of using the term social anthropology or cultural anthropology he used to prefer and popularise the term social-cultural anthropology at the University of Calcutta. He used to believe that society and culture are like content and container thus they are interrelated, intermingled, and inseparable.

He strongly believed that anthropology is not simply a discipline of tribal studies. It is not tribology, but anthropology i.e. the study of all human beings, all human societies, and all cultures, and above all entire humanities. The study of the structure, change, and continuity in respect to all societies and cultures was his special focus of anthropological interest. He was a structure-functionalist but did not ignore the historical perspectives and processes for understanding social organization. He was very much influenced by British, American, and French anthropologists, and those motivated him to go through almost all major classical anthropological monographs written by the veteran scholars of those countries. Many of those monographs he used to refer to his students for meticulous reading. But it is important to note that even though he had a vast knowledge of western anthropological traditions, but at the same time he evolved Indian perspectives to study the communities and societies of this country. This perspective he developed through his mentors and friends like Prof, K. P. Chattopadhyay, Prof.T.C. Das, Prof. N.K. Bose, Prof. S.C. Sinha, Prof. B.N. Saraswati, Prof. N.K. Behura and Prof. A.C. Bhagabati.

Biswanath Banerjee had a versatile knowledge of *Varna-Jati* concepts and their relations as well as on caste systems in India, which he acquired through readings of various classical texts and his studies and observations on caste communities in the empirical context. He did some excellent works on some caste groups of Assam and Bengal from the perspectives and dimensions of Indian civilization. Among them, the most important was the study of potters. To him, *Varna* is to be understood from texts (book views) and caste to be examined from empirical contexts (field view).

Biswanath Banerjee is well known in anthropology for his inclination towards a civilizational perspective for examining the Indian communities. He was highly motivated by the ideas of civilization as proposed and developed by Robert Redfield, B.S. Cohn and Milton Singer etc. In addition to the Chicago School of civilizational thought, he was also influenced by the civilizational thoughts of Tagore and Gandhi. On this aspect, he was highly motivated by the ideas of civilization as proposed by his mentors Prof. N.K. Bose and Prof. S.C. Sinha.

Biswanath Banerjee was known for his views on the *Varna-Jati* model of Indian civilization. His vision of the hierarchical model of the caste system in India is much closer to the views of Louis Dumont. According to him purity and pollution are the key attributes of the Hindu caste hierarchy. He holds the idea that the Varna system of India is grossly oversimplified as the real essence of the caste system lies in the concept of Jati. For him, the system of caste nowadays is much more representative of *Jati* instead of the *Varna* system. He also had the idea that castes in contemporary India are more of political affairs rather than the social and cultural of early days.

He used to believe that, India is a land of bio-cultural diversities and within these diversities, India emerged as a composite civilizational whole. The peoples living in this vast country have different ethnic and social backgrounds thus having different levels of cultures and lifeways. However, these diverse groups interact with each other in their everyday life and thereby share many common elements and traits of each other's cultures unconsciously or consciously. To him, the varied social-cultural groups of this vast country are like different followers in a garden and altogether made the garden glorious. In his view, this is the perspective to see Indian societies and cultures for knowing the great civilization of this vast country. Hence, the role of anthropology is to explore, examine and interpret the social-cultural mosaic of this great country. He opined that trusteeship, cooperation, interdependence, fellow feeling, sharing of selective cultural elements and values from each other, and coexistence are some of the significant attributes of the ways of life among the peoples of this country. All these bind those to live together and thereby play a great role in constituting a grand civilization of this country. To Biswanath Banerjee India is a land of varieties of the human population, having varieties of cultures, somewhere they are similar and somewhere they are different, as a result, both cohesion and contradictions are simultaneously taking place among them. Coexistence, cooperation, and occasional conflicts among different ethnic and social groups in India are a social reality of this country. In India, various peoples are living together for each other's needs and necessities. All these seem to be his prime attention towards anthropological studies of India. To him peoples, societies, and cultures of India are like a salad bowl, but not as a melting pot.

He was also very concerned about the social complexities, social inequalities, and poverty of India. Examining and understanding the social issues and problems of this country was his special focus of interest from the perspective of anthropology. In this context, he was much more influenced by the ideas of Gunner Myrdal. The book

Asian Drama: An Inquiry into the Poverty of Nations by Gunner Myrdal was his very favourite, which he used to refer to his students for mandatory readings.

Being a teacher of anthropology, he was also known for his unique strategy of doing fieldwork. He was an ultimate method field worker, who brought realism in fieldwork through his humanitarian approach of impression management and rapport establishment with the people (s) in field situations. Quite often, he told to his students that the art of fieldwork is to be known not simply by reading books or by attending classes but by doing field works. According to him, fieldwork is a lifelong learning process from the common peoples and for which listening to the people's voices, and observing the events of peoples doing, is the most important. His art of fieldwork was nearest and dearest to the people. He used to tell his students that fieldwork is to be learned better by doing field works.

Biswanath Banerjee himself did many fields works for his own and his teachers and friends. His major field works were among the Daflas of Arunachal Pradesh, Garos of Garo Hills, Potters of Assam, and many other tribal groups of the then Bihar and West Bengal are the most notable. In addition to tribal groups, he also did several important fieldworks among nontribal caste groups and other communities of rural and urban Bengal and other parts of India. His studies of towns and cities like Navadeep, Banaras, Haldia, and Calcutta (now Kolkata) need special mention. His study of *Sarbojonin Durgatsab* of Calcutta is considered as an example of the multidimensional and holistic approach of anthropological research in the context of the study of Indian civilization. He opined that fieldwork starts from knowing the phenomenons and their relations, followed by structure, then institution and culture, and finally the organization and change. He was very fond of intensive field works, comparative methods, and multisided ethnography. He was supportive of adopting multidisciplinary approaches in exploring anthropological knowledge.

Biswanath Banerjee had no hesitation to adopt the quantitative approach in anthropology in necessities. He was a strong believer in mixed methods. His interest in using statistics or quantitative data was developed out of his interaction with Prof. Ramakrishna

Mukherjee and his classmates Prof. Suhas Biswas and Prof. Kumar Chattopadhyay of the Indian Statistical Institute. In addition to the collection of intensive field data, his other emphasis was on data analysis and data processing from multiple dimensions. He used to follow a holistic perspective in data analysis as far as practicable. His ability of the art of interpretation and prediction on research problems out of field data has attracted the attention of many veteran anthropologists like Prof. N. K. Bose, Prof. S. C. Sinha, and Prof. P. K. Bhowmick.

The two most important lessons of Biswanath Banerjees' fieldwork training were the drawing of genealogy and the use of kinship data in the study of anthropological research problems and issues. He has drawn several extensive and long genealogies while he was studying and doing field researches at the initial stage of his academic carrier. The art of drawing exhaustive genealogy he learned from teachers Prof. K.P. Chattopadhyay, Prof. T.C. Das, and Dr. J. K. Bose. The present author learned the art of drawing long genealogy during his field studies on Muslims and their kinship systems in Bengal at the time of his M.Sc. dissertation work. Biswanath Banerjee's other concern was keeping and maintaining the field diary at the time of fieldwork. To him keeping a field diary and noting all the events of fieldwork within the diary is very essential in anthropological fieldwork. This is perhaps what he imbibed from his mentors Prof. T.C. Das and Prof. N.K. Bose.

Biswanath Banerjee devoted his entire life towards teaching and supervision of students and was able to produce several scholars as well as teachers of repute. He was known for his unique teaching style and research guidance. Open-air classes beyond classrooms; debates and discussions; agreements and disagreements on emerging social and cultural issues and human problems were unique to his teaching methods. He was a strong believer in the lab to land and land to lab approaches for the cultivation of true anthropological knowledge and its representation as well as application. About 15 scholars did their Ph.D.s under his active supervision. The most interesting fact is that most of his Ph.D. scholars did their researches on various nonconventional research problems and issues that were beyond typical anthropological stereotypes; ranging from the studies of agriculture to industry; tribal to nontribal communities; rural to urban studies; Hindus to Muslim societies; fine arts to performing arts; sacred to secular activities; and networks of social relations seem very notable in anthropology. He was an anthropologist whose concern was to study the contemporary social issues and challenges in Indian society.

He was highly concerned for the plight of marginal sections of society. Thus, very vocal about the social (human) responsibilities of the anthropologists (human/social scientists). He repeatedly pointed out that, the role of anthropologists is not simply to know the people but also to save them from social ostracism. He was one of the spokes-person who was in favour of relevance and representation of anthropology, and which he proved through his works and supervision of research works for his students.

Even though Biswanath Banerjee himself did not do much research and wrote much on anthropological issues, but he was highly engaged with the research works of his students and even his teachers and friends. At the initial stage of his academic carrier, he was deeply involved to assist the research works of his teachers of the department. Among them, the most important were Prof. K.P. Chattopadhyay, Prof. T.C. Das, Prof. M.N. Basu, Dr. D. Sen, Prof. G.S. Ray, Dr. J.K. Bose, Prof. N.K. Bose and Prof. S.C. Sinha etc.

He devoted almost his entire life to the success of the research of the students. He used to tell his students that research is a curiosity to know a fact or a phenomenon in depth. He had the ability of the art of questioning for the quest of knowledge. To him what you see is not important, but what are the things behind the acts or happenings are the most important to know for doing research. He taught his students to raise the questions in mind at the time of research like – what is there to know? Why know? How to know? What is the purpose of knowing? and for what we want to know (for people or power)? He was very much concerned with the ontology, epistemology, methodology, and ethics of doing anthropological field research. He had the idea that research requires a research mind to go deeper and deeper. Thus, for anthropological research, it is necessary to know what the people do? How are they so? Why do they do it? And how is the meaning produced out of their doing? To him, a relation of one social fact with other social facts needs to be known for a better understanding of Social-cultural issues and problems. The most motivating factor of anthropological research in his view as you start observing, then observing in-depth, and finally get an answer from your observance. He held the view that simply knowing of change is not important, but how and why the changes are taking place and what are their trends and directions needs to know through analytical research. Biswanath Banerjee was a unique personality who blended his scientific mind with the spiritual mind for understanding man and his life i.e. human nature. He raised and meticulously explained the most fundamental questions of anthropology like: (i) how man (humanity) came? Why did they come? And how do they live in their society? He always motivated his students to think and go beyond the conventional stereotype thinking of anthropology. He taught his student for logical disagreement on conventional ideas based on new facts for the growth of new knowledge.

One of his close friends Prof. Kumar Chattopadhyay remarked, once N.K. Bose told him that Biswanath is a wonderful field worker. He also remarked I was astonished by his imaginative understanding of the area of study and possible results predicted (Chattopadhyay, 2012).

[7]

Legacy of Biswanath Banerjee

The most important lesson that Biswanath Banerjee has left to us is to cultivate one creative mind. His main motive was to train the students not simply as a scholar, but as true human beings. To him, honesty, morality, and dedication have special meaning in life. Throughout his entire life, he never thought for himself, but did for his students, relatives, neighbours, friends, and society at large. Studying, listening, learning, and disseminating were his major interests. He left behind a rich tradition of teaching and supervision of research in anthropology. He had an innate art of selecting unique research topics for his students based on their interests on one hand and their social significance on the other. He was one of the proponents of doing anthropology of time in the Department Anthropology,

University of Calcutta. He had a notion that ethnography is as if true storytelling based on the facts gathered by the ethnographer (storyteller). Biswanath Banerjee earned his name for his historical and structural approach to examining Indian civilization. He was a great follower of Prof. K. P. Chattopadhyay, Prof. T.C. Das, Prof. N.K. Bose and Prof. S. C. Sinha and many others with whom he had close contacts. He was the imprint of a true last generation teacher of classical anthropological tradition, who learned the legacy of anthropology of the University of Calcutta. Biswanath Banerjee's anthropological ideas and thoughts grew out of his meticulous studies on the works of British, American, French, German, and Indian Anthropologists and Sociologists. In addition to such motivating factors, he was also very much influenced by social thinkers of India like Tagore, Gandhi, Ramkrishna Pramhansadeb, Swami Vivekananda, Pandit Nehru, etc. He had a vast knowledge of the literary works and literature of Bengal. He was a follower of Pandit Gopinath Kabiraj and his views on the social life of India. He was also very much influenced by the classical spiritual traditions of Kashi and Varanashi. All those together shaped the anthropological mind of Biswanath Banerjee. He was a strong believer in the existence of diversity and unity, sacred and secular, differences and similarity, social boundaries and they are overlapping, tradition and modernity, continuity and change in Indian social scenario. To him, all these are at the very core of Indian societies and cultures, which have given the shape of its unique civilization.

Biswanath Banerjee left behind the legacy of teaching, thinking, and research for the students of anthropology. He taught his students to think, to do fieldwork, and then write on them. He also taught them to disagree with the existing discourses but if there are logic and evidence. His main goal was to produce students and to grow them in they are ways to make them self-reliant. He meticulously carried the fieldwork tradition of anthropology of the University of Calcutta and has tried to strengthen it in his ways. He was a great field worker. He is known for his quadrangular perspectives of looking into the peoples and societies of India. These are environmental, historical, social-cultural, and civilization. To him, space, time, people, and ethics are very important for the anthropological understanding of all social events and problems. Time-space frames what he proposed for field studies for knowing the structure and organization of society have great anthropological relevance. He was a great storyteller and story maker of field situations but his stories were based on empirical evidence.

He was very much critical of the concept of development concerning the study of the social transformation of India. To him development means- freedom, self-determinism, democracy, equality, justice, rights, opportunities, social security, morality, peace, and attainments in life and those have to be felt and expressed by the concerned groups or peoples, but not by powers and agencies. To him in the name of development what we see is better to be called change. He advocated that for anthropologists changes are not much important, but the important are why and how the changes are taking place and what are their trends and directions.

Literature Consulted

Banerjee, Biswanath, 1965. An outline of the background, theory, and methods of social-cultural anthropology. *Bulletin of Cultural Research Institute,* Vol. 4, 1965.

Banerjee, Biswanath, 1968. The habitat and culture of primitive hill people of India, *The Proceedings of the 21st International Geographical Congress,* Kolkata, India.

Banerjee, Biswanath, 1973. *Sarbojonin Durgotsab* in Calcutta: A preliminary report of the pujas in 1969, in *Folklore,* September 1973, pp. 347-353. [Also published in D. Piplai (Ed.), 2012, *Mastermosai, The Teacher,* The Commemorative Volume of the Teacher – Biswanath Banerjee; *Kolkata: Prof. Biswanath Bandhopadhyaya Smriti Raksha Samity].*

Beteille-Andre, 2012. Biswanath Banerjee as I knew him, in D. Piplai (Ed.): *Mastermasai – The Teacher;* Kolkata: Professor Biswanath Bandhopadhyay Smriti Raksha Samiti, pp. 1-15.

Chattopadhyay, Kumar, 2012. Prof. Biswanath Banerjee: A Tribute in D. Piplai (Ed.): *Mastermosai – The Teacher,* Kolkata, Prof. Biswanath Bandhopadhyay Smriti Raksha Samiti.

Indian Anthropological Society, 2963. A brief history of the Indian Anthropological Society, in *Souvenir* on the occasion of Silver Jubilee (1957-1982), December 6-9, 1963, Calcutta.

Pillai, Dipak (Ed.), 2012. *Mastermasai: The Teacher* [Commemorative volume of the Teacher – Biswanath Banerjee] Kolkata: Professor Biswanath Bandhapadhyay Smriti Raksha Samiti, Kolkata.

Sankha Priya Ghosh, 2012. Biswanath Babu: The teacher of my Life, in D. Piplai (Ed.): *Mastermosai – The Teacher,* Kolkata, Professor Biswanath Banerjee Smriti Raksha Samiti.

Mandal, Sekh Rahim and Sarkar Amitabha, 2019. *Biswanath Banerjee* (1933-2009), in Amitabha Sarkar and Samira Dasgupta (Eds.): *Doyens of Indian Anthropology,* Delhi: Agamkala Publication, pp. 177-181.

Acknowledgement

For preparations of this write-up, I got academic support from Sri Dipak Piplai followed by Dr. Amitavaho Sarkar, Dr. Sakha Priya Ghosh, Dr. Nabakumar Duary, Dr. Shila Kundu Poddar, Sri Kamal Krishna Dey, and several others who were very close with him.

The present chapter is the revised version of the special lecture delivered on a digital platform for the occasion of celebrating Hundred Years of Teaching and Research of Anthropology in India. Therefore, the author intends to thank the Indian Anthropological Society, Kolkata, and the organizers of the lecture for enabling him to work for this write-up as a tribute to his teacher.

Chapter – 18

Life and Works of Prof. Bhuban Mohan Das

Sarthak Sengupta

Prof. Bhuban Mohan Das was the fourth son of eminent educationist of yesteryears of Assam, Late Haramohan Das who was Headmaster of Don Bosco High School, Guwahati, Assam. His mother was Late Jagaddhatri Devi. Haramohan Das was a great inspiration to Bhuban Mohan, besides; he was also greatly inspired by his elder brother Dr. Biraj Mohan Das. Prof. Das was born on 4th October 1933. His school education took place in Manik Chandra Middle English School and Cotton Collegiate High School, Guwahati, Assam. He graduated from Cotton College with honours in Anthropology in 1951. B.M. Das was an alumnus of the University of Calcutta where he obtained M.Sc. (1953), Ph.D. (1959; *Somatic Variability among Some Populations of South Goalpara, Assam*), and D.Sc. degrees (1973; *Studies on* I. *Variation on Physical Characteristics in the Khasi Populations of Assam,* II. *Anthropometry and the ABO Blood Groups of the Tribal Populations of Assam, and* III. *Head Hair from Some Caucasoid and Mongoloid Populations of Assam, India*). He completed his Ph.D. work under the direct supervision of a renowned anthropologist of Calcutta University; Dr. S. S. Sarkar. Dr. B.M. Das established himself as an accomplished anthropologist not only in India but also in the international field of anthropology, and there is no doubt that he has been an institution of North-east Indian anthropology.

Professor Das joined as a faculty member in the Department of Anthropology at Cotton College (1953) and then joined Anthropology Department at Gauhati University (1956). In 1973, he moved to the Dibrugarh University as Professor of Anthropology and remained there as Professor and Head of the Department till 1976. During his stay at Dibrugarh University, he builds up a well-equipped laboratory and investigated on globin gene in the North-east Indian population in collaboration with a renowned population geneticist – Prof. G. Flatz. He returned to Gauhati University again where he was Head (1976-1984) and Dean of the Faculty of Science. He was a recipient of Alexander von Humboldt Fellow and did post-doctoral research in the Institut fur Anthropologie, Freie Universitat, Berlin (1968-1970), Institut fur Humangenetik, Medizinische Hochschule, Hannovar (1975) and had visited Humburg, Bremen, Hannover, Harvard (Peabody Museum) for academic purposes delivering lectures in different Universities and Research Institutes. He also visited Italy (1982) to deliver lectures at Rome, Florence, and Pisa under the Indo-Italian Cultural exchange programme. He had the privilege of working in association with eminent anthropologists like Dr. S.S. Sarkar; Prof. E.C. Buchi; Prof. Gebhard Flatz; Prof. H.Walter, and many others. He was closely associated with Dr. Henry Field, Prof. F.Vogel, and also interacted with renowned anthropologists like Dr. Shapiro, Dr. Mandelbaum, Dr. Barnicot, Dr. Britinger, Dr. Sultz. He was superannuated from Gauhati University in 1993.

Some of his other academic recognition and distinction are that he has been President, Anthropological Society of North East India (1970-1974), National Lecturer, University Grants Commission, New Delhi (1979-1980), Co-Chairperson for the Session on Biological Variation at the 10th International Congress of Anthropological and Ethnological Sciences, New Delhi (1978); President, Section of Anthropology and Archaeology, Indian Science Congress (1979); President, History Section, Asom Sahitya Sabha organized at Diphu, Assam (1982); President, Assam Academy of Cultural Relations, Guwahati (1982-2008); Vice President, Srimanta Sankardeva Kala Kshetra (1992-2000); President, Assam Science Society (1992-1993); Emeritus Fellow, University Grants Commission (1996-1998);

Member, National Commission for Other Backward Classes (2000-2003); Founder President, Indian National Confederation and Academy of Anthropologists (2002-2008); President, S.S. Sarkar Society of Human Sciences (1993-2003); Chairman, Assam Text Book Production and Publication Corporation (1995-1996); President, Network of Practicing Anthropologists and Related Sciences (2001-2003). He was a recipient of the Annandale Memorial Award of Asiatic Society, Kolkata (2004), which was given to him for his outstanding contribution to the study of Anthropology of Asia. He has also served as a member of different advisory bodies and associated with the curriculum development of Anthropology in different Universities. Professor Das mentored some Ph.Ds and completed around fifteen major research projects sponsored by the University Grants Commission, Anthropological Survey of India.

Besides being an anthropologist of repute, Professor B.M. Das was equally endowed with academic and intellectual brilliance and gifted with the excellence of inimitable art of communication – oral and written, both in English and Assamese. He established himself as a prolific writer. Besides writing several books on anthropological research finding on the population groups of North-east India, he also contributed a lot to children's literature, like *Adim Jugar Adi Kotha* (1960), *Manobor Adi Kotha* (1960), *Amar Dore Sihoto Manuh* (1993), has fetched him National Awards. He has the talent of a historian, short story writer, and literature and earned fame for his flair for Assamese writing.

To encourage disseminating primary data-based anthropological research findings from the region, Prof. Das initiated the publication of an annual research journal entitled *Bulletin of the Department of Anthropology, Dibrugarh University,* and acted as its founder-editor which first appeared in 1972-1973, and is still publishing uninterruptedly.

Dr. Manjumala Das, his wife, is also a prolific writer, good orator, and noted scholar in Assamese literature, and well known for her skill in recitation. His daughter Dr Shrutimala Duara, a faculty member in the Department of English, Handique Girls College, Guwahati is a reputed writer, and anchor.

II

Professor Das was fully conscious of the holistic nature of anthropology as an academic discipline. For him, anthropology was the study of man in totality as a biological and social entity. He was a versatile scholar with rare distinctions. Prof. Das had single-handedly generated a considerable amount of data on physical anthropology in North-east India. His research contribution ranged from classical anthropology to highly technical gene technology.

In 1970, Prof. Das published his seminal work on *Anthropometry of the Tribal Groups of Assam,* where he included most of the available basic anthropometric data on the various population groups of the region reported by various researchers and compared these data with other Asiatic Mongoloid to find out the ethnic elements in the population groups.

Prof. Das examined the ABO blood group data of the Rabha (1958,1960); Khasi (1968); Ahom, Chutia, Deuri, Moran, Mishing, Karbi, Sonowal, Boro, Rajbanshi (Das et al., 1985a, Das et al., 1987); Assamese Muslims (Das et al., 1985b, Das et al., 1987); Brahmin (Das et al., 1986a, Das et al., 1987); Kalita (Das et al., 1986b, Das et al., 1987); Jogi, Hira, Kumar, Kaibarta (Das et al., 1986c, Das et al., 1987).

The dermatoglyphic characters of the Assamese Caste Hindu Populations (Brahmin, Kayastha, Kalita) were studied by Das and Das, (1965a, 1965b), Das et al., (1980a, 1986a, 1986b, 1986c), Das et al (1986c) examined the scheduled caste populations (Hira, Kaibarta). The Other Backward Classes (Jogi, Kumar, Koch) were studied by Das (1962), Das and Sengupta, (1972), Das et al., (1986c), Sengupta and Das (1987), Assamese Muslims also examined by him (Das et al., 1985b), Tai Mongoloid groups, (Das and Bhagabati, 1962,1967) studied the Ahom and the Khamiyang. Some of the Bodo tribes like Boro Kachari, Rabha, Garo, Moran, Chitiya, Lalung, Sonowal, Deuri, etc were studied by Das, 1959, 1960, 1963, Das et al., 1980b, 1985b), as well as four territorial groups of Khasi tribes (Das, 1978) of Meghalaya.

Credit goes to Prof. Das for his pioneering monograph on *Ethnic Affinities of the Rabha* (1960) where he concludes that the Rabhas were similar to the Garo who not only related with them linguistically but concerning many biological features. Studies on micro-evolutionary dynamics in North-east India were also initiated by Prof. Das when he compared the Garo population inhabiting two ecological settings based on somatometric traits. The study reveals how ecological differences and endogamy bring about variation in physical features (Das, 1960). Later on, he conducted a comprehensive study to understand the micro-evolutionary trends considering several Bodo tribes like Garo, Rabha, Kachari, and Rajbanshi of South Goalpara. These populations are in various stages of de-detribalization, the Garo as the baseline characterized by the strong preservation of their matrilineal culture and conservative tribal solidarity; the Rabha and Kachari occupy the transitional intermediate position by being Hinduised changing their food habits, customs, and manners, and the Rajbanshi as the most transformed end product of the process of detribalization (Das, 1964,1981). The study reveals that micro-variation was in different dimensions and different ways of operation of evolutionary forces in each of these four population groups.

Prof. Das also carried out a thorough bio-anthropological investigation among four Khasi territorial sub-groups namely, Khynriem, Pnar, Bhoi, and War (Das, 1978). Data comprise four different parameters, such as anthropometry, dermatoglyphics, ABO blood groups, and taste sensitivity to PTC. Although among the Khasis there is no restriction of intermarriages among the sub-groups, in practice intermarriages are rare. The study reveals that the Khasi population is no longer homogenous, and each territorial group deviates significantly from the original (pooled) stock with common Khasi characteristics. Such deviation is more pronounced among Bhois and Pnar compared to Khynriam and War, the latter two groups are very close to each other. Prof. Das suggested that these micro-evolutionary trends among the Khasi might be due to the pattern of gene flow and geographical factors.

Following the above model, studies were also carried out among the Assamese caste groups, namely Brahmin, Kalita, Vaishya, and Kaibarta of Brahmaputra valley, Assam. Further, the Hindu and Deuri Chutiya populations of upper Assam are also studied, which reveals that these two populations of Chutiya are heading towards the formation of two separate biological entities.

Group divergence of the Khasi, based on the anthropometric data published by Das (1978), the measure of Penrose distance (1947, 1954) was applied by a team of the researcher (Dutta et al.,1996) reported that the Khynriam and the War are very closely related, whereas the Pnar and the Bhoi are mutually widely apart from one another and each maintains a distant position from the former two Khasi territorial group, a very similar observation made by Das (1978) using simple descriptive statistics.

Several Assamese caste populations like Brahmin, Kalita, Hira, Kaibarta, Kumar Jogi; two Assamese Muslim groups – Sheikh and Maria; and five Mongoloid populations namely, Ahom, Chutia, Deuri, Mishing, and Moran have been investigated for the distribution of anthropometric, anthroposcopic, dermatoglyphics, ABO blood groups, and PTC taste sensitivity and reported in a series of research articles (Das et al., 1985, 1986). The study reveals that barring finger pattern, all the aforesaid variables considered showed a marked inter-group variability. A clear difference between population groups having Mongoloid ethnic affiliation on one hand and Hindu caste group on the other is discernible, the findings are also substantiated by the distance analyses. The Maria Muslims of Assam show more affinity with the former, whereas the Sheikh Muslims are closer to Hindu caste groups in phenotypic appearance.

Growth studies in North-east India were also initiated by Prof. Das. He supervised a good number of Ph.D. dissertations on human growth in varied population groups of North-east India. Under his able supervision, P.B. Das studied the growth of some somatometric characteristics among the Kalita caste (Das, 1967); ANZA Hazarika studied the growth pattern of the Ahom boys of upper Assam (Hazarika, 1981); A.K. Das studied the growth and body built of the Assamese and Rajasthani boys (Das, 1983); S. Devi studied the physical growth among the Meitei Kshatriya and Muslims of Manipur (Devi, 1985).

The current state of knowledge on the distribution and dynamics of the globin gene in North-east India is mainly due to the efforts of two great scholars – Professor G. Flatz (Germany) and Professor B.M. Das and their later collaborator Prof. Ranjan Deka (Cincinnati University), Prof. H. Walter and Prof. H. Delbruk (West Germany),

Prof. M. R. Chakravartti, Prof. Bijoy Gogoi (Assam Medical College, Dibrugarh), Prof. K. C. Malhotra (Indian Statistical Institute, Kolkata) and many others.

Haemoglobin E is highly prevalent in population groups of Southeast Asia and the distribution extends into South China and North-east India. Its distribution is connected with the distribution of the Mon-Khmer language. In North-east India, the oldest layer of the population is Austro-Asiatic, a label that covers Munda, Mon-Khmer, and Khasi-Khumuic groups of languages. Several population groups of North-east India have affinities with those populations of South East Asia. Intriguingly, the variant is highest in the periphery of distribution, in the populations of Eastern India.

Prof. Das and his associates (Das et al., 1971; Flatz et al., 1972) recorded a very high frequency of haemoglobin E among the Khasis of Meghalaya and the Ahoms of upper Assam. In Southeast Asia, there seems to exist a relationship between Austro Asiatic (Mon-Khmer) linguistic affiliation and a high prevalence of haemoglobin E. This hypothesis was tested in Assam, the North-eastern state of India, by examining three population groups: Assamese, Ahom, a Thai group related to the Shan in Myanmar, and Khasi, a matrilineal Austro-Asiatic group. The study reveals that there were no differences in the frequency of ABO blood groups and G-6-PD deficiency between the three groups. The frequency of the haemoglobin E gene differed significantly, and there was a reciprocal relationship between the frequencies of the haemoglobin E and the β-thalassemia genes. The high prevalence of the haemoglobin E gene among the Ahom led to much speculation as it was not reported among the Thai populations of South West China. Little or no Haemoglobin E was detected in any Tibeto-Burman groups of South East Asia. Thus, it was suggested that haemoglobin E was spread in the region through the migration of Austro-Asiatic speakers in prehistoric times. However, later findings (Das et al., 1975, 1980; Deka et al., 1987, 1988) records very high frequencies of haemoglobin E, ranging from 30 percent to 60 percent, in many Tibeto Burman populations of Assam.

The haplotyping study suggests a single origin of haemoglobin E variant in the Thai population, however, in Tripura, Arunachal

Pradesh, and West Bengal mutants reported being different. Recent studies, however, suggest a haemoglobin E variant with a different origin. In the Austro-Asiatic population, haemoglobin E haplotype is associated with framework-3, while a very recent study in Tripura and Bengal reported that it is linked with framework-2.

Some population living in similar environmental condition shows the existence of variant haemoglobin E while others lack. It may be due to the existence of dynamic interaction with other genetic abnormalities like ß thalassemia, G-6-P-D, and maintenance of some sort of reciprocal relationship may exist. It is reported that the pre-existing high frequency of ß thalassemia perhaps inhibited the rise of haemoglobin E gene frequency in the autochthones, whereas the virtual absence of ß thalassemia permitted a more rapid rise of the haemoglobin E gene frequency in the Bodo speaking population groups of Assam. The caste population of Assam also shows evidence of haemoglobin E which may be due to gene flow with their surrounding population. They opine that the migration history of the population also not be ignored. Similarly, the practice of village endogamy and a relatively high rate of consanguinity may be another important reason. A recent report says that malaria endemicity is less important than race in the maintenance of a high frequency of haemoglobin E in Myanmar.

Prof. Das was personally involved in several collaborative research projects with researchers from abroad amongst the population groups of North-east India. Prof. Water and his research team along with Prof. Das investigated the haptoglobin and for transferrin (Tf) and Gc subtype polymorphism among ten different population groups of Assam namely, Brahmins, Kalitas, Kaibartas, Rajbanshis, Muslims, Ahoms, Chutias, Kacharis, Karbis, and Sonwals (Walter et al., 1986). Transferrin and Gc allele subtype frequencies show considerable inter-population heterogeneity. From genetic distance analysis, it appears that the populations under study form some distinct clusters, which can be explained by the historical and ethnic affiliations of these populations. Especially the distribution of Gc subtype alleles reveals some Mongoloid admixture among Assamese populations, which is reflected by the presence of Gc^{1A8} alleles in them. Prof. Das also collaborated in a study to determine the distribution of the hemoglobin Constant Spring (Hb CS) gene in eight population groups in Southeast Asia, including Assam (Laig et al., 1990) using oligonucleotide hybridization. The study reveals Hb CS was absent in Assamese populations with a high prevalence of Hb E.

Samples of two populations in Assam (Assamese and Khasi) were examined for ten genetic polymorphisms of serum proteins (haptoglobin, transferrin, group-specific component, pseudocholinesterase locus E_1 and E_2) and erythrocyte enzymes (acid phosphatase, phosphoglucomutase, adenylate kinase, adenosine deaminase, and 6-phosphogluconate dehydrogenase).

Six Mongoloid and four Caucasoid populations of Assam, India, were examined for A_1A_2BO, Rhesus, Duffy, and Diego blood groups. The distribution of their phenotypes and allele frequencies are presented. In the perspective of the ethnographic background, the results have been discussed in terms of genetic variability among these populations and probable reasons for its existence. The major groups, namely Caucasoids and Mongoloids, appear to form two separate groups in terms of these blood groups, though the evidence is there to suggest intermixture (Das et al., 1987)

In Thailand, higher fertility in a female heterozygote for Haemoglobin E and reduced fertility in Haemoglobin E homozygote female and thalassemia heterozygote is reported, but in Assam high fertility has been reported in female homozygote for haemoglobin E. Women homozygous for haemoglobin E have late onset of menarche, and abortions are more frequent among them.

Prof. Das had single-handedly generated a considerable amount of data on physical anthropology in North-east India in general and Assam and Meghalaya in particular. These data although provide basic material to formulate various hypotheses and research questions and tested, however, scholars have given little attention to formulating meaningful hypotheses or research questions.

Prof. Das breathed his last on 22nd January 2008. On his death, the country has lost an intellectual, a distinguished academician, a creative writer, a good orator, and a dedicated and passionate social campaigner.

Some important research publications of Prof. B. M. Das

Books:

1960. *Ethnic Affinities of the Rabha,* Department of Publications, Gauhati University, Guwahati, Assam.

1961. *Outlines of Physical Anthropology,* Kitab Mahal, Allahabad, India.

1964. *Kaharpara: A Report on Socio-Cultural Survey.* Department of Tribal Culture and Folklore Research, Gauhati University, Guwahati, Assam.

1970. *Anthropometry of the Tribal Groups of Assam.* Field Research Series, Miami, USA.

1974. *Contemporary Anthropological Research in North East India,* Dibrugarh University, Dibrugarh, Assam.

1978. *Variation in Physical Characteristics in the Khasi Population of North East India.* Dutta Barua and Company, Guwahati, Assam.

1979. *On some aspects of variation and ongoing human evolution.* Presidential address, Section of Anthropology and Archaeology, Indian Science Congress Association, Hyderabad.

1981. *Microevolution.* Concept Publishing Company, New Delhi, India.

1985. *Children in North East India,* Anthropological Survey of India, Kolkata.

1987. *The People of Assam,* Gyan Publishing House, New Delhi.

1990. *North-East India: Its People and Culture.* Ethnographic and Folk culture Society, Lucknow, India.

1992-1993. *Physical Anthropology Practical* (jointly with R. Deka), Kitab Mahal, Allahabad.

1998. *Mor Prithivir Chinaki Manuh*, (in Assamese), Sahityaratna Prakasha, Guwahati, Assam.

2000. *Asomiya Sanskriti: Sangrakshan Aru Anannanya,(*in Assamese) Bani Praksh Private Limited, Guwahati, Assam.

2005. *Samayar Sotat Asomiya Sangskriti,* (in Assamese) Lawers Book Stall, Guwahati, Assam.

Research articles

1971. High prevalence of haemoglobin E in two populations of Assam, India, (jointly with MR Chakravartti, H. Delbruk, and G. Flatz), *Humangenetik,* 12: 264-266.

1972. Genetic survey in the populations of Assam: I. ABO blood groups, Glucose-6-Phosphate Dehydrogenase and haemoglobin type, (jointly with HW Goedde, HG Benkman, S.Singh, MR Chakravartti, H. Delbruk, and G.Flatz), *Human Heredity.* 22: 323-330.

1972. Genetic survey in the populations of Assam: II. Serum protein and erythrocyte enzyme polymorphisms (jointly with HW Goedde, HG

Benkman, S. Singh, MR Chakravartti, H. Delbruck, and G. Flatz), *Human Heredity*. 22: 331-337.

1975. Predominance of haemoglobin E gene in a Mongoloid populations of Assam, India. (jointly with R. Deka and G. Flatz), *Humangenetik*, 30: 187-191.

1985. Anthropological studies in Assam, India. I. Observation on five Mongoloid populations (jointly with PB Das, R Das, H Walter, and H.Danker-Hopfe), *Anthropologischer Anzeiger*, 43, 3: 193-204.

1985. Anthropological studies in Assam, India. 2. Observation on Muslims (jointly with PB Das, R Das, H Walter, and H. Danker-Hopfe), *Anthropologischer Anzeiger*, 43, 4: 299-310.

1986. Anthropological studies in Assam, India. 3. Observation on three Brahmin groups (jointly with PB Das, R Das, H Walter, and H. Danker-Hopfe), *Anthropologischer Anzeiger*, 44, 1: 35-43.

1986. Anthropological studies in Assam, India. 4. Observation on the Kalitas (jointly with PB Das, R Das, H Walter, and H.Danker-Hopfe), *Anthropologischer Anzeiger*, 44, 2: 105-115.

1986. Anthropological studies in Assam, India. 5. Observation on four further caste groups: Jogis, Hiras, Kumars and Kaibartas (jointly with PB Das, R Das, H Walter, and H. Danker-Hopfe), *Anthropologischer Anzeiger*, 44, 3: 239-248.

1986. Investigation on the variability of haptoglobin, transferring and GC polymorphism in Assam, India (jointly with H.Walter, BN Mukherjee, K.Gilbert, P. Lindenberg, A. Dannewitz, KC Malhotra and R. Deka), *Human Heredity*, 36: 388-396.

1987. Distribution of Gm and Km allotype among ten populations of Assam, India (jointly with H.Walter, H.Matsumoto, T. Miyazaki, BN Mukherjee, KC Malhotra, K. Gilbert and P. Lindenberg), *American Journal of Physical Anthropology*, 73: 439-445.

1987. Genetic variation of five blood group polymorphisms among ten populations of India (with H.Walter, K.Gilbert, P. Lindenberg, KC Malhotra, BN Mukherjee, R. Deka, and R.Chakravarty). *International Journal of Anthropology*, 2, 4: 325-340.

1987. Haemoglobin E distribution in ten population groups of Assam, India, (jointly with AP Reddy, R. Deka, BN Mukherjee, S. Banerjee, M.Toy, A. Dey, KC Malhotra, and H.Walter), *Human Heredity*, 38: 261-266.

1988. Anthropological studies in Assam, India. 6. Differentiation process among Assamese populations (jointly with H. Danker-Hopfe, H Walter, PB Das, and R Das), *Anthropologischer Anzeiger*, 46, 2: 159-184.

1989. Anthropological studies in Assam, India. 7. Socio-biological observations on Assamese populations. (jointly with H. Danker-Hopfe, H Walter, PB Das, and R Das), *Anthropologischer Anzeiger*, 47, 2: 129-143.

1990. The distribution of the Hb constant spring gene in South East Asian populations (with M.Laig, M.Page, J.Hundreisser, G.Flatz, T. Sanguansermisti, R.Deka, P.Yongvaint, and N. Mularlee), *Human Genetics*, 84: 188-190.

Note

For detailed research publications of Prof. B.M. Das, please consult his academic profile in S. Sengupta (Ed): *Studies in Anthropology: Recent Perspectives*, pp. 379-393, Inter India Publications, New Delhi.

References

Penrose, LS. 1947. Some notes of discrimination. *Annals of Eugenics*. London, 13: 228.

Penrose, LS., 1954. Distance, size, and shape. *Annals of Eugenics*. London, 18:337-243.

Chapter – 19

Life and Works of Dr. B. N. Sahay towards Anthropological Studies in India

Ragini Sahai

Dr. B.N. Sahay (1935-2017) a Social Anthropologist, an administrator, dedicated to applied and action anthropology, served for 35 years in the field of social development/ Rural development. He worked with the Government of India for 25 years, served under various positions, and retired in 1995 as a Senior Adviser (Social Development and Women's Programme), NITI AAYOG (then known as Planning Commission). A student of Late Prof L. P. Vidyarthi, a renowned anthropologist of India and abroad, Dr. Sahay received a Gold medal in his Masters for best thesis on the Political system of Maler. A doctorate in Anthropology from Ranchi University in 1967 on *Changes in the Leadership Pattern among the Maler and the Santhals of Santhal Parganas* was an example of ethnographic research in an Indian setting. He was also the recipient of Leverhume Visiting Fellow in 1966-67 for higher research and teaching in social policy, social development, social administration, and social welfare at University College of Swansea, University of Wales, United Kingdom.

Dr. Sahay started his career in 1960 as a Research Investigator in the Department of Anthropology, the University of Ranchi under the Research Project *Urban Patterns of Ranchi*, sponsored by the

Planning Commission, New Delhi. From 1961-1968 he served as a faculty member at Bihar Institute of Rural Development (BIRD). He joined as Assistant Professor of Rural Sociology in the Indian Agriculture Research Institute in the Department of Extension from 1968 to 1971. In the first decade of his career, he gained extensive experience in teaching, research, and administration. He also had an opportunity to conduct extensive training courses for personnel working in the tribal areas at the Tribal Orientation and Study Centre, Ranchi, and was also involved in organising the fieldwork.

For nearly 25 years (1971-1995) Dr. Sahay was engaged as an administrator in the Planning Commission for policy development, Plan Formulation, and Plan Evaluation processes from 1971-1982 under different capacities. During this major part of his career, he developed expertise in the social and rural development sector. He headed the Social Development Division, Rural Development Division, and Programme Evaluation Organization (PEO) and where he utilized and implemented all his anthropological knowledge in understanding and framing the programmes, policies, planning, implementation, field visits, evaluation, and critical appraisals. The Programme Evaluation Division (PEO) is a National Level Organization with Seven Regional Offices and 32 field teams spread all across the country. The main function of this organization is to evaluate the planned programme of national importance to provide feedback to the planning process.

His nature of work included planning, designing, directing, coordination, and supervising research projects and evaluation studies. He developed and applied methods and techniques of research, evaluation, guided, supervised, analyzed the data collected during studies and preparation of research and evaluation reports to provide feedback and inputs for the planning of the community, rural, tribal development programmes for the government. Also had been a trainer on community development, tribal development, rural development, and social development. The specialized areas of training were methods and approaches of working with people, social development administration, socio-economic research, methods, and techniques of evaluation. This involved his anthropological skills to provide learning on programme evaluation.

He also had an opportunity to work as Chairman and Member of faculty at Centre for Public Systems and Policy at Administrative Staff College of India, Hyderabad on deputation for one year (1982-1983) where has was extensively involved in training, teaching activities related to public policy. Further being an Adviser and Senior Adviser Evaluation at PEO, he had been the Principal Executive Officer, coordinated and supervised with seven subject matter divisions at headquarters, seven Regional Evaluation Offices, and thirty-two field teams spread across over the country.

He had also been the convener of different groups of Advisers appointed to develop the designs for the various evaluation studies. His role as Convener of Steering group on rural development, poverty alleviation programme for Five Year Plans, Annual Plans of Government of India, Mid Term Appraisal of Social Development / Welfare, Women and Child Development highlights his contribution as an action anthropologist as well as an administrator. Apart from this, he also had an opportunity to train various administrators during the training programmes of national importance on topics like social policy and administration, tribal development, community development, rapid rural appraisal, training in methods and techniques of designing evaluation studies.

While working with the Government of India he had the opportunity to interact and get advice from some eminent personalities like Dr. Manmohan Singh (Ex-Prime Minister of India), Shri Montek Singh Ahluwalia (Ex-Deputy Chairman of Planning Commission), Shri Pranab Mukherjee (President of India), Dr. Arjun K Sengupta (Ex Member Secretary, Planning Commission).

Fieldwork, grassroots experiences, and planning

Under the leadership of Prof. L P Vidyarthi, he developed strong skillsets for conducting ethnographic studies and fieldwork as a young anthropologist. His long stay among the tribal populations had equipped him with understanding the realistic aspects of their life. His quest for going to the field area since his younger days had strengthened him to capitalise on this skill in formulating major government programmes in his career.

Between 1960-65 when he was a research scholar in the Department of Anthropology, Ranchi University, Ranchi, and also an Instructor in Anthropology, Tribal Orientation and Study Centre, Ranchi. He could publish some of his ethnographic studies in various tribes like Maler, Pahariyas, Tangkul Nagas, Kukis, Mundas in the journal *Vanyajati.*

As an officer and an administrator in the Planning Commission at a major time of his career, he delve into development issues of underprivileged sections, related policies, programmes, and evaluation. He was one of the rare anthropologists, who could do immense contributions to anthropological knowledge in the development arena. He had an opportunity to visit field areas, analyze huge information, evaluate the programme implementation, design plans, and policies, and finally carry out these plans through action. In organizations like Planning Commission which is mainly dominated by Economists, his presence at various positions had helped in using the anthropological knowledge in framing and evaluating many government programmes and policies.

In one of his important contributions on *Approach to Tribal Development since Independence*, he discussed participatory approaches in Planning Process which can be summarized as follows:

1. A plan is not merely a reflection of desires but is a statement of possibilities, the extent to which it is possible to fulfill the felt needs within the available human material. It is efficient management of scarce resources. Integrated planning needs integrated machinery for development.
2. Planning is for the people, by the people and therefore it has to be of the people. People's participation has to be secured and sustained- a clear departure for the concept of charity to the concept of involvement so that development is achieved by a process that affords opportunities for the people to participate in the formulation and implementation of plans through a system of open and democratic decision making.
3. Choice of the scheme has to strictly follow the peoples own perception of their problems and their needs. Left to themselves people choose to satisfy infrastructural and immediate physical needs firstly, followed by the satisfaction

of other needs. Thus, given an assured opportunity, people can themselves create assets of great value and utility with minimum expenditure. They voluntarily contribute to the labour and material when it comes to satisfaction of their felt needs. The successive cooperative partnership between the government and the people for the all-round development of the people will be required. One of his famous quotes was *Jan Jagaran* (public awareness), *Jan Sangathan* (public union), *Jan Shakti* (public power), and *Jan Kalyan* (mass welfare).

4. There is an urgent need for skill planning at different levels *Zila Parishad, Panchayat Samiti* development so that needs are properly comprehended, objectives and goals pragmatically set, strategies suitably developed, schemes properly formulated, resources efficiently mobilized, and targets successfully.
5. According to his understanding, poverty and unemployment are primarily due to incapabilities of individuals and groups. Such capabilities have three dimensions—lack of comprehension, lack of competence, and lack of confidence.

One of his important articles on *Decentralization the Nagaland way* published in *Yojana* in 1989, discussed the development of Nagaland by the successful cooperative partnership between the government and the people for all-round development. The experiment of decentralization has helped in the development of the Village Development Council in which people from both traditional minds and modern outlooks sit together to plan and decide their course of action of growth and development. According to him the decentralization approach of Nagaland could be a suitable model for hill and tribal areas of Northeastern areas.

Chakriya Vikas Pranali (CVP) a unique drought-proofing published in *Kurukshetra* 1990, was an excellent model of participatory approach and innovative method to promote environmental security and rural self-reliance. It was also a reflection of holistic human growth with dignity, peace, and collective and cooperative ventures. He was an Adviser (Rural Development) Planning Commission at that time visited three villages of Palamu district of Bihar to interact with the participants (including the tribal *Parhiyas* and *Cheros*). He devised three broad principles:

1. All work, all protect, all receive, and all payments in the village system thus ensuring fuller participation of all in the development process.
2. The total harnessing of all basic resources that are available in plenty in all the villages viz sun, rain, soil, and human power in a multilayered planting system below and above the soil.
3. Equitable sharing of ever-growing produces among the landowners, the participants working in the systems, and village fund. The ever-growing village fund thus generated not only aims at all-round development of village but also makes the development self-perpetuating, self-sustaining, self-reliant, and self-financing. The most important part of this *Pranali* was that not even a single drop of water was being allowed to be wasted and thus every drop of water was being retained, detained, and used.
4. With the close interaction with people villagers developed immense confidence and sense of security which was reflected in their slogans in the local dialect: *Bachbo karab Bachaybo karab* (we shall save ourselves and also save others), *Khaibo Karab –Khilaybo Karab* (we shall feed ourselves and also feed others) *Parbho Karab –Parahibo Karab* (we shall learn ourselves and also teach others), *Sarkar ke Deb-Lev na* (we shall give to the government and not take). To develop greater confidence among participants he had the privilege of reversing these slogans like *Bachaybo Karab-Bachbo Karab* (we shall save others and then save ourselves) which was followed by participants. Especially the fourth slogan was modified as *Sarkar Se Lebo Karab-Debo Karab* i.e. we shall take from the government and also give to the government. *Leb Kam-Deb Jyada* i.e. we shall take less and give more.
5. The advantage of CVP created drought-proofing of the area, a democratic way of solving people's problems, and a sense of confidence, which was justified by saying that muscles

can do it and minds can be trained to do it. This model was replicable in similar situations.

Some of his contributions in planning, implementing, and evaluating important Government Programmes were mainly in areas of poverty, housing, nutrition, child development, water, and health were *Jawahar Rojgar Yojna, Indira Awas Yojna, Integrated Child Development Scheme, Rural Water Supply, Minimum Needs* and *Women Development Programme, Family Planning Programmes,* etc.

He had an outstanding contribution in the field of community and tribal development and Action Anthropology. His researches on tribes in different areas of India are extensive and he has lived and worked in many village communities. As an anthropologist, he always emphasised that research methods and discipline of social anthropology should contribute to village improvement. With his approach to interdisciplinary and rigorous scholarship, he could show the application of the subject in solving many human problems. In one of his conference papers in 1977, he discussed how social anthropology as an aid to tribal development explained the importance of understanding socio-cultural factors in development is crucial.

In his experience on intensive work at grass root levels, he developed a deep knowledge of the human situation and was able to devise suitable action plans for the development of the population. The States where he worked on tribal population and development programmes are Assam, Bihar, West Bengal, Manipur, Tripura, Odisha, Andhra Pradesh, Uttar Pradesh, Madhya Pradesh, Gujarat, Maharashtra. Apart from English, Hindi, Bengali, Bhojpuri, he was having a working knowledge of a large number of tribal dialects.

An attempt to show the applications of the subject of social anthropology to the solution of difficult, pressing problems and developing suitable action for social change and social development is evident from many publications like *Pragmatism and Development, Applied Anthropology in India, Research in Extension Education,* etc.

In his book on *Pragmatism in Development: Application of Anthropology* (1969) he had discussed how to relate the various theoretical aspects of social and cultural anthropology with that of the practical field situation i.e. linking the theoretical knowledge with that of the development and welfare programmes of our country.

In the above study amongst Oraons in Bihar, he adopted one village named *Murchu* which acted as his laboratory for the natural experimentation of theories. He identified that an action anthropologist mainly cares for insider's view in understanding the communities in operational programmes. For developing his natural personal identification amongst Oraons his rapport building at the village level, staying in their youth dormitories, learning local dialect *Sadri* was fruitful and helped in developing suitable intervention of the programmes.

On scientific lines, he implemented some of the development programmes himself and evolved twelve basic principles of an approach to tribal development.

1. Before starting work in tribal areas one needs to identify the different social groups in the community and understand the ways of life of tribal, which include different social institutions, customs, values, etc.
2. The worker must be sincere in gaining a working knowledge of the language or dialect.
3. Anthropologists must gain the confidence of people by a scientific approach and personal identification. He/She must go with humility and accept food and drink if offered and accept their way of life and participate in social, cultural activities. This would strengthen better identification.
4. After gaining confidence, one can assess the felt needs of people and prepare a village plan with people participation.
5. One should not try to introduce too many ideas at the same time, only a few selected ideas based on their felt needs are being introduced.
6. While introducing new ideas efforts should be made to work through and not in rivalry to, their traditional social institutions. One should try to revitalise the useful institutions, if necessary.
7. The right type of leader needs to be selected for the right type of work.
8. One should always watch that new ideas do not become contradictory to the traditional ones. If there were no

adjustments between the old and the emerging values, the zest for life would go forever.

9. The human and physical resources could be mobilized only when the programme is useful and appealing to the people. This aspect must be borne in mind.
10. Repeated persuasion needs to be made if the worker feels that a programme is congenial to the local condition.
11. Surveys and researches need to be conducted properly by the trained Block Staff, Tribal Research Institutes, and the University Departments of Anthropology and Sociology. The findings should be given due weight and implemented as far as possible.
12. True spirit and dedication on the part of the anthropologist are important. Genuine love, sympathy for tribal are pillars for success.

Having the expertise of social anthropology on using its techniques for the development process, it was interesting to find one of his articles on *Applicability of Sociological and Anthropological Research to the Tasks of Modern Banking* (1980) reflects on how this knowledge can be utilized for development banking. It was suggested by him that to revolutionise the rural economy and the social life bankers must be equipped with socio-economic, religious beliefs of the rural setting and understand human beings in totality. Highlighted the need for study on bankers as well as the study of potential customers, the article discusses the aspects of cultural survey, felt needs of people, communication pattern, gaining people confidence, social and economic process, etc.

His contributions on *Qualitative Dimensions of an Evaluation Study* in an edited volume entitled *Methods and Techniques of Programme Evaluation* (Das and Krishna, 1981) emphasizes the importance of qualitative data in programme evaluation. The analyst involved in this must attempt to measure intangible variables and changes in the behavioural aspects like habits, perception and motivation, attitudes, beliefs, and practices. Thus, the qualitative studies on evaluation should focus on whether the programme could help evolve the quality of human character and whether the implemented programmes could affect the other aspects of life and bring about a total or social change. One needs to identify the reasons for success and also find the bottlenecks of behavioural change. His publications also focused on the concept and definition of evaluation design and using case studies as a method of programme evaluation.

His doctoral work on *Maler and Santhals in Santhal Parganas* discussed the dynamics of leadership, which later came in the form of a book in 1969. It covered the details on the patterns and determinants of various types of leaderships viz traditional leaders, traditional emergent leaders, and emergent leaders. In this extensive study where he had stayed for months in various villages, he gave the applied aspect of this study. The various patterns of leadership, the roles, and importance of a various set of leaders in a given social structure, their needs, must be well understood by planners, policymakers, administrators, development, and welfare personnel. To implement tribal welfare programmes it is important to analyze the entire social situation and various patterns of leadership. Different types of leaders may be well suited for the implementation of welfare programmes as development can be done successfully after convincing the leaders.

His other work on *Research in Extension Education* 1970 (eds) where he highlighted agricultural communication and extension teaching methods like personal contact, group discussion, result demonstration were more effective methods in introducing improved agricultural implements, soil, and water conservation practices, improved seeds, fertilisers for agriculture practices. These methods also help in bringing relative effectiveness of various extension methods in changing the knowledge, skill, and attitude of farmers. With his anthropological knowledge, he could devise suitable methods of communication with farmers leading to more productivity.

A book *Role Performance and Role Prediction* (1981) discusses Village Level Worker (VLW) has been studied with the help of the model of the social system. VLW was an important link between the organization of the Intensive Agricultural District Programme (IADP) and the farmers and has an important role to play in the successful implementation of the IADP. Role expectations and role performance of VLW were important in fulfilling the goals of the IADP. The findings of the study are more useful for extension personnel working in research and field extension work in different organizations. These findings are equally helpful to extension administrators and planners in predicting the role performance of the VLW. This study provided a methodological approach to the understanding of the role of a functionary and can also act as a model for understanding the role of similar other functionaries.

One of his famous books with Late Prof Vidyarthi on *Applied Anthropology and Development in India* (1980) is a collection of eighteen research papers, which were contributed during the Centenary celebration of late Rai Bahadur Sarat Chandra Roy in 1971 in an International Symposium organized at Ranchi University. The whole volume is divided into four parts namely (1) Constitutional provisions, planning, development, administration and evaluation, (2) Social structure and stratification, (3) Problems and prospects of socio-economic development, (4) Cross-cultural adjustability and International understanding. This volume is highly useful for those interested in applied and action anthropology and is an important piece of literature on the subject. It is also being referred for Under-Graduate and Post-Graduate courses in anthropology in many Indian Universities.

Dr. B. N. Sahay was the author of nine books, more than 100 research papers published widely in professional journals of India and abroad, and about 90 All India Evaluation studies and research projects. He had also been the editor of a few professional journals like *Indian Anthropologist, Indian Journal of Extension Education,* etc and was also the life member of various scientific bodies like Indian Science Congress Association (ISCA), American Anthropological Association (AAA), Indian Society for Training and Development (ISTD), Indian Anthropological Association (IAA) and former Vice President and General Secretary of IAA. Some of his pioneering contributions received well in India and abroad included *Pragmatism in Development, Dynamics of Leadership, Communication Behaviour, and Social Change*, and *Role Perception and Role Prediction.* While finalising the book on *Pragmatism in Development* in 1966 and his visit to the University of Swansea, he also had an opportunity to get the benefit of the advice of eminent anthropologists of the U.K. like Prof E.E. Evans Pritchard, Raymond Firth, Haimemdorf, and Max Gluckman.

Many of his articles were focusing on planned development in India, approach towards tribal development, evaluation of programmes were frequently published in *Yojana* and *Kurukshetra* a monthly journal. His frequent visits to many North-east states to see the programme implementation have led to closely assessing the changes coming in the life of the tribal population. His contribution to Tangkul Nagas is an outcome of this. He contributed to many book reviews on books of diverse topics like tribal development, evaluation studies, ethnographic studies, etc.

Born and brought up in a family of Siwan (Bihar) Dr. B.N. Sahay was dedicated, hardworking, and a successful professional. He almost touched everyone's heart in a very special way be it his extended family or professional life. Because of his charismatic personality, humbleness, honesty he was a special figure amongst his near and dear ones. The Government of India and the field of anthropology would always be benefited from his excellent work.

Some of the programme evaluation reports contributed by him at the Government of India level are:

Programme evaluation reports (PEO) completed 1971-1982

- Family Planning Programme—Evaluation study of Maharashtra and Punjab
- Village Sanitation Scheme of Gandhi Smarak Nidhi, Maharashtra
- Study of Voluntary Agencies in Social Welfare
- Study of Special Schemes for Girls Education
- Study of Post Matric Scholarship for SC/ST
- Evaluation of the ICDS Projects
- Accessibility of the poor to water supply
- Report of the Committee for Training in Evaluation.

Programme Evaluation Reports (PEO) completed during tenure as Adviser (Evaluation), Planning Commission 1990-1994

- Evaluation Report on Dryland Farming
- Nehru Yuvak Kendra Scheme

- National Sports Coaching Scheme (Rajasthan and UP)
- Rural Functional Literacy Programme
- Jawahar Rojgar Yojna : A Quick Study
- Indira Aawas Yojna: A Quick Study
- Charwaha School in Bihar: A Preliminary Observation.
- Vishwa Programme in Karnataka
- Study of Desert Development Programme.
- Employment Guarantee Scheme in Maharashtra
- Western Ghats Development Programme in Tamil Nadu
- Study of District Industries Centre
- Scheme of Financial Assistance to Dance, Drama and Theatre Ensembles- A Quick Study
- Study of Drought Prone Areas Programme
- Impact of Fishing Harbour Projects on Living Conditions of Traditional Fisherman
- Revamped Public Distribution System—Quick Study
- Western Ghats Development Programme in Maharashtra.

Publications in Yojana, Kurukshetra, and others

1. Decentralization the Nagaland way- Feb1991 Vol. 7 *Gramin Vikas* Newsletter.
2. Chakriya Vikas Pranali - a unique drought-proofing Nov 1990 Vol. 6 *Gramin Vikas* Newsletter.
3. Vikendrikaran: Nagaland ka prayog *Yojana* January 1989, Vol. 32.
4. Nagaland experiment with decentralization *Kurukshetra,* March 1989 Vol. 37.
5. Follow Nehru approach for tribal upliftment Oct 1989 *Kurukshetra,* Vol. 37.
6. Samanvit Gramin Vikas Yojana (Integrated Rural Development Programme) Oct-Dec 1987 *Gramin Vikas Jyoti.*
7. Voluntary funding for rural development (Jt) December 1986 *Yojana.*
8. Integrated Child Development Services 1982 *Yojana,* Vol. 26.
9. Rural water supply 1980 *Yojana,* Vol. 26.
10. Tribal Development 1980 *Yojana,* Vol. 24.
11. Youth leaders for cooperation (Jt) 1970 *The Cooperator,* Vol. 17.
12. Village leaders and development programme April 1967, *Khadigramodyog,* Directorate of Publicity, Khadi and Village Industries.
13. Representation in Gram Panchayat 1969 *Kurukshetra,* Vol. 17.

14. Gram Panchayaton mein pratinidhitv 1969 *Kurukshetra,* Vol. 15.
15. Pahariyas and their customs 1966 *Vanyajati,* Vol. XIV, No. 1.
16. The Tangkul Nagas of Ukhrul T.D. Block, Manipur 1965, *Vanyajati,* Vol. XIII, No. 2.
17. A note on Kukis of Manipur 1964 *Vanyajati,* Vol. XII, No. 4.
18. Authority pattern in Maler Villages 1963, *Vanyajati,* Vol. XI, No. 1.

References

Kherde, RL and Sahay, BN 1981: *Role Performance and Role Prediction,* New Delhi, National Publishing House.

Sahai, Ragini 2018: In Memorium Dr. B N Sahay, in *Indian Anthropologist*: 48, 3, July-Dec.

Sahay, BN 1980: *Aspects of Social Anthropology in India*.New Delhi: Classical Publications.

Sahay, BN. 1969: *Dynamics of Leadership*. New Delhi: Bookhive Publishers.

Sahay, BN. 1969: *Pragmatism in Development: Application of Anthropology*, New Delhi: Bookhive Publishers.

Sahay, BN. 1969: *Vikas Mein Prayogvaad: Manav Vigyan Ka Vyawaharik Prayog* (Translation of Pragmatism in Development).

Sahay, BN. 1981: Case study and programme evaluation in Ed by BC Das, and K. Krishna (Eds*): Methods and Techniques of Programme Evaluation,* State Planning Institute, Government of Uttar Pradesh.

Singh, IB and Sahay, BN. 1972: *Communication Behaviour and Social Change*. New Delhi: Book Hive Publishers.

Singh, KN., Rao, CS and Sahay, BN. (eds) 1970: *Research in Extension Education for Accelerating Development Process,* IARI, New Delhi.

Vidyarthi, LP and Sahay, BN (eds) 1980: *Applied Anthropology and Development in India,* New Delhi, National Publishing House.

Chapter – 20

Prof. Priyabala Das: A Dedicated Teacher and a Passionate Researcher

Maitreyee Sharma

Priyabala Das, an anthropologist, a dedicated teacher, and a passionate researcher has immense contribution to the academics of anthropology and is well known within the community of anthropologists but her contribution is not much known outside the community of anthropologists. She was a Professor in the Department of Anthropology, Gauhati University, and was a brilliant student throughout her academic career. She was an active member of the Anthropological Society of North-east India, which was one of the pioneer organizations of Anthropology in India, and was also acted as the Chairperson of the Organization. She was known for her amiable and simple nature amongst her colleagues, students, and to the greater society as a whole.

Priyabala Das was born on 23rd November 1935, in the affluent and well-known family (well-known as the Uzir family) of Late Rajendra Lal Uzir who was her father, in the Uzan Bazar area of Guwahati. Right from the beginning, she had a brilliant academic career and was extremely motivated in her academic path, and had a clear focus on life. She secured a first-class Bachelor of Science degree with Zoology honours (Cotton College) from Gauhati University in 1956. When she was enrolled in a Bachelor of Science degree in Cotton College, Anthropology was introduced there in the year 1954. She then opted for Anthropology as one of her subjects in her Bachelor of Science degree. Interestingly, at the Post-graduation level, she chose Anthropology instead of Zoology in 1956 at Gauhati University (Choudhury, 1992). In this same year, Anthropology at the Post-graduation level started at Gauhati University. Here again, she passed Post-graduation with flying colours with First Class specialising in Physical Anthropology and joined the Department of Anthropology at Gauhati University as Lecturer in the year 1959. Therefore, she was one of the students of the first batch of Anthropology in the Department of Anthropology at Gauhati University. She completed her doctoral research under the guidance of Professor Bhuban Mohan Das, in the Department of Anthropology, Gauhati University in 1966. She was the first scholar who received a Ph.D. degree in Anthropology from Gauhati University. Due to her devoted teaching and dedicated research, she became Reader and from Reader to Professor very soon in the Department of Anthropology, Gauhati University. In 1990, it was her time to be the Head of the Department but due to sudden and serious health issues, she could not accept the position of Headship in the Department (from Bhuban Mohan Das Rachana Samagra, 2015, pp. 508-510).

In the 1960s, the studies and researches on human growth and development were on-trend in different parts of the world as well as in different parts of India. Priyabala Das at that time greatly understood the need to initiate human growth studies in North-east Indian population groups from the Anthropological perspective. She realized and focused on the fact that the Growth trend of children always acts as a mirror of the socio-economic and cultural conditions of a particular community. In Assam or rather in North-east India, she was the pioneer to initiate human growth studies from the Anthropological perspective. She achieved a doctorate degree doing research on the growth and development of the Kalita children of Assam. The title of the thesis was *A study of growth on some somatometric characteristics of a selected caste of Assam*. Her work was immensely appreciated by many anthropologists and in 1971 her doctoral dissertation was published in the form of a book, entitled, *Growth Studies of Kalita Children*, by Field Research Project, Miami, Florida, USA. She continued her research on growth studies throughout her life and published many research articles on the findings of her research. She was so involved and interested in growth studies that she had a habit of measuring the students of the University as well as in the University campus by taking into account different anthropometric variables related to growth and development (from Bhuban Mohan Das Rachana Samagra, 2015, page 508-510). She used to publish the data as well as findings of these measurements in the *Bulletin of the Department of Anthropology*: *Gauhati University* from time to time. These researches aim to know the variation in the growth amongst the children and adults belonging to different communities and to know the changes in growth year after year.

Research contribution

The research and contribution of Priyabala Das can be categorized into three major areas based on her research publications. These three areas of research are:

1. Human growth studies
2. Anthropological demographic studies
3. Studies on inter-population variation concerning the frequencies of ABO blood groups, dermatoglyphics pattern, colour-blindness, taste sensitivity to PTC (Phenylthiocarbamide), anthropometric and behavioural traits, and length of toes in the human Feet.

Studies on human growth

Priyabala Das was the pioneer in the area of human growth studies in entire North-east India. In her doctoral research on the Kalita children, she gathered anthropometric data by using the cross-sectional method of growth study and showed how the children grew and in what ways their growth was different in two genders. With this work of hers, the Descriptive Stage of human growth studies had begun in North-east India. Later, however, along with the cross-sectional method, she also used the longitudinal method and mixed-longitudinal methods in other growth studies.

Priyabala Das in her doctoral research studied growth concerning some somatometric characteristics of 442 boys and 423 girls of ages ranging from 6 to 21 years of the Kalita caste of Assam. The somatometric characteristics that attracted her were: stature, sitting height, the girth of thorax, weight, different dimensions of the head, face, and nose. She had highlighted the sexual variation in growth among the boys and the girls and revealed that the Kalita boys had longer heads, broader foreheads, lower jaws, and higher faces than that of the Kalita girls. The results also showed that the girls were heavier and taller during the early period of childhood but were later superseded by boys during the adolescent period. She also revealed in her study that in the Kalita girls the growth of the lower limb was more rapid than the trunk and it occurred before the attainment of puberty (Das, 1966). Priyabala Das along with B.M. Das (1969-71) measured 418 school-going Assamese boys of Gauhati from the ages of 6 to 16 years and also made a study on the growth of head dimensions in Assamese boys (1972). Priyabala Das (1973) studied the growth of Kaibarta boys concerning height and weight. Again in 1974, she compared the boys of four Assamese castes - Brahmin, Kalita, Baishya, and Kaibarta by taking into account the somatometric characteristics of height, weight, and chest circumference. In this study, she found that the Brahmin boys were slightly taller, heavier, and greater in their chest circumference than Baishya and Kalita boys up to 12 years of age but afterward, this trend was observed to get reversed. The reason cited by her research suggested that the Brahmin families observe different kinds of food taboos regularly as well as during certain rites and rituals which might have restricted the variety of food available to the Brahmin children. But such kinds of food taboos were not evident in the families of other castes under study. All the boys from different castes showed their adolescent growth spurts between 12 and 13 years. A research paper on the study of the growth of head dimensions of Baishya boys (1974) was published in the *Bulletin of the Department of Anthropology- Gauhati University*. She jointly (1978) studied and published the growth pattern of Khamti boys of Arunachal Pradesh concerning somatometric characteristics- their height, sitting height, and chest circumference.

The first mixed longitudinal study in North-east India (1982) was done by Priyabala Das and Bapukan Choudhury on growth in height and weight of the Assamese children from 1 to 7 years. They found that the growth in height was most rapid from 1 to 3 years in both the boys and the girls which was followed by a slower and constant increase for the boys between 3 and 4 years, while among the girls it was between 4 and 5 years. The girls were taller than the boys at 4 years but between 5 and 7 years the height for both the sexes becomes almost the same, the boys were slightly taller than the girls. No significant population variation was found in this study (Das and Choudhury, 1982). The second mixed longitudinal study of growth in height, weight, and sitting height vertex was also done by Priyabala Das and Bapukan Choudhury (1992) among the urban Assamese children from 8 to 16 years of age. The adolescent growth spurt was found to occur at 13-14 years among the boys whereas in the girls the adolescent growth spurt occurred two years earlier than the boys (Das and Choudhury, 1992). Priyabala Das (1977) did the first longitudinal growth study in the entire North-east concerning growth in height, weight, and sitting height of five siblings for ten years. She also conducted the second longitudinal growth study (1978) that encompassed the study of the growth of head and face dimensions of four sisters for twelve years. These two studies revealed the individual rates of growth and its variation and the growth spurt at the adolescent period of each of the siblings.

Priyabala Das continued her area of interest in human growth studies through her Ph.D. scholars. She produced the first Ph.D. (Dr. B. Choudhury) in the year of 1979. The title of the work was *A cross-sectional study of the growth of some somatometric characters of Rabha boys of Kamrup district Assam,* the study revealed that the adolescent growth spurt in all the somatometric measurements excepting in head breadth, bizygomatic breadth, foot breadth, and height Spherion occurred between 12 and 13 years of age. A high positive correlation was observed between different body segments at all age levels. On comparing with the sexes, the study revealed that the Rabha boys had a broader and longer face than the Rabha girls, but the latter had greater skinfold thickness almost throughout the age period. During the early age period, the Rabha boys remained shorter than the Ahom and the Khampti boys and taller than the boys from different caste groups, but at adulthood, the Rabha boys reported to be the shortest of all, including the groups. The study suggested that the shorter stature of the Rabha boys may be due to their genetic factors (Choudhury, 1979).

Priyabala Das produced another work on human growth studies. Under her guidance, Dwijendra Kumar Duarah worked on, *A Study on the Physical Anthropology of the Monpas of Arunachal Pradesh with Special Reference to the Growth of Monpa Boys* (1985), which revealed many interesting facts on the physical growth of the Dirang, Tawang and Kalaktang Monpas. In Somatometric characters, the three groups reported having monocephalic, hypsicephalic, and metriocephalic heads. However, in somatoscopic characters, all the groups of Monpas resembled one another. In ABO blood groups, the Dirang and Kalaktang Monpas exhibited the highest frequency of blood group A but in the Tawang Monpas, blood group B was more frequent. The frequency of defective colour vision was reported to be higher in the Dirang Monpas followed by the Kalaktang and Tawang Monpas. The study revealed that concerning the physical characteristics all three groups differ from each other. In addition to this, the Kalaktang Monpas were found to deviate more from the other groups of Monpas (Duarah, 1985).

Anthropological demographic studies

Priyabala Das initiated the anthropological demographic studies with the study of the age at menarche of Kalita girls in Assam. The results were published jointly in 1967. Later she studied the variation in age at menarche of Assamese girls (1987) which reported that the mean age at menarche varies from 12.53 + 0.08 to 12.83 + 0.12 years among the Assamese girls of different castes. She also reported the decreasing trend of the menarcheal age from the higher to the lower age groups in this significant study. Priyabala Das (1973) jointly studied the incidence of child mortality in a Kachari village as well as in 1975 she studied fertility and child mortality among the rural Assamese (Das and Devi, 1975). A study on the fertility of the Mishmi women of Arunachal Pradesh was studied and published jointly by Priyabala Das (1979). This study revealed that the Mishmi women had higher fertility as well as higher infant mortality due to the faulty feeding habits of the infants. She co-authored many other papers on infant and child mortality on several other castes and tribes. Priyabala Das (1982) as a co-author reported that the child mortality rates among the Mongoloid, Muslim, and Hindu populations of Assam were 11.43 percent, 14.24 percent, and 15.49 percent respectively. They had also found that the frequency of reproductive wastage was comparatively higher among the Assamese Hindu castes than among the Mongoloid populations and the Muslims of Assam. A series of papers were published on demographic studies on Hindus, Muslims, and Mongoloids from 1985-1989, as a part of the UGC project of the Department of Anthropology, Gauhati University jointly with B.M. Das, R. Das, H. Walter, and H. Danker-Hopfe. These studies reported that the girls belonging to the Mongoloid fold attained puberty earlier than that of the Hindus and Muslims. They explained this to be genetic or ethnic affiliation. Though the Mongoloid girls attain puberty earlier, their mean age at marriage, as well as the time of birth of the first child were found to be higher than those of the other two groups (1985). The pregnancy wastage was reported to be much higher among the Hindus in comparison to that the other two groups, but the rate of infant and child mortality was reported lower in them. The study suggested that as the Hindu upper-caste women particularly the Brahmin women did not take part in agricultural operations in the field; and hence less physical labour was done by them in comparison to women of other castes and the Mongoloid and Muslim women. It was said that regular physical labour helps in maintaining normal health causing normal delivery, and in such women, the percentage of pregnancy wastage would be less. The Hindus of the sample were observed to be more educated. They knew and took better care of their babies for which the postnatal mortality was reported less in the Hindus than in the Muslims and Mongoloid population groups.

Under her supervision, two more doctoral theses on anthropological demography had been completed - *A study on certain problems of fertility among the Khasi women of Meghalaya*: This doctoral work was done by Sunil Kumar Baruah in 1980. The study examined the fertility performance and various problems related to fertility among the Khasi (Khynriam) women, differentiated by place of residence (rural and urban), religion (Christian and non-Christian), and family type (nuclear and joint). The study reported no difference in fertility performance among the Khasis living in rural and urban areas. The pregnancy wastage due to stillbirth and abortion among the rural non-Christians was found to be higher than among the Christians but it was found to be higher among the urban non-Christians than among the Christians. The neo-natal, as well as post-natal mortality, was reported higher among the rural Khasis than among the urban Khasis. While infant mortality was observed to be higher in rural areas and child mortality was higher in urban areas. It was also observed that among the Khasi couples, the rate of fertility increased as the level of education decreased (Baruah, 1980). Another doctoral thesis on anthropological demography was completed by Rumi Sarma on, *Fertility among the Rabhas of Kamrup district, Assam* (1991). The study was undertaken among the Pati Rabhas of the Boko area, Kamrup district, Assam. The study examined the fertility, infant and child mortality, and knowledge, attitude, and practice of family planning among the Pati Rabhas. The study revealed that the majority of women got married before reaching 18 years of age. The highest percentage of women experienced their first conception at 15 years of age and more than half of these women had their first birth below 18 years of age. Child mortality was reported to be highest in the first 2 years of life in both the non-acceptor and acceptor mothers. In both acceptor and non-acceptor mothers the overall percentage of mortality of female infants and children was higher than their male counterparts. The highest percentage of induced abortion was observed at the 6th order of pregnancy in the study population and induced abortion (as indigenous ways/institutional) was considered by one of the family planning measures by the couples (Sarma, 1991).

Studies on inter-population variation

Priyabala Das conducted studies on finger dermatoglyphics of the Kumar population (1972). She also studied the Kalita (1986), Kaibarta, and Brahmin (1986) populations of Assam jointly as a part of the UGC project. Among the Kumar population, the frequency of loops was reported to be the highest followed by whorls in both the sexes. The same was observed among the Kalitas and the Brahmins of Assam. Priyabala Das was part of an important project lead by

Prof. B.M. Das. The project (1980) was undertaken with financial assistance from the University Grants Commission, New Delhi. A series of papers were published as a part of this project from the 1980s onwards under the main heading Anthropological studies in Assam, India. The papers attempted to look at the genetic differentiation processes among the populations as well as to ponder about the biosocial characteristics of all the populations under study. Mongoloid population groups from Upper Assam like Ahom, Chutia, Deuri, Mishing, and Moran were investigated (1985) for the distribution of anthropometric and dermatoglyphic traits as well as ABO blood groups and PTC taste sensitivity to show genetic distances among these populations. The results were discussed with special reference to the extent and causes of intergroup variability. Altogether 12 population groups were studied: five Mongoloid groups and seven Caucasoid groups (six caste populations and one Muslim group). They took four categories of anthropological variables into account: anthropometric traits, behavioural traits, dermatoglyphic traits and ABO blood groups, and PTC taste sensitivity. It was observed from the anthropological data presented by the investigators that the five Mongoloid populations under study show marked and statistically significant differences in the distribution of anthropometric, behavioural, and dermatoglyphics traits as well as in the distribution of ABO blood group and PTC gene frequencies. The reasons for these heterogeneities according to them suggested that all these populations were endogamous units with no or at least minimal genetic contacts or gene-flow amongst them. So, genetic differences that emerged over time by factors like genetic drift and/or founder effects or geographical and especially the social isolation could preserve the uniqueness of gene frequencies (1985). Four Assamese caste groups—Jogis, Hiras, Kumars and Kaibartas (1986) were also analyzed for the distribution of anthropometric and dermatoglyphics traits as well as for the distribution of ABO blood groups and PTC taste sensitivity. The differences among these four caste groups concerning anthropometric and dermatoglyphics traits were found to be statistically significant, which they stated could be connected with the history of these groups and their genetic isolation from each other. In 1985, Priyabala Das as a part of this project studied six Assamese

Muslim groups that showed more or less marked and statistically significant differences. One of the Muslim groups under study consisted of the so-called Marias, who were said to be the descendants of the prisoners captive after the unsuccessful Muslim invasion in 1533, and who had a low position in the Assamese Muslim society (Das et al., 1985). They used to marry among themselves and considering these historical and sociological facts, the study found anthropological peculiarities with unique gene frequencies ABO blood groups, PTC taste sensitivity, and dermatoglyphics traits among this group. The results assumed that due to no gene flow from the other Muslim groups, the Marias, could maintain their anthropological peculiarities. Thus, the obvious biological distance of Maria from the Sheikhs, according to them, could be attributed to their social isolation. In another article, *Anthropological studies in Assam, India: observations on the Kalitas* (Das et al., 1986), they suggested that among the five Kalita groups (data were collected during the years 1977-1979 from five different districts of Assam, namely Goalpara, Kamrup, Nowgong, Darrang, and Sibsagar) under study more or less marked and statistically significant variations observed in the distribution of head and face measurements, stature, behavioural and dermatoglyphic traits, ABO blood groups and PTC taste sensitivity. The reason for this intergroup variability as they reported was that these Kalita groups were endogamous, hence marriages occurred mostly between members of these groups, and thus, the anthropological variability of the Kalitas according to them could be the result of their geographic isolation from each other. Similarly, the *anthropological studies in Assam, India: observations on the Brahmins* (Das et al., 1986), suggested that a marked and statistically significant variability existed among the three Assamese Brahmin groups (Kamrup, Darrang, and Sibsagar); was observed only regarding some of the anthropological traits: upper facial index, total facial index, nasal index, behavioural traits (except tongue rolling) and PTC taste sensitivity. The study showed that the intergroup variability among the Brahmins was much lower as compared to Mongoloid and Muslim population groups from Assam. This study tried to observe genetic distance among these three Assamese Brahmin groups. It is interesting to state that for indices, behavioural traits, and dermatoglyphics as well as for ABO and PTC gene frequencies the greatest distance was seen between the Brahmin groups from Darrang and Sibsagar. That meant that regarding these variables the Kamrup and Sibsagar Brahmins were rather close, and they were found to be relatively distant from the Darrang Brahmins. Priyabala Das co-authored a paper on population and region-wise variation in the distribution of ABO blood groups in Assam in 1973 (Das et al., 1973). They observed that the Kaibartas stand apart from other castes of Assam in respect of the ABO blood group with a high frequency of B and low A and with blood group O below 0.6 percentage. In this paper, an attempt had been made to measure the genetic distances in respect of ABO blood group genes among four castes, namely, Brahmin, Kalita, Baishya, and Kaibarta, in Assam, India. The results reported that the Kaibarta stood distinct from the other three castes.

Priyabala Das co-authored a research paper on the foot type of the Rabha population (Das and Uzir, 1959). On comparing their Rabha data with that of the Juang, Pahira, Oraon, and Mundari found that the Rabha differ from each of these tribes in having higher frequencies of the type fibular (F) and O and a lower frequency of the type tibial (T). The Khasi foot was studied by her in 1961 (Das and Uzir, 1961) and measured only foot length, foot breadth, and foot index. The foot types of 56 Khasi males were studied and found that the majority showed type, T followed by type F and O.

The frequency of colour blindness was also studied by Priyabala Das jointly with other scholars (Choudhury and Das, 1974) among some tribal populations of Arunachal Pradesh like Padam, Minyong, Wancho, Dirang, and Khalaktang Monpa, Tagin, and Gallong, the incidence of colour-blindness was observed to be relatively low. She also published a joint paper on the frequency of colour blindness in five groups of Assam (Das and Das, 1973) and found that in Lower Assam, the frequency of colour-blinds (particularly the deutan form) was comparatively higher among the Brahmins than among the Kalitas and Kaibartas. She also studied hand-clapping, arms folding, earlobe attachment, and colour-blindness among the Gallong of Arunachal Pradesh (Das and Choudhury, 1975) and tongue-rolling and tongue-folding ability among the Ahom, Deori, Chutia, Mishing, and Lalung populations of Assam as a part of the UGC sponsored project mentioned earlier and reported low frequency among the Chutia, Mishing, and Moran (Das et al., 1985).

One of the Ph.D. theses on a very new and least studied area of research that she guided in her last years of life was on the *Association of duodenal ulcer with some anthropogenetic parameters among some selected sections of the population of Assam* (1991) by Meenakshi Das. The results indicated that blood group O is closely associated with duodenal ulcers. The Hindus were more affected by duodenal cancer than Muslims. The risk of developing duodenal ulcers was found to be higher in males than females and its occurrence was observed to be more frequent among the Kalita and Kayastha caste groups than the other caste groups.

Priyabala Das made Anthropology rich by co-authoring five valuable books on Anthropology which proved very useful to the students as well as to the teachers at the undergraduate and the post-graduate level. These are:

1. *Nritattva Parichaya* (Part I), Text Book in Assamese, University Coordination Committee for Production of Text Books in Regional Language, Gauhati University, 1972.
2. *Prathamik Abayabik Nritattva.* Text Book in Assamese, University Coordination Committee for Production of Text Books in Regional Language, Gauhati University, 1974.
3. *Jibashma Manab*. Text Book in Assamese, University Coordination Committee for Production of Text Books in Regional Language, Gauhati University, 1977.
4. *Nrideh Mapatattva* Text Book in Assamese, University Coordination Committee for Production of Text Books in Regional Language, Gauhati University.
5. Goswami, MC, and PB. Das, 1990, *The People of Arunachal Pradesh: A Physical Survey.* Directorate of Research, Government of Arunachal Pradesh, Itanagar.

The last years of her life

In the early part of 1988, Priyabala Das was diagnosed with an incurable disease. Her health was deteriorating fast but despite this condition, she remained mentally and psychologically strong though she was physically weak. At that time, she made a plan to complete all her half-done works. In the last few days of her life, she was bedridden and started to do all her academic works at home. She continued to supervise her last three doctoral students and made them complete and submit their thesis in the department. Under her able guidance, a total of seven students received doctoral degree and all these research works received utmost appreciation. She breathed her last on 18th April 1992, at the age of 56 years. She left behind her husband and daughter. Priyabala Das is still remembered fondly by everyone whom she met in her life. She was known for her amiable and sweet-spoken nature. Everyone remembers her for her dedication to teaching and research, a woman with a soft yet strong personality and an ideal human being. She came to the department putting on Assamese *Mekhela-Sadar* with a fine border. Her works are still being carried over by most of her research students and her works are still referred to and cited in the most recent research publications.

References

Baruah, SK. 1980. *A study on certain problems of fertility among the Khasi women of Meghalaya*. An Unpublished Ph.D. Thesis, Department of Anthropology (Faculty of Science), Gauhati University.

Choudhury, B. and Das PB. 1974. Frequency of colour blindness in some populations of Arunachal Pradesh. *Journal of Gauhati University* (Science), XXIII–XXV, 2: 1-7.

Choudhury, B. 1979. *A cross-sectional study of the growth of some somatometric characters of Rabha Boys of Kamrup, Assam*. Unpublished Ph.D. Thesis, Gauhati University.

Choudhury, B. 1992. A tribute to Priyabala Das. *The Sentinel*: April 30.

Danker-Hopfe, H., Das BM., Walter H. , Das PB. and Das R.. 1988. Anthropological studies in Assam, India. 6. Differentiation process among Assamese populations. *Anthropologischer Anzeiger*, 46: 159-184.

Das, BM. and Das PB. 1973. Frequency of colour blindness in five groups of Assam. *Man in India*, 53, 4: 363-367.

Das, PB. and Choudhury B. 1975. Hand clasping, arm folding, earlobe attachment, and colour-blindness of Gallong of Arunachal. *Bulletin of the Department of Anthropology, Gauhati University*, 4: 65-70.

Das, PB. and Sengupta NN. 1972. Finger dermatoglyphics of the Kumar of Assam. *Journal of Assam Science Society*, 15, 1: 36-43.

Das, BM. (Reprinted in 2015). Priyabala Das. In Manjumala Das (Ed.)- *Bhubanmohan Das Rachana Samagra*, Vol. II, 2015, Katha Publications,

Guwahati, pp. 508-510.

Das, BM., and Uzir P. 1959. Relative length of the first and second toes of the Rabha foot. *Journal of Gauhati University* (Science), 10: 153.

Das, BM., and Das PB.1969-71. A study on some aspects of growth of the Assamese boys. *Journal of Gauhati University* (Science), 20-22: 51-65.

Das, BM., and Das PB. 1972. A study of growth of the head in Assamese boy. *Bulletin of the Department of Anthropology: Gauhati University*, 1: 88-86.

Das, BM., and Das PB. 1982. Child mortality among rural Assamese. *Bulletin of the Anthropological Survey of India*, 31: 14-29.

Das, BM., Das PB and Das R. 1973. Genetic distances in respect of AB0 blood groups among four castes of Assam, India. *Humangenetik*, 20: 179-181.

Das, BM., Das PB, Das R, Walter H, and Danker-Hopfe, H. 1985. Anthropological studies in Assam, India. 1. Observations on five Mongoloid populations. *Anthropologischer Anzeiger*, 43: 193-204.

Das, BM., Das PB, Das R, Walter H, and Danker-Hopfe, H. 1985. Anthropological studies in Assam, India 2. Observations on Muslims. *Anthropologischer Anzeiger*, 43: 299-310.

Das, BM., Das PB, Das R, Walter H, and Danker-Hopfe, H. 1986. Anthropological studies in Assam, India: 3. Observations on three Brahmin Groups. *Anthropologischer Anzeiger*, 44, 1: 35-43.

Das, BM., Das PB, Das R, Walter H, and Danker-Hopfe, H.1986. Anthropological studies in Assam, India: 4. Observations on the Kalitas. *Anthropologischer Anzeiger*, 44, 2: 105-115.

Das, BM., Das PB, Das R, Walter H, and Danker-Hopfe, H. 1986. Anthropological studies in Assam, India. *Anthropologischer Anzeiger,* 44, 3: 239-48.

Das, Meenakshi. 1991. *Association of Duodenal Ulcer with some Anthropogenetic Parameters among some Selected Sections of Population of Assam.* An Unpublished Ph.D. Thesis, Department of Anthropology (Faculty of Science), Gauhati University.

Das, PB. 1966. *A Study of Growth on Some Somatometric Characteristics of a Selected Caste of Assam*. Ph.D. Thesis. Gauhati University.

Das, PB. 1971. *Growth Studies of Kalita* children. Field Research Project. Miami, The U.S.A.

Das, PB. 1973. A cross-sectional study of growth in height and weight of an endogenous caste of Assam. *Bulletin of the Department of Anthropology: Gauhati University*, 2: 24-31.

Das, PB. 1974. A comparative study of growth in respect of height, weight, and chest circumference of rural Assamese boys. In B.M, Das (Ed): *Contemporary Anthropological Research in North-east India*, (Bulletin of the Department of Anthropology: Dibrugarh University), 3: 43-55.

Das, PB. 1974. A study of growth of head dimensions of Baishya children. *Bulletin of the Department of Anthropology: Gauhati University*, 3: 52-57.

Das, PB. 1977. A longitudinal study of growth in height, weight, and sitting height of five siblings for a period of ten years. *Abs. Proc. 64th Indian Science Congress.*

Das, PB. 1978. A longitudinal study of growth of head and face dimensions of four sisters for twelve years, *Abs Proc. 64th Indian Science Congress.*

Das, PB. 1987. Variation in age at menarche of Assamese girls. *Journal of Science*, Gauhati University, XXIX: 1-8.

Das, PB. and Das BM.1967. Age at menarche of Kalita girls in Assam. *Man in India*. 47, 2: 113-117.

Das, PB., and Choudhury B.1979. A study on fertility of the Mishmi women of Arunachal Pradesh. *Abstract published in the Proc. 66th Session of Anthropology and Archaeology Section. Indian Science Congress*: 3-4.

Das, PB., and Choudhury B.1982. A mixed longitudinal study on growth in height and weight of Assamese children from 1 to 7 years. *Bulletin of the Anthropological Survey of India*, 31, 3 and 4: 37-42.

Das, PB., and Choudhury B.1992. A mixed longitudinal study on growth in height and weight of Assamese Children from 8 to 16 years. *Bulletin of the Department of Anthropology, Gauhati University*, 6: 61-69.

Das, PB., and Das BM. 1973. Incidence of child mortality in a Kachari village. *Journal of Society and Culture*, 4, 1: 127-129.

Das, PB., and Devi R. 1975. A study of fertility performance among three rural populations of Kamrup, Assam. *Bulletin of the Department of Anthropology, Gauhati University*, 5: 75-81.

Duarah, DK. 1985. *A Study on the Physical Anthropology of the Monpas of Arunachal Pradesh with Special Reference to the Growth of Monpa Boys.* Unpublished Ph.D. Thesis, Gauhati University.

Duarah, DK., and Das PB. 1978. A cross-sectional study of growth in four somatometric characters of Khamti boys of the Arunachal Pradesh. *Resarun,* 10: 15-24.

Sarma, R. 1991. *A study of some demographic aspects of the Rabhas of Boko area, Kamrup District.* An Unpublished Ph.D. Thesis, Department of Anthropology (Faculty of Science), Gauhati University.

Chapter – 21

Dr. Rebati Mohan Sarkar

Atul Chandra Bhowmik

Rebati Mohan Sarkar was born on 4th May 1937 in the Birbhum district of West Bengal. He obtained M.Sc., Ph.D. from Ranchi University, Bihar, and D.Lit. in Anthropology from Patna University. He served around 40 years as a teaching faculty member and Head of the Department of Anthropology at the Bangabasi College in Kolkata (1961 – 1997). He was editor of the reputed journal *Man in India* (1987 – 2018).

He wrote books on both Cultural Anthropology and Physical Anthropology in the Bengali language published from Knowledge House, a publisher of repute at Kolkata. His book entitled *Fundamentals of Physical Anthropology* (1965) which runs 4th edition is very informative. To date, these books are considered praiseworthy and these have a consolidated glossary of technical terms for easy understanding. During his class teaching, he explained all anthropological issues very lucidly citing examples from the common surrounding niche which are very helpful to students to understand the things mentioned in his lectures. Being specialized in Cultural Anthropology, he had deep knowledge in anthropometry and the instruments used in the topic and their working method, identification of constituent bones in the skeleton of man, somatometric landmarks, and field methods in Anthropology and other social sciences indicating his versatility in Physical Anthropology. He was very popular among the students for his inborn ideas. He was an expert in primitive and rural technology and was being governed by the tribal and rural folk sphere of food production, hunting, shelter, fuel, and spoiling and damaging the ambient environment. He mentioned very pinpointing the interrelationship between indigenous knowledge of the folk masses and their sustainable development. Readers are surprized to feel his depth, orientation, and sagacity of the indigenous knowledge contrived by the local communities in the tribal-folk panoramas.

His important published articles are *Sanskritization among the Sutradhar caste - A case study* (1969); *The Santhal insurrection through ballads* (1971); *Tribal folklore of the Santal Parganas* (1975); *Study of sacred complex and the Bakreswar temple* (1976); *National integration and the tribal people of Chotanagpur* (1973); *Tribal life in Birbhum district* (1976); *From nomadism to sedentism: Adaptation and response as exemplified by the Birhors of Chotanagpur* (1992); and many more besides well-knitted books entitled *Fundamentals of Physical Anthropology* (1976); *Regional Cults and Rural Traditions* (1986); *Bauls of Bengal: In the Quest of Man of the Heart* (1990); *Land and Forest Rights of the Tribals Today* (2006); *Dalits in India: Past and Present* (2006); *Primitive Tribal Groups of India: Tradition, Development and Transition* (2008); *Sunderban Fisherman in the World Heritage Setting: A Community Striving in the Mystic Mangrove Ecosystem* (2009); *Indigenous knowledge in Traditional Folk Panorama: Genesis, Development and Application* (2011); *Anthropology of Development – An Integrated Appraisal* (2018) etc.

He was well-known to the global intelligentsia for inter-disciplinary research. In his exalted attempt to focus the discernible light of an investigation into the rural-tribal philosophy and inter-relatedness cognizance, he had delved deep into the rural and tribal communities and their tradition through his direct and integrated field investigation which was resulted in a close relationship between the folklore and anthropology in the conventional Indian soil. His indigenous knowledge system was based on the basic understanding of the native communities' life and activities. He closely observed their thought pattern. This particular venture had instigated him to acquire the specific potentiality for genuine comprehension in grasping the very bedrock of the primitive and indigenous lifeways and thought-ways, Dr. Sarkar had been editing the premier

International Journal *Man in India* for long twenty-seven years with full devotion and seriousness. He curved out his name as a renowned Anthropologist.

He was associated with many research organizations and folk-culture assemblies. He was an active member of the syllabus of the Indian Committee of Anthropology and Social Sciences of the University Grants Commission, New Delhi, and an advisory member of the Anthropological Survey of India.

Important Books and research articles

1. 1965. *Fundamentals of Physical Anthropology*, (1976, 3rd Edition); Blackie ECIS Ltd, Calcutta.
2. 1986. *Regional Cults and Rural Traditions.* Inter India Publishers, New Delhi.
3. 1992. From nomadism to sedentism: Adaptation and response as exemplified by the Birhors of Chitanagpur, *Man in India*, 72, 3: 253-270.
4. 2000. *Through the Vistas of Life and Lore: Folkloric Reflections of Traditional India,* Puthi Pustak, Calcutta.
5. 2003. *Bauls of Bengal: In Quest of Man of the Heart.* Gyan Publishing House, New Delhi.
6. 2006. *Land and Forest Rights of the Tribal Today*. Serial Publications, New Delhi.
7. 2006. *Dalits in India: Past and Present*. Serial Publications, New Delhi.
8. 2008. *Primitive Tribal Group in India: Tradition, Development, and Transformation*. Serial Publications, New Delhi.
9. 2009. *Sundarban Fisherman in the World Heritage Setting: A Common Striving in the Mystic Mangrove*. Serial Publications, New Delhi.
10. 2011. *Indigenous Knowledge in Traditional Folk Panorama: Genesis, Development, and Applications*. Serial Publications, New Delhi.
11. 2018. *Anthropology of Development: An Integrated Apprisal.* Sahajatri, Kolkata, West Bengal.

Chapter – 22

Prof. Ashesh Kumar Haldar: A Man of Simplicity

Kakali Chakrabarty

It was sometime in the year 1996 when I got introduced myself to Professor Ashesh Kumar Haldar over a telephonic converzation. He was then associated with the Department of Anthropology at Ranch University as a professor. I had no prior idea about him and his personality. So, being on the other side of the telephonic cord, I was a little bit scared and of course a bit nervous to introduce myself. But as soon as the phone got connected a soft voice was heard and my instant feeling was that the man on the other side was a person of a different kind. I spoke much and he was mostly a listener with minimum words. After the converzation, I was a bit confused whether he is a kind-hearted person or avoids talking much with the people less acquainted with him. However, his soft voice gave me some kind of relief from my anxiety. Afterward, whenever I talked to him the same soft and kind voice attended all my queries, and gradually, I did realise that he was a person with extraordinary politeness and gentleness. He was extremely amiable too. Following the telephonic converzation, I arrived at Ranchi University to meet him in person, and on this very first meeting, my immediate impression was that he is a man of simplicity. This impression remained unchanged even after years of interaction with him. He was a mine of knowledge but never wanted to show himself off rather always maintained a silence amidst the roars of anthropologists around him. He was perhaps an offbeat in the stardom craze within the periphery of anthropology. This very nature kept him away from the limelight always and he was happy with that.

This meeting with Professor Haldar was the commencement of a long amicable relationship with him and the period was the golden opportunity for me not only to learn from him but also to discover how a person can contribute so largely to develop and nurture the intelligentsia of the young scholars and students of the discipline without being loud in presenting himself as a giant in the field. By his very nature, he was a soft-spoken and quiet personality. Among the students, he was one of the most wanted and loved teachers. Among the scholars, he was a revered one. Among his colleagues, he was popular and trustworthy. In his family, he was an affectionate and homely person.

Prof. Haldar was born on May 1, 1943. He was hailed from a village named Shyamganj in the district of Medinipur (West) of West Bengal. The simplicity of Professor Haldar was an integral part of his nature, a character, perhaps, that was naturally imbedded into his conscious because of his rural linkage. Once one of his scholars told me that he looks like a village school teacher with very simple attire and he never bothered about that. I also noticed his carelessness about his attire and appearance as he never attached any extra value to all these outer showoffs. With his most simple outfits, he comfortably presented himself in meetings, seminars, selection committees of different universities, among the well-dressed elites of the universities and academic committees. His intelligentsia and expertise in the discipline were so well recognized among his associates and colleagues that no one ever minds for his attire. He was highly respected in his field. Professor Haldar lived happily in his world submerged into the ocean of knowledge and academics and surrounded by his students, scholars, friends, and family. He was a rare breed in the society of anthropologists.

In his academic carrier, Professor Haldar was a bright star. He stood first with first-class marks in his post-graduation (in 1967) and was awarded a gold medal by Ranchi University. He was adjudged as the best field researcher in his academic batch (1966-67) by the University and was awarded B.N. Sahay Gold Medal. He carried out his doctoral research under the guidance of Professor L. P. Vidyarthi of Ranchi University, a stalwart in the field of anthropology. Professor Vidyarthi liked and trusted this quiet and promising scholar of him and their amicable relationship lasted forever. Vidyarthi used to rely on him for his academia. In any academic publication by Professor Vidyarthi, the active presence of Ashesh Kumar was inevitable in editing, compilation, and finalization of the volume. He was such a trustworthy associate of Professor Vidyarthi. Professor Haldar had in his mind a special place of respect for his teacher, the expression of which frequently came out in his converzation with his students and scholars. When I was doing my doctoral research under him, he often spoke of his experiences with Professor Vidyarthi. He used to talk about his teacher with pride.

Professor Haldar was a hardcore field worker. Having subject specialization in the Social-Cultural branch of anthropology, he took interest in varied fields of research from ethnographic study to developmental issues in urban and industrial societies and from research methodology to theories and dimensions of civilization. He roamed at ease into this vast domain of anthropology and the outcomes were several publications in the form of books and articles. He had seven books and more than fifty articles in his credit. His doctoral thesis was on *The Mining Labourers of Chotanagpur: A Comparative Study of the Coal and Iron Ore Mining Labours* for which he was awarded a doctoral degree (Ph.D. in Anthropology) in the year 1978 by Ranchi University. From Professor Vidyarthi he inherited a theoretical bent of mind. He was on the editorial board of several Indian journals on anthropology. One of his well-known works was *The Artisan Tribes of Jharkhand and West Bengal*. The book was co-authored by G. Pandey. He underwent a special training course on Tribal Welfare and Culture from a reputed institute at Hyderabad because of his keen interest in tribal development issues.

The book *The Artisan Tribes of Jharkhand and West Bengal* was an outcome of in-depth ethnographic research and dealt with the socio-economic problems of the artisan tribes of Jharkhand and West Bengal. These artisan tribes were traditionally engaged in making agricultural implements and related crafts and used to supply to the agriculturist tribes and castes at the local level. Interestingly he found a kind of *Jajmani* relationship existed between these artisan tribes and the local Hindu agriculturist castes of the area. But with the introduction of machine-made products in the market at a cheaper rate, these tribal craftsmen were in a back step and found it hard to compete in the modern competitive market system. Consequently, there was not only breakage of the traditional linkage between the tribes and the castes but also a large-scale shift of occupation from craftsmen to daily wage labourers. The book revealed the situation in detail with empiricism. Besides pure academics, the book also unveils to its readers the human feelings and emotions of the authors for the hard struggle of these marginal artisan tribes in maintaining their bare existence. The findings and the analysis were arrayed in thirteen chapters and besides ethnographic details on family, marriage, kinship, economy, religion, and political organization separate chapters were devoted to dealing with children, women, and aged persons, one chapter on each. This shows independent thinking of Professor Haldar different from the stereotype. He observed that, it is beyond doubt that before the emergence of industrialization, the artisan tribes occupied a significant position in the agricultural economy. He further observed that their craft items were also popular among the agricultural societies. In this work, he followed the concept of Artisan as a Cultural Type as proposed by L.P. Vidyarthi in 1966. According to Vidyarthi, there are five Cultural Types in Tribal India (with special reference to Bihar) and they are hunting-gathering type, hill cultivation type, plain cultivation type, artisan type, and industrial and urban labour type. Following Vidyarthi's concept, he selected four tribal communities who represented Artisan Cultural Type in Jharkhand and West Bengal and they were Lohara, Karmali, Mahali, and Chik Baraik. This work was, perhaps, a tribute to his late teacher.

Professor Haldar was keen on focusing on tribal society. Another well-known contribution was a joint venture with Professor Kanchan Roy of Ranchi University on Sauriya Paharia, one of the forest-dwelling tribes of Santal Parganas. This anthropological work was focused on ethnomedicinal practices of the Sauria Pahariyas and interpretation was done in the light of the Nature-Man-Spirit Complex, the famous theory proposed by L.P. Vidyarthi. The book titled, *The Sauria Paharia: A Study of Ethno-Medical System* contains 96 pages and was published in 1998 by Rarh Samskriti Sangrahalaya, Fulgeria, Medinipur (West Bengal). It was an empirical study undertaken during 1987-88 in the Sahebgunj district of Bihar. The book is an important contribution in understanding the Ethno-medicinal practices of the community as well as their concept of health and related beliefs and behaviour. The concept of disease, traditional remedies for healing, and magico-religious practices of the traditional tribal medicine man as well as nutritional aspects was also discussed. Interestingly, food items were classified functionally into three types: Energy producing, bodybuilding, and productive. Disease and diagnosis had been considered as negative health and cognitive approach had been taken into use for interpretation. In this work also he was very much within the legacy of Professor Vidyarthi, his friend, philosopher, and guide.

As an ethnographer, he relied upon empiricism for understanding the tribal societies. His contribution to the tribal study is worth acknowledging. He had a theoretical orientation too and tried to interpret theories through empirical work. He was an inspiration for his students and scholars. I remember the day when I came to Ranchi to submit the draft of my doctoral thesis to him for his suggestions. Being residing in Kolkata I could only depend on telephonic contact but that was not much helpful always as he had a low voice and used to be very brief in communication over the telephone. So, the discussion used to be one-sided always, I kept on talking and he used to offer a patience hearing. Realising my problem he called me to Ranchi, thus, I arrived. I wanted him to go through my draft thesis and offer necessary suggestions. But instead, he proposed that I should read out the whole draft and he will listen. Accordingly, the reading session started and it continued for three successive days. He did not utter a single word on my thesis while I was reading out. I was a bit nervous and disappointed too as he was silent while listening. No remark, no suggestion at the end of the session. The only instruction was that the session would start at 4 p.m. the next day i.e. after his routine classes would be over. During the session, he only needed a steady supply of tea and smoking. After three days when the whole draft was read out, he spoke out. To my surprise, he remembered every line and each chapter even after three days. He suggested me to shift a portion of the introduction to the conclusion as the observation was conclusive and some portions from other chapters to the introduction, some to the conclusion, and the like. He was satisfied with my draft and after necessary shifting, the thesis might be finalized. It was a great experience for me to fathom his intelligentsia and height of academic excellence. At the same time, all his suggestions were so simply uttered with so much politeness as if he was dealing with a friend. This attitude was natural to him. He discussed in detail my introduction part where theories were referred to and reviewed and it was an academic class for me. I realized his depth of knowledge in the vast realm of theories and their applications in the field of research. The whole discussion was held in a casual mood with his usually smiling face. He was a teacher of an exceptional brand. He was always a source of courage for the students.

In *Some Aspects of Indian Society and Culture, Essay in Honour of Prof. A. K. Haldar*, (ed.) Pradip K. Bhowmick and Nabakumar Duary (2005), a felicitation volume for Professor Haldar, Y.K. Jaiswal, the then Head of the Department of Anthropology, Ranchi University observed, 'He (Professor A. K. Haldar) combines the image of one man, and integral man of singleness of mind and purpose…we cannot afford to forget and work without such a rare combination of a great scholar and good soul'.

Ashesh Kumar Haldar was a humanitarian from his inner soul. In his humble way, he tried his level best to promote his students and younger colleagues whom he found promising. He had a soft corner for those students who were hailed from downtrodden or economically and socially deprived families especially the tribal students who were meritorious and looking for an opportunity to prove themselves in academics. He always tried to extend his helping hand to them; most important was that he did all these in silence and never wanted any credit out of that. Perhaps, very few knew all his welfare activities. He was loved and respected by his students, scholars, and university colleagues. He hardly had any enemy and negative critic among his associates, a rare happening indeed in the society of anthropologists.

In his academic field, he was a meticulous worker and a voracious reader. Whatever responsibility was assigned to him he completed it meticulously. He was the person who designed and organized the M.Phil course in Social Science at Ranchi University under the auspices of the Department of Anthropology in 1985. He was associated with several academic activities in the department and contributed effectively to the development and smooth functioning of the department with which he had an emotional attachment. It is revealed from various sources that he was holding charge of several academic curriculums and maintained an amicable relationship with the students of all strata like post-graduation, M.Phil, Ph.D, and D.Litt. He also extended his academic support with utmost sincerity to other universities in opening up the course of anthropology in their curriculum as and when he was requested for. He never bothered for publicity and fame and preferred to keep his usual silence.

In his anthropological contribution, he wandered easily into the vast field of research from the empiricism of the mining labourers of Chotanagpur, demographic aspects of Oraon and Kharia tribes of Ranchi District, the impact of industrialization in Middle India (Economic life of the Bharia tribe of Patalkot, Madhya Pradesh), students unrest in Chotanagpur, artisan tribes of Jharkhand and West Bengal (a research project sponsored by the Ministry of Welfare, Government of India), working of voluntary organizations in Chotanagpur, patterns of South Asian culture to the theoretical domain of the rise of anthropology in India (*The Rise of Social Science in India: An Anthropological Orientation*) and the trends in world anthropology besides conceptualising the cultural pattern of Bihar and tribal leadership in Chotanagpur. He took a keen interest in understanding the socio-economic problems of the Particularly Vulnerable Tribes of Jharkhand and West Bengal. Unfortunately, the contribution of this self-reliant anthropologist has not been noticed by most of the drumbeaters of the anthropological society.

It is learned that after his masters in anthropology he started his academic carrier as Research Officer of two mammoth research projects of the Department of Anthropology, Ranchi University, one was on the Tribal Leadership and the other was an Indo-Japanese joint venture on the economic life of the tribes of Madhya Pradesh, and joined as Demonstrator to the Department. In 1976, he joined as a Lecturer in the same Department and superannuated as a Professor from the same university with thirty-four years of uninterrupted teaching experience. About twenty-four doctoral thesis and one D.Litt.

had been submitted under his guidance and all of them were awarded Ph.D. and D.Litt. respectively from Ranchi University.

His intelligentsia and concomitant interest in the vast field of anthropology attracted students towards him to discuss their topic of interest. To him, all students were welcomed and he spent all his life building up good students. Here lies the beauty of his personality as a teacher and as humane. I feel fortunate that I came in contact with Professor Ashesh Kumar Haldar and he kindly agreed to be my guide in my doctoral thesis. I take this opportunity to pay my homage to this great teacher and a great soul, who preferred to be in silence and kept himself away from showoff and drumbeating of himself and lived with dignity with his inherent quiet and humble nature combined with a strong decisive personality.

Prof. Haldar moved to his heavenly abode on May 17, 2018.

Acknowledgement

I am extremely thankful to Dr. Nabakumar Duary of Anthropological Survey of India for his wholehearted cooperation in this write-up. He provided me with the information I required and published materials. Professor Rahim Mandal of North Bengal University shared his experiences with Professor Haldar and that became a great help for me.

Some important research works of Prof. A. K. Halder

Haldar, AK and Aurora S, 1991. The religious observances of the Artisan tribes of Chotanagpur. In B. Choudhuri (ed): *Tribal Transformation in India: Religious, Ritual, and Festivals*. Vol. 5, New Delhi, Inter India Publications.

Haldar, AK. 1997. Prospect of development of tribal untouchables of Chotanagpur. In G. Pfeffer and D.K. Behera (Eds): *Contemporary Society: Tribal Studies*, Volume II, pp. 266-274, Concept Publishing Company, New Delhi.

References

Bhowmick, Pradip K. and Duary Nabakumar (ed.) 2005: *Some Aspects of Indian Society and Culture, Essay in Honour of Prof. A. K. Haldar*, R.N. Bhattacharya, Kolkata.

Duary, Nabakumar, 1999: Book Review (*The Sauria Paharia: A Study of Ethno-Medical System*, authored by A. K. Haldar and Kanchan Roy,1998: Rarh

Samskriti Sangrahalaya, Fulgeria, Midnapur) in *South Asian Anthropologist*, 20, 2:105.

Duary, Nabakumar, 2018: Obituary: Professor A. K. Haldar (1.5.1943-17.5.2018) in *Anthropos India*, 4,1 and 2: 357-359.

Haldar, A. K. and Pandey, G. 2001: *The Artisan Tribes of Jharkhand and West Bengal*, R.N. Bhattacharya, Kolkata.

Chapter – 23

Contributions of Prof. H.C. Sharma towards Prehistoric Anthropological Studies in North-east India

Bhabani Kumar Borah

Dr. Harish Chandra Sharma was born in Belbari village of undivided Kamrup district on 28th February 1945. He had lost his mother after a few days of his birth and consequently, his paternal aunt take all the responsibility to up-bring him during his childhood. His father, Pandit Aniruddha Dev Sharma, was a well-known Sanskrit teacher in Vella Sanskrit School situated in Barpeta district. As such, Dr. Sharma also completed his primary schooling in Vella Sanskrit School. Then he moved to Sarthebari High School and completed Matriculation there in 1959. For the higher study, he came to Dhubri College and passed his I.Sc. Examination there and finally moved to Arya Vidyapeeth College, Guwahati and from there he completed B.Sc. examination. Harish Chandra Sharma had a keen interest in Anthropology and completed his M.Sc. with Prehistoric Anthropology as a special paper from Gauhati University and then started research works continuously.

He had been carrying on Ph.D. research since 1967 as a UGC research scholar in Prehistoric Archaeology and the degree of Ph.D. was awarded to him by the University of Gauhati on his thesis entitled '*Prehistoric Archaeology: Stone Age Culture of Garo Hills*' in May 1973. He was fortunate enough that after completing his master's degree, he was appointed as Curator in the Museum of Anthropology Department, Gauhati University in 1970, which is later on named as *Madhab Chandra Goswami Museum* of Anthropology Department. While working as a U.G.C research scholar, he has been given the opportunity of undergoing a training course in Prehistoric Archaeology covering explorations and excavations at Inamgaon under the guidance of Professor H.D. Sankalia, Deccan College Post- Graduate and Research Institute, Poona. He was also permitted to take classes of P.G. students in Prehistoric Archaeology in the Department of Anthropology by the then Head of the Department, Professor Madhab Ch. Goswami. He worked as a Museum Curator till 1973.

In the year 1973, Dr. Harish Chandra Sharma got married to Smt. Geetanjali Goswami from the Amranga village, Chaigaon. It is said that the then Vice-Chancellor of Gauhati University had handed over him the letter of his appointment as Lecturer in the Department of Anthropology, Gauhati University on the wedding ceremony day.

Dr. Sharma had conducted intensive fieldwork in Garo Hills for several years with other scholarly workers from different parts of India. His initial exposure in the field of archaeology began in 1966 at Garo Hills, Meghalaya and that year he had explored the Rongram - Asannenggiri area and collected numerous valuable prehistoric archaeological materials. In December 1967, he accompanied the departmental exploration team to the district of Garo Hills and discovered a few innovative Prehistoric sites. He along with his team unearthed many valuable prehistoric antiquities from Selbalgiri sites in Garo Hills and published the findings in *Indian Archaeology - A Review* in 1967- 1968.

Dr. Sharma had carried out another exploration in the Hahim area in the border of Kamrup and Garo Hills districts during 1969 and extensively studied the Hahim river terraces and their sections to understand the geology and geomorphology of the area for further research works. His investigations were extended further among Garos, who inhabits in the proximity of the Khasis, Rabhas, and Hajong as neighbours.

In March 1969, he got the opportunity to accompany Professor K. De B. Codrington of the University of London in his exploration trip to Garo Hills during which they examined the prehistoric sites at

Rongram and Thebronggiri (*Indian Archaeology - A Review* - 1968-1969). Again in December 1969, while exploring various prehistoric sites in the district of Garo Hills, Meghalaya, discovered a large number of prehistoric antiquities (tools) of Palaeolithic periods.

In January 1970, Dr. Sharma left for Garo Hills accompanying Dr. H.D. Sankalia, for an archaeological trip and collected some important information about geological data regarding the Pleistocene Stratigraphy of the region, and collected a good number of stone tools.

In January 1971, he carried on field investigation along with the departmental team (Anthropology) of Gauhati University and studied different river valleys of Garo Hills, Meghalaya and successfully located some sites containing Palaeolithic tools.

Dr. Shama put forward active participation in various archaeological excavations in different archaeological sites. In 1970, he took part in the excavation conducted by the Archaeology Department of Deccan College, Poona at Inamgaon, a notable Chalcolithic site in Maharashtra. Dr. Sharma continued his exploration and excavation in the Selbalgiri area, an important Stone Age Site in Garo Hills, Meghalaya. He also oversees the Ambari excavation conducted by the Department of Anthropology, Gauhati University in 1969 and 1970- 1971 sessions (*Indian Archaeology - A Review*, 1968-1969 and 1972- 1973). Further, he has been nominated as Director of Ambari Excavation by Gauhati University, and subsequently, he has excavated the site with his team namely, Prof. A.A. Asraf, Dr. Hari Chandra Mahanta, Dr. Bhabani Kumar Borah, Pranati Barman, etc. in 1991- 1992, and prepared a report. Exploration in 1977 at Nangalbibra, Garo Hills, resulted in the discovery of an important Early Palaeolithic Site. The work was financed by the University of Gauhati. A report was published in *Indian Archaeology - A Review* - 1977- 1978. In 1978, a joint expedition was conducted with Dr. S.N. Rajguru of Deccan College, Poona in Garo Hills, Meghalaya. Further, in the same year in April, another exploration was conducted in the Darrangagiri area, Bhutan with Dr. S.N. Rajguru.

In September 1978, he has done successfully his exploration in the Nangalbibra area in Garo Hills and resulted in the discovery of an important and unique flake tool industry, the report was published in *Indian Archaeology - A Review,* 1978- 1979.

Dr. Sharma along with the team of Deccan College Post Graduate and Research Institute, Poona made a joint expedition in 1979 in Assam, Meghalaya, and Manipur and found some stone tools. In the same year, he explored Umium river valley, Borapani, Shillong, Meghalaya, and discovered a Stone Age Site on the bank of the Umium River. This is the only site so far discovered in the Shillong area *Indian Archaeology - A Review*, 1979- 1980.

He had conducted another excavation in 1982 at P.W.D. Inspection bungalow, Rongram, and he continued his explorations in Rongram, Ganol, and Ringgi river valleys. He salvage several hoabinhian types of tools besides many more palaeolithic tools collected from the sites. Besides, he also studied the geomorphology of the river valleys.

In 1983, he conducted investigations into the Prehistoric Archaeology in the Mahanadi river valley, Burla; and Kharla river valley, Kuchinda in Sambalpur district, Odisha. This results in discovering numerous stone tools from both the valleys, some of which are preserved in the Prof. M.C.Goswami Memorial Museum, Anthropology Department, Gauhati University.

An ethnoarchaeological investigation had also been conducted by him in 1984 among the Kabui Nagas of Tamenlong district, as well as in the Imphal valley, Manipur. Under his able supervision a team of the researcher of the Anthropology Department, Gauhati University conducted an extensive exploration in Garo Hills district in 1985 and collected a good number of palaeoliths which are now exhibited in the museum of Anthropology, Gauhati University. In 1986, he had conducted exploration in Central Garo Hills and excavation in the Selbalgiri II (Gawak Abri) site. Two new palaeolithic sites (Didami II and III) have also been discovered and collected enumerable stone tools. Further, in 1987- 1988, Dr. Sharma conducted explorations in the Rongram- Ganol valley and two new sites – one is palaeolithic (Ganol II) and the other one is Neolithic (Chibragiri II) in the valley of the river Ganol. In 1989 and 1990, he conducted archaeological and geomorphological investigations in the valleys of the river Ganol, Rongram, Ringgi, and Simsang and their tributaries besides some valuable data for geomorphological interpretation. An important ceramic-Neolithic site at Daojali Hading in North Cachar Hills, Assam with Dr. Abdullah Ali Ashraf revealing three stratigraphic cultural layers yielding Neolithic Celts (broken and fresh) and cord impressed, stamped potshards of typical types.

It may be mentioned here that Dr. Sharma had supervised a good number of small-scale excavations at Rongram, Selbalgiri, Mikir Hills district Jalukbari (bat-shaped terracotta sites), etc. at different places of North-east India with Prof. M.C. Goswami, Prof. H.D. Sankalia, Prof. T.C. Sharma, Prof. A.C. Bhagabati, and Prof. S.N. Rajguru.

Research Projects undertaken by Prof. Sharma

1. The Stone Age Cultural Sequence of Garo Hills with a Special Reference to their Geochronology. Sponsored by Gauhati University under UGC Vth Plan (1977- 1979).
2. The Stone Age Cultural Sequence of Nangalbibra, Garo Hills, Meghalaya. UGC Minor Research Project. (1981-1982). The project records valuable evidence of Palaeolithic as well as Neolithic periods of the prehistory of Garo Hills.
3. Excavations at Ambari. Sponsored by Gauhati University (1992).
4. Craft specialization and occupation mobility of Hira Potters of Kamrup District, Assam. Sponsored by Ministry of Social Justice and Empowerment, New Delhi (1997- 1998).

Dr. Sharma had participated various seminars and conferences in many places in India like *Trend of Researches in Archaeology in India* (1974), *Recent Advances in Indo- Pacific Prehistory* - Indo-Pacific Prehistory Association, Post Plenary Symposium Xth ICAES, University of Poona (1978); *Recent Trend of Researches in Prehistory*, Andhra University (1981); *Biological and Cultural variation*, Gauhati University (1982); *Man and Ecology with special reference to North-east India*, Gauhati University, (1983); *Dimensions of Contact among Tribal and other Communities of North East India*, Gauhati University (1984); *Necessity of Preservation of Nature and Cultural Heritage of Assam*, Directorate of Museum, Nagaon, Assam (1984); *Cultural Identity, Development, and Integration with special reference to*

North-east India, Arunachal Pradesh (1987); *Application of Science and Technology for Tribal Development*, Guwahati (1987); *Ramkatha in Tribal and Folk tradition, with special reference to North-east India*, Gauhati University (1988); *Anthropological Perspectives on the Tribes of Assam Hills, Karbi Anglong* (1988); *Cultural Heritage of Northeast India*, Guwahati (1993); *Traditional Customs and Rituals of Arunachal Pradesh as practiced by different ethnic groups*, Guwahati (1994); *Traditional Customs and Rituals of Assam*, Guwahati (1996); *Tribal Tradition and its Relation to Development in the Hill Areas of Assam,* Guwahati (1996); *Forest Resource of Hills Districts of Assam, Constraints of Development*, Guwahati (1996); *Archaeological Heritage of North-east India*, Guwahati (1996); *Utilization, Plantation and Conservation of Medicinal Plants*, Gauhati University, (1997); XVth Convention on Indian Association of Sedimentologists, Gauhati University (1998); *Anthropology in North-east India*, Shillong (1999); *Urban Anthropology*, Gauhati University (2000) and many more.

His association with a few of the academic bodies includes – Indo-Pacific Prehistory Association (IPPA); the Indian Society for Prehistoric and Quaternary Studies (ISPQS); the Indian Archaeological Society; Assam Science Society, Guwahati; Indian Science Congress Association. Kolkata; Assam Research Society, Guwahati; Northeast Indian Museum Association; Anthropological Society of Northeast India, Guwahati; Anthropological Students' Forum, Gauhati University; Indian Anthropological Society, Kolkata.

He was invited as a Visiting Professor, Department of Anthropology, Dibrugarh University and delivered lectures for 25 days in February 1994; delivered a series of lectures as Resource Person in '*Refresher Course in Anthropology*', organized by Academic Staff College, Gauhati University, 1995; and again delivered lectures as a Resource Person in '*Refresher Course in Anthropology*' organized by Academic Staff College, Gauhati University from 23rd March to 11th April 2000.

He successfully supervised four Ph.D. dissertations on different archaeological topics with emphasis on the investigations and studies on potters and pottery, prehistoric Stone Age cultures, and ethnohistory and ethnoarchaeology of indigenous populations of

North-east India.

1. Bandita Medhi, 1992. *The Potter and Pottery of Nalbari District of Assam: A Study in Ethnohistory and Ethnoarchaeology*. Unpublished Ph.D. Thesis, Anthropology Department, Gauhati University.
2. Hari Chandra Mahanta. 1995. *A Study on the Stone Age Cultures of Selbalgre, West Garo Hills, Meghalaya*. Unpublished Ph.D. Thesis, Anthropology Department, Gauhati University.
3. Preeti Rekha Sarmah. 2001. *The Hira Potters and Pottery of South Kamrup: A Study of their Ethnography and Occupational Mobility*. Unpublished Ph.D. Thesis, Anthropology Department, Gauhati University.
4. Borah, B.K. 2002. *Settlement Subsistence Patterns of the Nah of Arunachal Pradesh: An Ethnoarchaeological Approach*. Unpublished Ph.D. Thesis, Anthropology Department, Gauhati University.

Some important research publications

1968. A report on the investigations into the prehistoric archaeology of the Garo Hills (with T.C. Sharma). *Journal of the Gauhati University*. 16-17, 2: 73-84.

1971. On the discovery of stone age sites in central Garo Hills (with T.C. Sharma), *Journal of the Assam Science Society*, 14, 1: 18-26.

1972. *Prehistoric Archaeology: Stone Age Cultures of Garo Hills, Meghalaya*. Unpublished Ph.D. Thesis, Anthropology Department, Gauhati University.

1972. A typological study of some prehistoric tools from the Kameng district of NEFA (Arunachal), (with M.C. Goswami and R. C. Das), *Journal of Assam Science Society,* 15, 1: 129-135.

1975. Archaeological findings in Meghalaya. *Bulletin of the Department of Anthropology, Gauhati University,* 4: 20-25.

1976. Stone age sites in Garo hills. *Bulletin of the Department of*

Anthropology, Gauhati University, 5: 82-93.

1983. On the occurrence of stone age industries in the valley of Barapani river, Meghalaya. *Journal of Assam Science Society*, 25, 2: 41-49.

1985. On the discovery of a pebble tool industry in the Garo Hills, Meghalaya. In V.N. Mishra and P. Bellwood (Eds): *Recent Trends in Indo-Pacific Prehistory*, pp. 89-91, New Delhi; Oxford and IBH Publication.

1993. A fresh light on the stone age cultures of Rongram Selbal valley, Western Garo Hills Meghalaya (with H.C. Mahanta), *Bulletin of the Department of Anthropology, Dibrugarh University*, 20-21: 49-57.

1993. The stone age cultures around Selbal river, Western Garo hills: A reappraisal (with H.C. Mahanta). *Bulletin of the Department of Anthropology, Gauhati University,* 7: 61-72.

1993. Transition in basic economy: Consideration on a small population group of Arunachal Pradesh, (jointly with others), In S.B. Roy and A.K. Ghosh (Eds): *People of India: Bio-Cultural Dimensions*, pp. 298-304, New Delhi, Inter India Publication.

2003. Prehistoric archaeology of North-East India. In T.B. Subba and G.C. Ghosh (Ed): *North East India: A Handbook of Anthropology*. pp. 3-21, New Delhi; Orient Longman Private Limited.

Prof. Sharma was a great teacher, hardcore researcher, compassionate mentor, friend, philosopher, and guide to his students. His untimely demise on 24th September 2002 at the age of 57 years only created a void in the academic field of teaching and learning, particularly in the field of prehistoric archaeological research in Eastern India.

Chapter – 24

Life and Works of Prof. Surinder Nath

Deepali Jain and O.P. Jasuja

The Genesis

In the decades preceding the independence, when our country was under the colonial regime, many political disturbances ran across the nation. It was the City of Lahore where, once a tiny cell, fully developed as a newbie. On the day of 13 September 1945, Mr. J.N. Grover and Mrs. Premlata were blessed with a baby boy, and they named him Surinder Nath. He was the youngest among siblings. He, later on, became a famous anthropologist, researcher and did exemplary classical work in science, with many research articles, books, and many more.

At that time the city of Lahore was part of the erstwhile British India, which now is part of present-day Pakistan. Further, it was not that buttery smooth for the parents to be in Lahore during the days of the partition of India and Pakistan. So in 1947, they decided to migrate from the sub-tropical steppe semi-arid climate of Lahore to the mountainous state of Himachal Pradesh in the mid of Pir Panjal ranges of the lesser Himalayas. His family had witnessed emasculating and debilitating realities of human existences as they had left behind the huge agricultural land, a big ancestral house in Lahore. Here they spent almost a year in the search of stability.

As said by folks, God always has a way of getting us to our destiny. Now, the family shifted to Mohiuddinpur, Uttar Pradesh in 1948. His family stayed there for around five years, where Surinder

Nath got his early schooling. And from there, they again shifted to Kamla Nagar, Delhi, in 1954. There he was admitted to R B Ram Roop Vidya Mandir, managed by R B Ram Roop Trust, founded in 1951. He completed his higher secondary education by 1962.

With the completion of his higher secondary education, the turning point of his life arrived. As he had developed a keen interest in the contemporarily unconventional field of Anthropology, so he joined for Bachelors of Science program in Anthropology (Hons) at Kirori Mal College, New Delhi, an institution of academic excellence, established in 1954. Being one of the premier institutes within the University of Delhi, it strived to set and maintain a global standard in academic parlance and so was evident from its influence on Surinder Nath.

We recall, often he used to say, being youngest in the family; he had been hard-working, obedient, and sincere in family affairs. He completed his graduation in Anthropology in 1965. After graduating, his curiosity grew and he joined the Master of Anthropology course in the Department of Anthropology at the University of Delhi. In 1967, the day of convocation arrived and he threw his hat in the air with joy. The hat might have fallen on the ground under influence of gravity, but nothing could hinder the path of Surinder Nath thereafter; his eagerness to acquire more knowledge and proficiency in quality education pumped him towards research and academic excellence.

His search for excellence and yearning for knowledge conclusively culminated in 1972. He had been awarded a Doctorate of Philosophy (Ph.D. in Anthropology) under the supervision of Dr. Abhimanyu Sharma. It's the highest academic level award.

The only thing that does not reduce if shared is knowledge. So, from the journey of acquiring knowledge now, it was the time to transfer knowledge to the new budding generation.

The skirmish

To pursue this thought on one cold fine day on March 26th, 1975, he stood proudly in the temporary lecturer position in Physical Anthropology at Delhi University. Impressed by his passion and dedication towards his job, just within six days, he was appointed as an Ad-hoc lecturer in the Anthropology Department, Delhi University. His work period had also been extended for some more months. Besides he received special pieces of training in Forensic Science and serological investigations at crime sites in Central Forensic Science Laboratory of CBI, New Delhi. There he kept on expanding his knowledge boundaries to newer limits. His studies on forensic science, human growth, and development there, later on, proved to be the cherry on the cake.

Further, it was on February 22nd, 1978, when he was interviewed for the permanent post at the University of Delhi. The result was almost certain, and on March 11th, 1978, he had been appointed as the permanent Faculty in the Department of Anthropology, Delhi University. It was the same year when he published *A Study of Physical Development among Tibetan Boys* by S.C. Tiwari, M.K. Basin, and S. Nath.

Furthermore, in 1979, his solo publication *'Lanthropologie', Extrait Direction de la croissance differentielle et de la maturation des jats du Nord de Linde, de sexe masculin* got internationally published in Paris, Milan, Barcelona, and New York.

It was the leap year of 1984 when he published his book on *Fingerprint Identification.* Thereafter, he never looked back on hitting new books after another, which was extremely helpful for the students to gain new insights. In the year 1985, he was promoted as a Reader in the Department of Anthropology, Delhi University.

Prof. Ravinder Singh said that his association with Prof. Nath had begun in November 1987 during his M.Sc. fieldwork in Baiga-Chak, Mandla District of Madhya Pradesh. He recalled that he was collecting anthropometric data for the physical growth and development of Baigas and Gond male children of Baigas-Chak, a reserve forest land. While working in Baiga-Chak Prof. Nath used to move on foot with their things for fieldwork and was a constraint to identify those primitive tribal people to help them in getting those subjects available. As tribal people were more scared of them hence never came closer and remained away whenever they heard or saw them, they disappeared. It became difficult to get subjects for physical anthropology data of these people. Whereas Dr. V K Srivastava was guiding five girl students for fieldwork in social anthropology for different aspects - medical anthropology, the trans-possession state of the local traditional healer, *Gunia*, healed common alignments of those tribal people.

Prof. Nath had worked on *Issues and Trends in Rehabilitation Research* with N.K. Chadha and S.S. Phulia in 1994. Prof. Ravinder Singh recalled when they went to Srinagar, Gharwal with Prof. Nath for a seminar where Prof. N. K. Chaddha, President and Founding Member of AASTHA, organized a Seminar on Health in collaboration with the Department of Anthropology, Hembati Nandan Bahuguna University, Srinagar, Garwhal which Dr. P. C. Joshi, Head of the Department coordinated that Seminar. Most of the research scholars - Ravinder Singh, Abhik Ghose, Satish Kedia, Ms. Bharati, and others with Prof Nath and Dr. Chadha participated in the Seminar.

It was his tender love and care for his students, most of the girls of the time has attracted to work with him. Some of the women students who worked for Ph.D. were Prabha Badkur (1985); Reita Jain (1989); Kavita Jain (1993); Shivani Aggarwal (1997); Sunita Roy (1997); Shivani Chhibber (1998); Sumider Kaur (1998); Preeti Jain (1999); and girl students under his co-supervision were Deepali Jain (2015); Shruti Aggarwal (2015); Renu Devi (2015); Puja Mittal (2015). Three boys who received Ph.D. under his supervision were: N.Satish Chandra (1989), Swetansu Shekhar Rath (1994), and Ravinder Singh (1995).

In the year 1991, Prof. Nath wrote a book *Fingerprint Identification in Crime Detection*, which describes the usability of fingerprints in establishing a shred of perfect judicial evidence by detecting crime. Again in 1992 he worked on and published *Application Areas of Anthropology* along with Anil Mahajan. Soon after, he co-linearly authored *Criminology - A Psychological and Anthropological Analysis* with N.K. Chadha and S.S. Phulia.

In the preceding year, 1995, he became a Professor at the Anthropology Department and published another book *Forensic Anthropology*. Prof. Nath had created an indispensable niche for himself in his chosen field in the country. He developed a curriculum for M.Sc. Forensic Science, optional paper of Forensic Science for the post-graduation programme in Anthropology or Human Biology. He had started Certificate Course in Forensic Science and remained several years as the Chief Coordinator of this course in the Department of Anthropology, Delhi University.

In 1995, the name of Professor Nath was in news in the National leading dailies in Delhi. Central Forensic Science Laboratory of CBI, New Delhi consulted him for his opinion in the Naina Shahani Murder case, popularly known as *Tandoor Kaand*. His opinions were recorded for ageing and sexing of the partially burned skull cap of the victim.

He was an eminent teacher and was in demand for the guest speaker in the Police Training Academy or such training colleges. He has invited faculty to the Lok Nayak Jayprakash Narayan National Institute of Forensic Sciences and Criminology, New Delhi. Besides they used to visit often to lecture in Academic Staff College of various Universities in Delhi, Gorakhpur, Chandigarh, Amritsar, Jodhpur, Patiala, and Manipur. Further, he had been faculty of Life Sciences and Forensic Sciences, Punjabi University Patiala.

He had been a member of various committees such as the Departmental Research Committee, Institute of Forensic Science, Bundelkhand University, Jhansi, and Members of the Board of Studies, Amity Institute of Biotechnology, Amity University, Uttar Pradesh. In 1997, he published *Nutritional Anthropology,* where he not only focused light on the study of food and nutrition from evolutionary and behavioural perspectives but also from social and cultural perspectives. Finally, he began with a new publication in 2001, *Advances in Forensic Science* with M.K. Bhasin. By the time this book was published, he was already 57 years old. His health was dwindling and as a result, he faced a heart attack and had to go through heart bypass surgery.

On December 31st, 2004, he joined the University, as the Head of the Department and Dean Faculty of Science. Not only this, but he also became a member of the Academic Council of the University of Delhi, along with a membership of the Executive Board of the University of Delhi. He successfully handled his work pressure there and carried on research work, and published some more books.

Further, in 2005, he published, *Society, Crime, and Prosecution* and another *Forensic Anthropology Science and Medicine*, both of them were with M.K. Bhasin and V.N. Sehgal. Later on, *Anthropometry – The Measurement of Body Size Shape and Form* and *Forensic Science and Crime Investigation*, where Ramesh Chandra was Chief Editor, and one of the Editors was Prof. Surinder Nath.

One of his famous books, which is still readily available on popular e-Commerce websites, *Encyclopaedic Dictionary of Food and Nutrition* (Volume One) was written and published in 2006. The book addresses an obvious need, and the interest generated in the subject had never been higher. The book is enriched with highly referred, simplified, and lucid style to make it more understandable and straightforward. The entries range from the most common to those more clinical, and it contains an extensive definition in non-technical language. Again, in the same year, he published *Personal Identification through Fingerprints* and *Modern Trends in Forensic Science* by Ramesh Chandra, Surinder Nath, and Praveen Janjua.

In addition to this, he participated in numerous National, International Seminars and conferences and presented many research papers there. He also organized six Seminars and Conferences, as Organising Secretary.

During his last days as Head of the Department, he published *Human Blood Analysis* with M.K. Bhasin, V.N. Sehgal, and ended his tenure as Head of the Department on 30 December 2007. After getting a little free time from the long journey of being an educationalist, he went further to publish a book in Hindi, *Vayaktigat Pehchan Mein Ungaliyon Ke Nishaan*. Afterward, on September 30th, 2010, he took retirement.

His health condition was again dipping down. But still, his love for the subject never faded, and in 2011 he published one of his famous books *Fingerprint Identification*. His last published book was *Forensic Science and its Related Issues* with V.N. Sehgal.

He got a vast area of research starting from Forensic Anthropology, Anthropometry, Optometry Craniometrist Forensic Science, Biological Anthropology Human Growth, Health and Nutrition, Identification of Skeletal Material (determination of sex, age, and stature), identification through Fingerprints, and Sports Performance, and many more.

Life after retirement

After his superannuation, he kept himself busy in giving guest lectures in the institution as mentioned above. His life was nice after retirement and enjoying with extended family members. He also used to travel often with family members to other places as Member experts of the Committee in different places like Chandigarh and Patiala.

In late 2012, while in the market nearby his house, he suffered a Stroke. He was admitted to Hospital. He was in ICU being treated for the Stroke, right side full arm and leg paralyzed, slurring in speech, writing skills, and memories affected drastically. It was a hard time for him as well as for his family.

On 4th November 2016, he was admitted once again to the hospital for his uncontrollable anxious behaviour and later shifted to Neurosurgery ICU. Since then, he never returned home after a wait of one month of technocratic and ventilator suffering in ICU.

He fought a long battle with his health condition and left us in deep sorrow on *Krishna Paksha Chaturthi, Pushya Nakshatra*, according to the Hindu calendar, and 16 December 2016 according to the Georgian calendar. He was the longest-serving Coordinator for the Certificate Course in Forensic Science; a programme that runs in the evening in the Department of Anthropology, University of Delhi. We still miss the imperial enlightened soul in his proclaimed name Prof. Surinder Nath.

The conclusive culmination

He has contributed, over 130 scientific and popular articles in National and International Journals. His thirteen books of which five were authored and eight edited. He was not only a prominent academician but he was equally proficient in managerial and administrative activities as well. He served as the Chairman of the Management Committee at D.S. Kothari Hostel, University of Delhi, and International Students Hostel, University of Delhi both. Likewise, he also provided his service as a Member of Research Panels of important bodies such as UGC, CSIR, DMRC (Jodhpur), NIFT, ICMR, Sports Authority of India, Ministry of Tribal Affairs.

As part of administrative work, he served as Provost in Gwyer Hall for two years, University of Delhi. Also, for three years as Head, Department of Anthropology, the University of Delhi (2004), and again two and a half years as Dean, Faculty of Science, University of Delhi. He was also the Chairman of the Internal Ethical Committee at Pt. Deen Dayal Upadhaya Institute of Physically Handicap and Physiotherapy.

His proficiency in the field of academics is evident from his contribution towards developing Syllabus for M.Sc. Forensic Science and Degree Course of the Institute of Forensic Science and Criminology, Bundelkhand University, Jhansi. He also Developed Syllabus for P.G. Diploma Course in Forensic Science for Amity Institute of Behavioral (Health) and Allied Sciences, New Delhi. He was also a Member of the Committee, which helped in the modernization of the Lok Nayak Jayprakash Narayan Institute of Criminology and Forensic Science, Ministry of Home Affairs, Government of India, and Guru Govind Singh Indraprastha University, Delhi. Additionally, he also developed a teaching curriculum for M.Sc. and prepared various examination papers such as a partially optional paper on Forensic Anthropology and a compulsory paper on Human Growth and Development for the Department of Anthropology, University of Delhi.

He also earned the membership of various academic bodies and societies such as Life Member of Indian Academy of Forensic Sciences, Forensic Science Society of India, Ethnographical and Folk Culture Society, and Indian Anthropological Association. He was also the Founder Member and Vice-President-AASTHA. Likewise, he also became a Member of the Faculty of Life Sciences, Punjab University (Patiala); Member of Board of Studies, Punjab University, Patiala (Forensic Science); Member of Departmental Research Committee, Institute of Forensic Science and Criminology, Bundelkhand University, Jhansi; and Member, Board of Studies. Institute of Biotechnology, Amity University, Noida. In addition to these, he also served various institutions as a Guest Faculty such as NICFS, MHA; Guru Govind Singh Indraprastha University, Delhi. He had forty years of research experience, 37 years of teaching experience, and had numerous students supervised for their doctorate, M.Phil, and other researches. He always tried to give his best despite having a severe illness in the last years.

Acknowledgements

The authors would like to express their sincere gratitude to the immediate family of Professor Surinder Nath who granted an interview on the life and works of Prof. Surinder Nath and their assistance for the completion of the research article.

We are thankful to Dr. Ravinder Singh, Department of Medical Anthropology, Institute of Human Behavior and Allied Sciences Hospital for providing me information regarding college days, initial working years, and health issues of Prof. Surinder Nath and Dr. Ankit Srivastava, Asst. Professor, Institute of Forensic Science and Criminology, Bundelkhand University, Jhansi for providing the relevant information.

Special thanks to Biswamitra Parua, M.Sc. Forensic Science, Babasaheb Bhimrao Ambedkar University, Lucknow for arranging the data and the completion of the write-up.

Chapter – 25

Prof. Abdullah Ali Ashraf

Anamika Gogoi Duarah

Prof. Abdullah Ali Ashraf was an eminent Prehistorian of North-east India. He was born in the year 1956 in Machkhowa, Guwahati, Assam. He was the son of Renowned Educationist Ashraf Ali and Syeda Sakina Ashraf. He did his schooling at Cotton Collegiate and graduated from Arya Vidyapeeth College. He Post graduated from Gauhati University and was awarded a Ph.D. in the *Prehistoric Archaeology of Meghalaya* from Gauhati University in the year 2004. In the year, 1982, he got PG Diploma in Archaeology from the School of Archaeology, Archaeological Survey of India, New Delhi. He joined the Directorate of Research in, Arunachal Pradesh as Technical Assistant and was subsequently promoted to the post of Assistant Director during the decade 1981-90. He worked there for 9 years. In the year 1990, he joined as Lecturer in the Department of Anthropology, Gauhati University, and was promoted to the post of Professor in the year, 2016. He passed away on 4th August 2019.

Ashraf's contribution to the field of prehistoric archaeology

Dr.Ashraf, the eminent Prehistorian of North-east India was the Professor of Anthropology at Gauhati University. He pursued the comprehensive and holistic study of Prehistoric man and his culture particularly in the process of continuity and variation of prehistoric traditions operating in various parts of North-east India. He has made a tremendous contribution to the field of Prehistoric Archaeology.

He conducted several Archaeological explorations and excavations in various parts of North-east India such as the Parsi Parlo Neolithic site, Kurung Kume Valley, Arunachal Pradesh (1990); Meghalaya Sumer Neolithic site, East Khasi Hills (2002), Nakshaparbat Medieval site, East Kameng District and Bambooti Neolithic settlement site (2012-13). Based on intensive exploration and excavation, we are gifted with his valuable published books like *Ethnoarchaeology of Kamla Valley* (1990), *Prehistoric Archaeology of Lower Subansiti*, Arunachal Pradesh (1990), *Medieval Life at Nakshaparbat* (1997), *Nritatwa Sopan, Stone Age Traditions of Meghalaya: A Study of Variation and Continuity* (2004). His book on *Stone Age Traditions of Meghalaya* was on his Ph.D. work which was published by the British Archaeological Report, Oxford (2010). During his doctoral work, he identified two technical traditions in the lithic industries of Meghalaya in the Hoabinhian context and these are Cobble Tool Tradition (Peeble Flake) as found in Bibra Gre and Stone Block Tool Tradition as found in Makbil Bisik and Sumer stone tool tradition in Meghalaya. According to Prof. Ashraf, North-east India is an area where, if the clock of time is wound in an anticlockwise direction, then one may discover that the number of archaeological elements still survive in the analogous form (Ashraf and Roy, 23: 2012). Taking into consideration this fact Prof. Ashraf has made several valuable contributions to the Prehistoric Archaeology and Ethnoarchaeology of North-east India through his minute observations, tedious explorations, and excavations in different parts of North-east India.

It is to be noted that he is the pioneering authority who has established the absence of the Acheulian tradition in the North-eastern region although it was believed earlier. His research findings are known through National and International print media.

Prof. Ashraf excavated the Neolithic site of Parsi-Parlo which is situated on the northern slope of the Terrace at a height of 12 m from the river bed of Kamla on its right bank. Excavation at Parsi-Parlo during 1982-83, revealed about the 50-100 cm thick cultural deposit. Scrapers and large cutting tools with the rudiments of pecked and ground techniques characterize Phase 1 at the site. Phase 2 represents layer 2 and is characterized by pecked and ground stone implements, wasted blades/axe, and faceted tools with hand-made pottery. It is the continuation of the preceding phase with the conspicuous absence of scraper and other large cutting tools and also the emergence of pottery. The toolkit, in general, provides hafting facilities and is mostly agriculturally based. At the site of Parsi-Parlo, a small number of potsherd represent square-grid and honeycomb (web) beater impressed pottery. Navigation is poor and it contains a high percentage of gritty particles. The pottery represents a bowl with a featureless rim and constricted neck, a lipped pot with a globular body made for culinary purposes. Again, potsherd discovered at this site of Taba is coarse in texture and these were handmade and comprise plain (thick and coarse) ware, stamped (grid pattern) ware, and irregular corded ware. (2011-12:98).

The archaeological studies of North-east India entered into a completely new arena with the technometric and morphometric study of the lithic evidence in anthropological perspective through his doctoral work which was undoubtedly the pioneering work in this field. This study was based on the lithic tool tradition of Garo and Khasi hills which has opened a new approach to the study of cultural variation and continuity. This study followed conventional typo-technological methods as well as the non-conventional study of edge angle, use wear, grip axis, handedness, etc. This pioneering work is significant in respect of the systematic assimilation of conventional, non-conventional archaeological methodology and anthropological theoretical formulations and ideas in the history of the study of North-east Indian prehistory. Ashraf has brought the lithic assemblages of Meghalaya under the broad spectrum of southeast Asia and developed a chronological framework about Southeast Asian prehistory. He has considered that Mesolithic nomads inhabited the higher altitudes of eastern Meghalaya in the early Holocene period. By around the 7th to 8th millennium B.C., the western part of Meghalaya was occupied by the people of Hoabinhian culture. The study has shown some distinct morphological similarities between the Hoabinhian of Southeast Asia and Meghalayan Hoabinhian especially in respect of truncation character. The appearance of edge grinding tools before the appearance of pottery in both regions has been considered a common sequence. He has considered these two as a common cultural zone due to their undetectable geo-cultural homogeneity and closes a sequential continuum of material cultures. This study has developed a new structured model for further study of this kind.

It is to be noted that the person behind the discovery of Bambooti, the Late Neolithic site of the Assam-Meghalaya border near Damra of Goalpara district was Prof. Ashraf. He was doing some preliminary exploration in this region for several years before the proper discovery of the site. The site proper was discovered by a group of students of Gauhati University under the supervision of Prof. Ashraf in the year 2010 where the present author worked as an assistant investigator. Bambooti, geomorphologically a sloping site and culturally a habitation site is located on the right bank of the Bambooti Chiring-(stream) III towards the north of the village Tengasoth, East Garo Hills. The site is located some 500 meters away from Assam–Meghalaya political boundary that passes through Tengasoth village. Bambooti is quite significant in the sense that for the first time in North-east India it yielded artifacts consisting of pottery and ground lithic tools from a Kitchen Midden. The Bambooti excavations exhibit a 45 cms thick cultural deposit divisible into three layers. The dating of the pottery was done by the present author in the Wadia Institute of Himalayan Geology, Dehradun, and the findings were analyzed under his supervision.

The presences of the highest numbers of platters especially from the excavated site of Bambooti suggest that the area was inhabited for a long period. The earthenware that was clustered with the stone artifacts, stands as strong supporting pieces of evidence to understand the actual utilization of the stone artifacts. The context of its occurrence indicates that the stone artifacts were used as household implements. At the same time, the presence of platter among the ethnic groups living in the neighbouring areas of Bambooti and their utilization especially for the making of rice cake indicates the continuity of this tradition since the Neolithic age in this region. This postulates an early phase of pottery culture as suggested by the OSL date.

Prof. Ashraf was such a dedicated and extraordinary teacher who produced four Ph.D. scholars despite his severe illness. He was such a nice personality who was always ready to serve others with a sweet smile on his face. He was a person of exceptional quality of positivity who fought with the real truth of life the death very bravely. He was the God Father of several students including me who taught us not only about our subject but also envisioned us with honesty, sincerity, truthfulness, and dedication towards our duty. He was a tower of encouragement for all of his students who were inspired in innumerable ways. Although, it will be difficult to work without his academic support, however, his valuable ground-breaking research contribution and blessings will always show us the exact way of working in the field of research.

Few Important Research Publications

1986. Through the eastern gateway: An ethnoarchaeological approach. *Resarun*, XII (I) 14-18.

1990. *Prehistoric Arunachal: A Study on the Prehistory and Ethnoarchaeology of Kamala Valley*. Itanagar. Directorate of Research.

1994. Anthropo-archaeological background of Nishi material culture. *Bulletin of Department of Anthropology*, Gauhati University, Vol. VIII.

1997. *Medieval Life at Naksaparbat,* Directorate of Research, Arunachal Pradesh, Itanagar.

1998. Archaeological remains and further prospects in Arunachal Pradesh. (*Puratattva*): *Bulletin of Indian Archaeological Society* (K.N. Dikshit and K.S. Ramandran eds), 28: 64-76.

2001. North-East India through the windows of the past. *Souvenir. Gauhati University Science Forum,* Gauhati University.

2006. Conundrum of past culture of North-east India through the windows of the present in G. Sengupta, S. Roy and S. Som (Eds): *Past and Present: Ethno Archaeology of India*. pp. 235-250, Pragati Publication, New Delhi.

2006 Autochthons of Meghalaya in anthropo - archaeological perspective *Humankind,* Vol. 2: 31-36, 164.

2010. Stone age traditions of Meghalaya: A study of variation and continuity, *BAR International Series,* 2176. 203, Oxford, John and Erica Hedges Ltd.

2011. On the Discovery of Prehistoric Sites in North-east India in Tiluttoma Baruah (Ed): *People of the Contemporary North-east India*. Pratishruti Publication. Guwahati, Assam, pp. 268-280.

2011. Perceiving the spatial distribution of stone tools: A case study from Ida Bifek of West Garo Hills, Meghalaya. *Bulletin of the Department of Anthropology, Dibrugarh University,* 39: 29-44.

2012. Ethno-archaeology of North-east India. in T.B. Subba (Ed): *North-East India: A Handbook of Anthropology*, pp. 22-33, Orient Balck Swan, New Delhi.

2011-2012. The comparative analysis of the ground tools of highlands and foothills region of Meghalaya and Assam. *Bulletin of the Department of Anthropology. University of Gauhati.* 13: 138-159.

2015. Wheel to hand: A strategic reversal of pottery technology in Majuli, Assam. *Humankind*. 2: 1-29.

2015. Bambooti: A late Neolithic site in the foothills of southern Assam. *Bulletin of the Department of Anthropology, University of Gauhati*. 15: 23-32.

Index

D

E

H

I

J

K

N

T

U

V

W

Y

Z